Congressional Control of Administration

CONGRESSIONAL CONTROL
of
ADMINISTRATION

by Joseph P. Harris

The Brookings Institution, Washington, D.C.

113352

Foreword

THE ALL-IMPORTANT FUNCTION of Congress is to legislate—as is set forth so clearly in Article I, sections 1 and 8, of the Constitution. The legislative power of Congress to authorize programs, to create agencies, and to appropriate funds for them, however, implies some control of administration (which is primarily the function of the Chief Executive). But how much and what manner of control has remained a perennial question.

The exercise of appropriate control has become increasingly difficult with the growth of executive functions and the need to enlarge the discretionary powers of administrative officers. In an effort to extend the control of administration, Congress has made use of traditional means and has also developed new devices that go well beyond control through general legislation. These varied congressional efforts to control administrative operations in detail (rather than the clash of President and Congress on broad issues) are the subject of this book.

The author, a professor of political science at the University of California, Berkeley, has long been recognized for his authoritative books on election administration, California politics, and the United States Senate. He also has had extensive experience in public service with the President's Committee on Economic Security and the President's Committee on Administrative Management in the formative years of the New Deal, with the Social Science Research Council's Committee on Public Administration, as an administrator in UNRRA, and in military service during both World Wars. He brings to this present study a long perspective on the American scene—and also a wide knowledge of foreign governments. His not uncritical view of congressional control of administration is thus an informed judgment that deserves full and careful consideration.

The Institution and the author are grateful to the members of the committee who reviewed and criticized the manuscript in its final stages. These included Paul T. David of the University of Virginia, who was Director of Governmental Studies at Brookings when the book was commissioned, and George A. Graham, who succeeded him; H. Field Haviland, Jr., Director of Foreign Policy Studies at Brookings; Rowland Egger of the University of Virginia; Rufus E. Miles, Jr., Administrative Assistant Secretary of the Department of Health, Education, and Welfare; and James H. Rowe, Jr., of the Washington law firm of Corcoran, Foley, Youngman, and Rowe. The Institution and the author are also indebted to others who read all or parts of the manuscript and who made many valuable suggestions for its improvement: Herman Finer of the University of Chicago; Laurin L. Henry of the Brookings Institution; Harvey C. Mansfield of Ohio State University; Carl Tiller of the U.S. Bureau of the Budget; and Kenneth Sprankle and Paul M. Wilson of the staff of the Appropriations Committee of the House of Representatives. The Honorable Joseph Campbell, Comptroller General of the United States, graciously read and criticized the chapter on the audit, though differing fundamentally with its findings and conclusions. Robert Pranger, Eugene Poschman, and William Rhoades greatly aided the author as research assistants during the study's preparation. Special thanks are due to Kathleen Sproul, who edited the manuscript.

During the course of the study the author consulted and was aided by many federal officials in various departments and agencies, by a number of members of Congress, and by members of the congressional staff. He also wishes to express his appreciation to the Institute of Social Sciences of the University of California, Berkeley, for research assistance during the early part of the study.

The opinions expressed in this work are those of the author and do not purport to represent the views of the trustees, officers, or other staff members of the Brookings Institution, or of those who reviewed the manuscript.

ROBERT D. CALKINS
President

January 1964
The Brookings Institution
1775 Massachusetts Avenue N.W.
Washington, D.C.

Contents

1

Introduction

CONTROL OF ADMINISTRATION is one of the most important functions of legislative bodies in all modern democracies. We live today
in the age of the administrative state, with immense power and sums
of money entrusted to public officials who serve, defend, and regulate us in innumerable ways. Authoritative prescription of the purposes and programs to be carried out by those officials is the primary
function of legislatures. The actual conduct of programs is left to the
executive arms of government. In practice, however, it is difficult if
not impossible to make a perfect separation between the concerns of
legislative and executive officers—between the declaration of ends
and the devising of means.

The authority to prescribe the objectives of executive action implies at least some authority to see that appropriate steps are taken
to achieve those objectives. And the means of government are not
politically or philosophically neutral: they are closely related to, or
sometimes become, ends themselves. Therefore legislatures must concern themselves with the *how* as well as the *what* of executive
action. It is not enough for a legislature to enact policies and programs into law; it must check to see how those policies are being
executed, whether they are accomplishing the desired results, and, if
not, what corrective action the legislature may appropriately prescribe. Such activity on the part of legislatures is what we mean by
"legislative control of administration," and its purposes may be stated
as follows:

1. To determine whether legislative policies are being faithfully,
effectively, and economically carried out, so that appropriate legis-

1

lative action may be taken to correct any shortcomings of administration.

2. To determine whether legislative programs are accomplishing their desired objectives, and if any further legislation is needed.

3. To ascertain that the laws are being administered in the public interest, and to encourage diligence on the part of administrative officers.

4. To discover any abuses of discretion, arbitrary actions, or gross errors of judgment by administrative officers.

5. To check on the systems of internal management and control established by the department heads and the chief executive, to ascertain that they are adequate and effective.

6. To hold responsible executive officers accountable to the legislature for their use of public funds and other resources put at their disposal.

The methods of legislative control of administration have much to do with the effectiveness, acceptability to citizens, and survival power of any given governmental system. If control of administration is weak or incomplete, there is a danger that executive agencies will misinterpret or misapply legislative intent, that they will become inefficient or wasteful of public funds, or act in an arbitrary or unlawful manner. However, legislatures should not—and by their very nature cannot—undertake detailed supervision of administration or effectively substitute their judgments for those of executive officials in all matters. Effective administration requires that executive officials have appropriate discretion to apply the expertness that they have but legislatures do not, and to pursue the intent of the law in varying circumstances that legislatures cannot possibly anticipate. Legislative controls which are unduly detailed stifle initiative; make for inflexibility and inefficiency in the conduct of governmental programs; sometimes result in imposing the will of individual legislators, or small groups, in matters in which they do not speak for the entire legislature and which are best left to executive officials; and end in frustrating the basic will of the legislative body.

A perennial problem, then, in all except authoritarian regimes, is to devise and maintain methods of legislative control that keep things in proper balance—that keep the activities of executive officials under effective scrutiny and control while at the same time preserving the values of administrative flexibility and discretion. The problem becomes especially critical under modern conditions of big government, with both governmental programs and administrative methods undergoing rapid change.

This book is a study of legislative controls as applied by the Congress of the United States to the administration of the departments and agencies of the Executive branch of the federal government. We shall be concerned with what those controls are, how they work, and how they might be improved. We shall not be concerned with the broader subject of congressional-presidential relations, except as those relations are involved in the congressional interest in administration. The problem is of course analogous to the problems of control of administration in the fifty American states, and incidental reference will occasionally be made to state experience. More frequent comparisons will be made with Great Britain, which has forms of legislative control that differ in many respects from those of the United States but offer much to instruct the American observer.

Constitutional and Political Setting

In any governmental system, the particular constitutional and political setting strongly conditions the legislative-executive relations involved in control of administration. This can be demonstrated by examining some characteristics of the American system as compared with the British.

The writers of the Constitution of the United States established a separation of powers by providing for a Congress and a President on the same legal plane, then blurred the separation by giving each certain rights to check or influence the activities of the other. The Founding Fathers knew perfectly well what they were doing. In a great exposition in *The Federalist*, James Madison claimed that neither in the British constitution nor in the writings of "the celebrated Montesquieu" where the separation of powers maxim had been elaborated was it ever contemplated that the legislative, executive, and judicial departments should be "totally separate and distinct from each other."[1] The correct interpretation of the doctrine was that the same hands must never exercise the *whole* power of more than one department. This, pointed out Madison, "did not mean that these departments ought to have no *partial agency* in, or no *control* over, the acts of each other."[2] In fact, he went on to argue "unless these departments be so far connected and blended, as to give to each a constitutional control over the others, the degree of separation which the maxim requires, as essential to a free government, can never in practice be duly maintained."[3]

Following this theory, the Constitution vested the executive power in the President but gave to Congress certain specific functions, including authority to provide for executive departments and their officers, to advise and consent to (or reject) the President's nominations to the principal offices, and to provide the funds for the departments to spend. From these rights, and from the implied right of inquiry in connection with the exercise of its substantive legislative power, Congress has developed a complex variety of controls on the Executive branch. Controversy over the evolution and exercise of those controls has been, and remains today, one of the principal manifestations of the broader rivalry for political supremacy between Congress and the President that was built into the Constitution.

Congress, having no direct responsibility for administration and being institutionally jealous of the President's increasing influence in legislation and national policy-making generally, has usually sought to extend and tighten its controls over administrative activity. Most congressmen see nothing improper or unconstitutional about forms of control that involve review of administrative action in great detail, or that enable the Senate and the House or their committees—or sometimes even individual members—to influence quite specific executive decisions. But the President and other executive officials acting in his shadow have resisted what they have regarded as improper legislative encroachments on executive functions, basing their arguments both on practical administrative necessity and on constitutional doctrine: the President, too, takes his powers directly from the Constitution and (with the eclipse of the Electoral College as an

---

[1] *The Federalist*, No. 47 (Max Beloff, ed., 1948), p. 246.
[2] *Ibid.*, p. 247. (The italics are Madison's.)
[3] *Ibid.*, No. 48, p. 252.

autonomous body) is directly elected by the whole people. Thus legislative control of administration is one of the checks and balances of a constitutional system deliberately designed to produce legislative-executive compromise, but also conflict—and, according to Madison, to protect our liberties.

It is at first glance paradoxical but on reflection quite understandable that in Great Britain, where the chief executive is not constitutionally independent but is politically responsible to the legislature, control of administration in modern times has not been a subject of controversy as in the United States. In fact, Congress and the British Parliament represent opposite extremes: Congress exercises the greatest degree of direction and control of administration found in any major democratic country, while Parliament exercises the least. Nevertheless, Parliament has the most effective arrangements of any legislative body for holding executive officers responsible for the policies and administration of the departments. Control of the executive in Great Britain is grounded on the principle of ministerial responsibility. Parliament grants maximum latitude and discretion to executive officers, and does not attempt to dictate their day-to-day decisions, for to do so would destroy the responsibility of the Prime Minister and the other ministers who head the departments. Being politically one, the parliamentary majority and the government of the day are not impelled to the sort of conflict over the details of administration that arises in the United States, where Congress and the President are constitutionally independent and represent differently composed constituencies.

Why the British political system works as it does is a very subtle matter, but without attempting to distinguish cause and effect it can be said that the high degree of unity and discipline that prevails within the majority party in Parliament is essential to an explanation of the scheme of legislative control of administration—and, for that matter, to almost everything else about British politics. The parliamentary majority has elected the party leader who becomes Prime Minister and has acquiesced in his choice of the ministers who comprise the Cabinet and head the major executive departments. If the parliamentary majority is dissatisfied with the conduct of the government, it has various ways of letting the Prime Minister and the Cabinet know, which may lead to changes of policy, to changes of ministers, or in extreme cases to a new party leader and Prime Minister. But such changes are worked out within the framework of a party that stands or falls together.

The political career of the individual member of Parliament depends in large measure on the success of his party and on his own service to the party leadership. If he is of the majority party he wants enough legislative checks on what the executive departments are doing to be sure that trouble is not arising which might lead to loss of public favor and an eventual party overturn. But as long as his party is in, he is motivated to stand firm with other party members to defend its conduct of the government against partisan criticism or meddling by the opposition, and to support the ministers against any legislative encroachment on their authority as department heads. The Cabinet members—who are also powerful party leaders and have come up through and still hold seats in Parliament—demand this kind of support, and it is in the member's interest to provide it. Neither committees nor individual members are permitted to participate in or exercise influence over specific executive actions. Although there are parliamentary committees for the oversight of administration, there are no standing legislative committees exerting influence comparable to that exercised by committees of the U. S. Congress.

In contrast to the high degree of party unity in Britain is the low degree of party cohesion in the United States. Members of Congress owe their political lives and primary allegiance to their own state constituencies. Although congressmen wear Democratic and Republican labels and may vote with their fellow partisans most of the time, both parties include men of widely differing points of view and there is likely to be much crossing of party lines on any given issue. Individual members can be and frequently are indifferent or hostile to the national party organization, to a President of their own party, and even to their own legislative leaders. Leaders of the President's party in Congress ordinarily make some effort to rally support for the President and protect an appropriate amount of executive discretion in the conduct of the government. Legislative controls and investigations tend to wane when the President and the congressional majority are of the same party, and to wax when one or both houses of Congress are in the hands of the President's opposition.

However, the President's legislative leaders often support executive discretion with no great enthusiasm, and neither they nor the President have strong disciplinary measures at their disposal. Party cohesion is insufficient to overcome the vagaries of individual members, dissident factions, and congenital suspicion of the executive power. Members of the President's party often join with the opposition in criticizing the operations of the executive departments, for either good or bad reasons, and feel no hestitation whatsoever in trying to extend and tighten legislative controls on administration. Along with low party cohesion go traditional Senate and House rules of internal procedure which put great power in the hands of the chairmen and senior members of the standing committees, who achieve their posts, not by service to the party, but strictly by seniority. Those who have risen to positions of leadership in these committees usually favor controls on the executive which are effective in detail, enabling Congress or the committees to pass on specific executive decisions and enhancing their personal influence over the decisions.

The factors of perennial legislative-executive rivalry, low party cohesion, and limited control by Congress of its own committees permit legislative control of administration to be used as a strategy in the continuous struggle among political, economic, regional, and personal-interest groups for power and legislative achievement. When interests associated with the President propose new governmental programs, the opponents often assert that this would amount to giving a "blank check" to the administration, and summon the legislature to do its duty and block this dangerous extension of executive power. If opponents cannot stop such legislation, they try to write in provisions for legislative checks which they hope will limit its impact. Supporters of new ventures, however, discount predictions of executive tyranny and seek legislation allowing ample executive discretion, in the interest of vigorous and effective implementation of the program. Having failed to block its adoption, opponents of a program often can work with a like-minded committee chairman and press for investigations and restrictions designed to hamper its administration. The reverse of all this occurs when supporters of a program are strong in Congress but have reason to doubt the President or department head's enthusiasm. In such cases they may seek, sometimes in connivance with subordinate executive officials, to insert detailed legislative mandates intended to allow little room for executive modification or maneuver.

Types and Trends

Congress exercises control over administration in a variety of ways, formal and informal. The predominant formal means of control is by the passage of statutes which create executive departments and agencies and sometimes prescribe their form of organization; provide for their principal officers; authorize their programs and activities; prescribe their objectives and major policies; regulate their personnel; prescribe certain of their procedures and methods of work; impose limitations and restrictions on their activities; and appropriate funds for them to spend. The appropriation process is perhaps the most important single control over the departments.

Control is also exercised through investigations of administration conducted by the standing and select committees of Congress. Such investigations have been conducted since the early days of the Republic, but with increasing frequency in recent times. Under the Legislative Reorganization Act of 1946, every standing legislative committee is authorized and directed to exercise continuous oversight of the executive agencies and programs within its jurisdiction. The Senate exercises a special control over the Executive branch through its power to advise and consent to the President's nominations to high federal offices. In recent years a new form of control, commonly known as the "legislative veto," has arisen. In this form Congress passes a statute authorizing the Executive to do or to propose certain things, but requires that the consequent decisions or plans under the statute be laid before Congress before they go into effect; the plans then must be approved or, within a certain period, disapproved by the two houses, by a single house, or by a designated standing committee.

Informal legislative controls are exercised by committees and individual members through their consultations with executive officers, and may take the form of suggestions, advice, inspections, oral commitments, and instructions. The questions asked and opinions expressed by members of legislative committees during hearings have important effects on administrative action. Statements of legislative intent in committee reports on proposed legislation are treated by the departments as having almost the force of law. Behind the informal controls lies the sanction of formal controls through investigations, restrictive statutes, or reduced appropriations. Informal controls are more pervasive than the formal types and, because they are not subject to review and approval or disapproval by the whole Congress, are more subject to abuse by legislators seeking to advance personal or provincial interests.

A distinction is sometimes made between legislative "control" and legislative "oversight" of administration. "Control" in the narrow sense refers to legislative decisions or activities prior to the relevant administrative action. Thus it includes legislative determinations about departmental policies and activities, examination of proposed executive actions in view of a possible legislative veto, and the issuance of authoritative instructions to guide executive officers in the performance of assigned functions. Such controls are expressed in provisions of statutes or appropriation acts, in committee reports, and in various informal ways. "Oversight," strictly speaking, refers to review after the fact. It includes inquiries about policies that are or have been in effect, investigations of past administrative actions, and the calling of executive officers to account for their financial transactions.

In Great Britain, legislative checks on the executive mainly occur in forms classified as oversight. Principal among them are the question hour in the House of Commons, when ministers are required to respond to members' inquiries about activities of the departments, and the review of department expenditures by the standing Public Accounts Committee assisted by the Comptroller and Auditor General, a legislative officer. As indicated above, the United States Congress has ways of touching administration both before and after the fact, and the two forms are commonly lumped under the heading of "legislative control." In describing United States practice in this book we shall take advantage of the prevailing loose usage, although when we speak specifically of "oversight" it will mean examination of existing policy or completed actions.

Congressional control of the executive departments has substantially increased in extent and importance in recent years, and has taken new forms as well. These developments have been due in part to the great increase and expansion of federal government activities. On the one hand, the new activities have required unprecedented kinds of government operations and greater delegations of authority and discretion to the administrative establishment; on the other hand, Congress has been extremely concerned that control of the government was slipping away from it, and has sought new means of keeping a finger on those activities it regards as the most sensitive politically. Thus Congress tends to be no longer content to exercise control by prescribing statutory guides or standards of administrative action, but has looked for further ways to participate in, if not control, particular executive decisions, through such devices as the legislative veto. Another reason for the increase in congressional influence on administration is that Congress is becoming far better equipped to exercise control. Since the Legislative Reorganization Act of 1946, Congress has greatly increased and strengthened its staff and improved its committee organization. Investigations by the committees have become more frequent, and staff aid has enabled both committees and individual members to become informed on the details of administrative matters and exert influence in various formal and informal ways.

These trends have created new problems in legislative-executive relations. They raise anew the issues of what is the proper role of Congress, and what methods it shall use in exercising control and oversight. Many students—including the author of this book—have felt that Congress, although overlooking some possibilities for exercising salutary types of check on executive action, has in the main extended its activities in ways that threaten to defeat its own ends by involving itself in excessive detail, limiting executive discretion unduly, and interfering inappropriately in specific administrative decisions. Some have gone so far as to assert that unprecedented uses of congressional power are threatening to upset the constitutional balance of powers and could bring about a fundamental change in our system of government.[4] The problem today is not how congressional

[4] It is interesting that James Madison, in the exposition already referred to, argued that in the sort of constitution being set up the principal danger of upsetting the balance of powers would be from legislative aggrandizement: "But in a representative republic, where the executive magistracy is carefully limited, both in the extent and the duration of its power; and where the legislative power is exercised by an assembly, which is inspired by a supposed influence over the

control of the Executive branch may be increased, but rather how Congress may exercise appropriate kinds of authority and influence without impeding administration or weakening executive authority.

Criteria for Evaluating Controls

By what criteria may we judge the suitability, effectiveness, and wisdom of various types of congressional control of administration? It may not be easy to establish criteria on which all would agree, particularly those who are most closely involved. Although most executive officers recognize in principle the essential role of the legislature and cheerfully accept some limitations on their own discretion, their natural tendency is to minimize the need for detailed control; and some officials frankly regard all legislative control as a necessary evil, to be avoided or circumvented whenever possible. Legislators, on the other hand, commonly look on control of administration as a legislative prerogative, to be extended whenever feasible; they regard themselves as guardians of the public's freedom and are not inclined to see constitutional problems in extending their control of administrative detail. Those who have risen to positions of leadership in Congress are especially likely to take this view, and to evaluate any form of control by the extent to which it enables Congress or its committees to control particular executive decisions.

In considering the several kinds of control which will be discussed in subsequent chapters, seven criteria or tests are suggested.

1. The test of constitutionality may be applied by asking this question: Is the kind of control being considered authorized or implied in the Constitution, and is it in conformity with the basic division of powers between the two branches? The debates in the Constitutional Convention of 1787 show that the founders considered and rejected various proposals that would have established a parliamentary

people, with an intrepid confidence in its own strength; which is sufficiently numerous to feel all the passions which actuate a multitude, yet not so numerous as to be incapable of pursuing the objects of its passions, by means which reason prescribes; it is against the enterprising ambition of this department, that the people ought to indulge all their jealousy and exhaust all their precautions." See *Ibid.*, p. 253. *Cf.* Walter Lippmann, *Essays in the Public Philosophy* (1955), especially Chaps. 3 and 5.

system, with the Executive branch subordinate to Congress. Instead, a distinction was made between the framing of laws, which was assigned to Congress, and the execution of laws, which was placed under the President. Although the founders intended that Congress have certain authority to check the Executive, they were fully aware of the tendency of legislative bodies to encroach on executive authority and sought to establish safeguards. The manner in which Congress should exercise its powers was carefully prescribed in the constitutional document. Congress was to act through the enactment of statutes. Exceptions, such as the Senate's participation in appointments and its approval of treaties, were specifically provided for. The veto power was granted to the President primarily as a shield to protect his office against legislative encroachment. For the first 140 years of the Republic, Congress in general exercised control over the departments in a manner clearly sanctioned by the Constitution, that is, through statutes, appropriations, and investigations of administration. Recently it has adopted other methods, including devices to circumvent the President's veto, which raise serious questions of constitutionality.

2. Do the controls provide Congress with the information it needs to discharge its basic responsibilities? Congress must know if its legislative policies are being faithfully, competently, and economically carried out, and if they are having the desired effects. If they are not, Congress may wish to enact new legislation or take other steps, as in voting appropriations, to correct shortcomings.

3. Are the legislative controls effective in bringing to light administrative abuses or arbitrary actions that have occurred in the past, and in preventing them in the future?

4. Do the controls operate in a way that allows executive officers the discretion and flexibility they need if they are to administer government activities effectively and be held responsible for results?

5. Do the controls, as applied in specific cases, reflect the policies and wishes of Congress as a body rather than the wishes of a small segment of Congress? Control by standing committees or committee chairmen is not the same thing as control by Congress itself. As will be seen in the following chapters, certain controls are often utilized to advance personal, local, and provincial interests without regard to the national interest.

6. Do the controls tend to strengthen and enforce the internal disciplines of the Executive branch, or do they duplicate and weaken them? Legislative control is not a substitute for firm direction and supervision by the President and the principal executive officers responsible to him. Congress should seek to ascertain that the internal management controls exercised by the department heads and the central agencies of the President are adequate, yet not overly restrictive on subordinate officials.

7. Finally, is a specific control a suitable one to be exercised by a legislative body? There are some kinds of decisions, principally those relating to major public policies, which a legislature is ideally qualified to make—and must make—in a democratic government. But there are certain other types of decisions for which legislative action is unsuitable. A large proportion of governmental decisions are of the kind that can be made wisely and within an effective time span only by officers who have appropriate information, expertness, and experience. Executive officers are supposed to have these qualifications, and it is highly appropriate for Congress to make sure that they do, since Congress and its committees do not have the requisite knowledge—and, even if they did have it, are not organized to put it into action.

A classic example of a legislative body that went beyond its competence was the joint committee of Congress on the conduct of the Civil War, which interfered to the serious detriment of the Union cause (see Chapter 9). More commonplace examples of the kind of decisions legislatures are not qualified to make include the design of work methods and procedures, the planning and programming of specific activities, internal organization of administrative units, the location of field offices, and day-to-day operation problems. Legislative controls that seek to influence or determine decisions on such matters are very likely to be influenced by personal and provincial considerations of individual members and tend to deprive executive officers of the authority and discretion they must have if they are to be held responsible for results.

WITH THESE CRITERIA IN MIND, we shall examine several types of congressional control. Chapter 2 is devoted to a discussion of the types and patterns of statutory control that Congress customarily utilizes, with observations concerning the effects of those controls and their impact on administration. Control of the purse, which has become of equal (if not greater) importance to control through statutes, occupies Chapters 3, 4, and 5. Subsequent chapters deal with the audit of financial transactions, the legislative veto and committee control, regulation of the civil service, and the use of investigations.

Competent, effective, and responsible administration of the programs of the federal government was never so important as it is today. The United States cannot meet its responsibilities for leadership in world affairs and cope with increasingly complex domestic problems unless it is assured of strong, able administration. The primary concern of Congress is, or should be, to secure effective administration of its legislative policies, to hold executive officers accountable, and to correct mismanagement and abuse of authority. Properly devised and applied, legislative controls can do much to secure these ends, but controls are not ends in themselves.

2

Control of Executive Organization and Activities

SINCE THE BEGINNING of the Republic, except in wartime and other periods of crisis, all administrative departments and agencies have been created, and their objectives and policies authorized, by statute. In many cases detailed statutes have also prescribed their internal structure, activities, and methods of work. The power to determine the executive organization is nowhere expressly allotted to Congress by the Constitution but is implied in the general enablement of the last clause of Article I, Section 8:

> To make all Laws which shall be necessary and proper for carrying into Execution the foregoing Powers, and all other Powers vested by this Constitution in the Government of the United States, or in any Department or Officer thereof.

Zealously guarding the authority so implied, Congress has always been reluctant to delegate it to the President or to the heads of departments.

The statutes through which Congress over the years has regulated the ever enlarging administrative establishment amount by now to a vast accumulation. Summary of them here would not only be impossible but in fact not serve the purpose of this study. In this chapter we shall be concerned, then, with the emerging pattern of statutory determination of administration and with typical provisions that illustrate the scope, character, and impact of congressional control.[1]

---

[1] Legislative control of the Executive by statutes is discussed by John D. Millett, *Government and Public Administration* (1939), Chaps. 4-7, and Charles S. Hyneman, *Bureaucracy in a Democracy* (1950), Chaps. 2, 6, 8.

The Pattern Begins to Form

On May 19, 1789, the House of Representatives of the First Congress began deliberation and debate on the establishment of executive departments for the new government; on May 21 an eleven-member committee was appointed to prepare organization bills.[2] Although the Constitution's only mention of such agencies was the vaguely worded assumption that there would be a principal officer "in each department," both House and Senate appeared to be in agreement with President Washington on the urgency of creating an administrative structure to assist him in going about the business of government. There is little doubt that the identity of the President made the task more readily acceptable. As Alexander Hamilton had remarked soon after the Constitutional Convention adjourned in September 1787, the probability that George Washington would be elected President if the Constitution was ratified would "insure a wise choice of men to administer the government and a good administration. A good administration will conciliate the confidence and affection of the people and perhaps enable the government to acquire more consistency than the proposed constitution seems to promise for so great a country."[3]

All concerned seemed also to be agreed that the departments which had existed under the Articles of Confederation should be continued. Nevertheless, long and involved debate ensued before the first department was created by law late in July. In a very real sense, as Charles C. Thach has pointed out, the first session of Congress was an extension of the Constitutional Convention.[4] Eighteen of the newly elected congressmen had been members of the Convention —notably among them James Madison—and a majority of the others had served on state ratifying conventions. Further, to make a start

[2] *Annals of Congress,* Vol. 1, p. 412.

[3] H. B. Learned, *The President's Cabinet* (1912), p. 110. The influence of Washington on the Convention debates was mentioned by Pierce Butler in a letter to England on May 5, 1788: "Entre nous, I do [not] believe . . . [the executive powers] would have been so great had not many of the members cast their eyes toward General Washington as President; and shaped their Ideas of the Powers to be given a President, by their opinions of his Virtue."

[4] Thach, *The Creation of the Presidency, 1775-1789* (1922), pp. 141-142.

on the job of transforming a documentary government into a government in fact, these men and the other members of the First Congress were unavoidably faced with examining those numerous implications of the Constitution that needed clarification.

Thus the debate that revolved around presidential power in relation to the tenure of department heads—a point on which the Constitution was silent—illuminated many facets of the doctrine of separation of powers and was important for all time. Specifically—did the power to remove executive officers rest in the President alone, or was he to exercise it "by and with the advice of the Senate"?

The struggle was prolonged, but when the House finally sent the organization bill for the Department of Foreign Affairs to the Senate several vital issues had been given clear interpretation. The President's power to remove his appointees was seen as part of the explicit executive power granted him by the Constitution and should therefore not be granted or qualified by legislation that would interfere with his direct responsibility to the people for his administrative assistants. By implication, the Senate was debarred from assuming the status of an executive council. To make the implication explicit, Section 2 of the bill was deliberately phrased to avoid any suggestion that the removal power was a legislative grant.[5] The President alone was to be the head of the administrative departments, which were construed as agencies subject to his choice and direction.

> Congress would indicate the field of the secretary's activities, but it would not go further. In the vivid phrase of Representative Sedgewick, the officer was to be "as much an instrument in the hands of the President, as the pen is the instrument of the Secretary in corresponding with foreign courts."[6]

The Senate, after discussion that left no doubt that it knew what the implications of the removal issue were, voted for the House bill as it stood. On July 27, 1789, the Department of Foreign Affairs was established by law.

Successive acts organized the War (and Navy) Department

[5] *Annals of Congress*, Vol. 1, p. 525; also see 1 Stat. 28-29.
[6] Thach, *op. cit.*, p. 161. The debate throughout was specifically on the Foreign Affairs Bill, but the principles advanced were clearly applicable to other departments and to executive organization in general. For further accounts of the debate see Leonard D. White, *The Federalists* (1948), pp. 20-25; Joseph P. Harris, *The Advice and Consent of the Senate* (1953), pp. 30-33.

(August 7) and the Treasury Department (September 2). A bill for a department of "Home" or "Domestic" affairs failed of passage, as a result of which Congress redesignated the Department of Foreign Affairs as the Department of State and assigned home affairs to its jurisdiction. The Office of Postmaster General was temporarily established as a branch of the Treasury (September 22), with the officer to be subject to the direction of the President. On September 24 the Judiciary bill, on which the Senate had started work early in April, became law, making provision for the Supreme Court and thirteen district and three circuit courts; its last section included a very brief provision for an Attorney General, who was to be federal prosecutor and legal adviser to the President and the department secretaries.

The statutes for the three departments all contained identical provisions respecting the removal power, but differed from each other in several other respects. The Foreign Affairs and War departments were termed "executive," Treasury was not; however, in the title of the act of September 11 that provided salaries, the three secretaries were all termed "Executive Officers of government." The duties and powers of the Secretary of Foreign Affairs and of the Secretary of War were left to the discretion of the President; the duties of the Treasury Secretary were defined in detail and circumscribed, since the department was created to carry out the money enactments of Congress, and, although the Secretary was responsible to the President, he was specifically required to report to Congress. This Janus-faced organization was destined to make the Treasury the center of stormy arguments—was it or was it not an "executive department" —and through the years there were a number of attempts to amend the Constitution so that Congress might choose the Secretary.

The President sent his nominations for the three Secretaries, the Attorney General, and the Postmaster General to the Senate at various times in September, and all were quickly confirmed. The foundations of the executive establishment had thus been laid. From the beginning Washington considered Hamilton, Knox, Jefferson, and Randolph his assistants, consulting them often, but it was not until 1792 that what would later be called Cabinet meetings were held with anything like regularity. Meanwhile, the relationships between the secretaries and Congress seemed to reflect exigencies of the moment and individual personality traits more than an intent on either side to set precedents. Shortly after the second session of Congress convened, however, there was a glimpse of a new pattern.

When Hamilton, who had for some time been assuming a posture in the government not unlike a Premier's, informed the House that he was ready to report on the financial program Congress had instructed him to prepare, it was obvious that he expected to make the presentation in person. The House decreed that he should submit a written report. In so doing, although at the time perhaps without such specific intent, it was taking a further step toward rejecting the British concept of ministerial participation in legislation. The decision was also an early indication of the preference of Congress for its own internal leadership—a preference that would soon become a trademark of congressional procedure, to be guarded jealously whenever threatened by interference from without.

For the time being, however, Congress was in general willing— even eager, according to contemporary accounts—to take advice from the brilliant Secretary of the Treasury and others in the administration. President Washington continued to be the balance wheel, and the more troublesome aspects of the constitutional system of checks and balances were only dimly revealed, although the political factionalism which would later highlight the trouble spots was rapidly taking shape. This was a period of feeling the way—the learning period for all new roles. It was also a time when innovations that worked assumed very quickly the aspect of custom, and a time that provided a remarkable demonstration of the truism that society is governed not by law as abstraction, but by laws interpreted and applied by men. The development of the unwritten Constitution had begun.[7]

Authorization of Government Programs

One of the basic principles of the constitutional system had been confirmed in the establishment of the first departments: executive agencies have only those powers granted to them by law, and hence can carry out only the programs authorized by Congress. Such au-

[7] For a detailed account of this period, see James Hart, *The American Presidency in Action, 1789* (1948), especially Chap. 7.

thority may be granted in broad terms, or in detailed provisions that in some degree circumscribe agency activities and limit the discretion of the officers in charge.

The statutes of 1789 that authorized the first three departments, the Attorney General's duties, and the Post Office establishment were simply worded and brief. Subsequent legislation tended to be much more detailed; throughout the years, however, the pattern of such statutes has varied widely between very broad authorizations and those that are highly specific. But in general the increasing complexity and length of the statutes which have ordained and governed the operations of the executive agencies during the past century seem to indicate that Congress has avoided broad general grants of authority whenever it was feasible to do so. It is also true that this statutory trend is in large part attributable to the vast increase in the size, activities, and complexity of the federal government over the same period.

Whatever the reason, the intricacy and lengthy detail of modern legislation are undeniable. Regulations for the armed services occupy four volumes of the *United States Code, Annotated*, that total approximately 2,500 pages, and there are additional volumes on the National Guard and Pay and Allowances. The volume dealing with the work of the Department of Agriculture has 940 pages; one of its chapters deals with insect pests, another with the golden nematode. The Federal Aviation Act of 1958, which created the Federal Aviation Agency to regulate airspace and the movement of planes and codified the body of federal statutes regulating commercial and private aviation, is 81 pages long—totaling approximately 50,000 words.

The typical bureau operates under perhaps a dozen statutory authorizations of specific programs and activities. The wording of the statutes and the interpretations of them determine in large measure the policies, the range of activities, and often the methods to be followed. It is the view of some observers of the federal scene that the bureau whose activities are prescribed in detail is likely to regard its function as the limited one of administering only the specific prescriptions, while the bureau with a broad grant of authority has greater latitude in the formulation of programs to carry out the objectives of the legislation.

The breadth of grants of authority, as well as the substance or re-

ality of the powers conveyed, vary with a number of factors, such as the current state of legislative-executive relations, the traditional policies of the committee handling the legislation, the standing of the executive agency with its legislative committee, the field in which action is to be taken, and the degree of consensus upon the action needed. Without considering the circumstances, it is difficult to predict whether a grant will be general in terms or carefully prescribed, substantial in power or weak, clear or vague. In general, it can be said that Congress tends to be cautious in conveying authority to the administrative agencies, and ordinarily legislates in considerable detail concerning the objectives, policies, and content of authorized programs, but the authority granted actually varies from time to time, from agency to agency, and from one section to another of the same law.

Congress is continually faced with the necessity of steering a middle course between excessively detailed legislation that hampers efficient administration, and broad legislation that fails to enunciate legislative policies and objectives and thereby places important policy decisions in the hands of executive officers. Wide discretion is usually granted to the executive officers in charge if a program is urgent and requires vigorous administration, if it is strongly supported and has achieved a high degree of consensus, or if the officers have the confidence of Congress. In the case of a new activity, such as the atomic energy program in 1946 or the space exploration program in 1958, Congress may not have sufficient information to legislate in detail, but may later enact more detailed legislation on the basis of accumulated experience. At times Congress is unable to reach an agreement on important policy issues when new activities are being authorized and for this reason may delegate the determination, at least initially, to executive officers.

The issue of broad or detailed authorization does not always signify a struggle between the Congress and the Executive branch for control. Members of Congress who advocate considerable administrative discretion for programs they are personally sponsoring must often fight the narrow authorizations favored by other members who oppose the programs and hope by such means to impede them. Further, bureau chiefs sometimes welcome detailed prescription for the policies and programs they administer, since such legislation reduces

the supervision exercised by the department head and by the President. The Comptroller General, who is at times consulted, almost invariably favors restrictive statutory provisions, which may be strongly opposed by Administration spokesmen.

Determination of Internal Structure

Under the empowerment to "make all Laws which shall be necessary and proper for carrying into Execution . . . all other powers vested . . . in any Department or Officer," Congress can, if it desires, prescribe the internal organization of departments and agencies in the most minute detail. To do so, however, would be neither practicable nor wise. Considerable discretion is usually accorded to most department and agency heads, especially in adapting organization to keep it current with changing tasks, needs, and problems. Nevertheless, it is Congress that decides where the dividing line between statutory prescription and executive discretion lies.

In applying the dividing line Congress seems to have followed no uniform rule. Of the 124 bureaus and other major operating units within the executive departments of Cabinet rank in 1960 (not including such staff units as accounting, personnel, etc.), 68 had been provided by statute, 56 by executive action; the bureaus of the regulatory commissions and other so-called independent agencies had practically all been established by agency heads. The longevity of a department is apparently not a criterion: Secretaries of State and Postmasters General, for instance, have traditionally determined much of the inner organization of their departments, while the bureaus within the Treasury and Navy departments have usually been prescribed by statute; of the 13 bureaus in the Department of Agriculture, only 4 have been created by law.[8]

When Congress writes bureaus within a department into law, it does so, as a rule, to accomplish a specific legislative policy. In 1952, for instance, Congress departed from its traditional practice for the State Department and created the Bureau of Security and Consular Affairs, in which it placed the Passport and Visa offices. The provision (included in the Immigration and Nationality Bill of 1952,

[8] The statistics have been compiled by the author from an examination of the *U. S. Government Organization Manual* and the *U. S. Code*.

which was subsequently vetoed by President Truman) was intended to bring passport and visa activities more closely under the control and protection of certain congressional committees, which at the time were dominated by members not in accord with the Administration. The head of the new bureau was directed by the statute to "maintain close liaison with the appropriate committees of Congress in order that they may be advised of the administration of the Act by consular officers."

The principal officers of departments are customarily provided for by statute. In the 1789 organization acts, the positions of Secretary and of Chief Clerk were prescribed for the departments of State and War; for the Treasury Department, those of Secretary, Assistant Secretary, Comptroller, Auditor, Treasurer, and Registrar. Other variously titled top offices have from time to time been created—Under Secretary, Deputy Under Secretary, Assistant to the Secretary, Special Assistant to the Secretary, and the like; occasionally their powers and duties have been stipulated by law.

In some instances such newly created positions are a part of executive reorganization plans. Following the recommendation of the first Hoover Commission in 1949, the office of Assistant Secretary for Administration was established by executive reorganization plans in the departments of Treasury, Commerce, Agriculture, Justice, and, in 1953, in the Health, Education, and Welfare Department.

Statutes creating top executive positions in the departments are usually requested by the departments concerned, but in some cases are a response to pressure from outside organizations. The Office of Special Assistant for Health and Medical Affairs in the Department of Health, Education, and Welfare was created in 1953 to give recognition to the importance of public health activities in the new department and to placate organizations that had pressed for a separate public health department.[9] To satisfy demands of commercial fishing and sportsmen groups, the Fish and Wildlife Act of 1956 provided Interior with both an Assistant Secretary for Fish and Wildlife, which the department said it did not need, and a Commissioner to head the Fish and Wildlife Service, thus placing two intermediary officials between the Secretary and the bureau chiefs.[10]

Besides the numerous and variously titled sub-secretaryships,

[9] 67 Stat. 18.
[10] See House Report No. 2519, 84th Cong., 2d sess. (1956), p. 5.

many other departmental positions have been written into law. A glance through a *U. S. Government Organization Manual* of any recent year reveals a bewildering array of titles such as Comptroller, General Counsel, Commissioner, Director, and Chief, Vice Chief, and Deputy Chief for various bureaus, Budget Officer, Administrator— and, often, assistants and/or deputies for each office. The Navy Department may be cited as an outstanding example of statutory prescription of internal department organization. Chapters 501-515 of the *U. S. Code* establish and prescribe the duties of no less than 44 top Navy executive officers, plus an indeterminate number of assistant bureau chiefs. The officers range from the Secretary to the heads and assistant heads of bureaus and the heads of some divisions. It is unnecessary to point out that such a high degree of statutory prescription of the top organization of the department seriously curtails the discretion of the Secretary.

The point has been increasingly made in recent years that Congress, in making excessive use of its power to prescribe the internal organization of departments by placing bureaus and many of the principal officers on a "statutory pedestal" (Woodrow Wilson's term), is moving counter to sound principles of administration. If an executive head is to be held responsible for the operation of a department's program, he must be permitted reasonable discretion to determine the organization of its bureaus and other line and staff units and the assignment of their activities; this is an essential element of dynamic executive management. Especially should he have freedom to make changes as needed from time to time to promote better planning, coordination, and efficiency.

In 1949 the first Hoover Commission recommended that "each department head should receive from Congress administrative authority to organize his department and to place him in control of its administration."[11] Nine years later Senator Stuart Symington, during the debate on the President's reorganization plan for the Defense Department, put the same view directly before the Senate:

> We can, if we choose, put the Department of Defense in a strait-jacket by prescribing every meticulous detail of how the Armed Forces shall be composed, organized, and led. . . . The mere fact

[11] The Commission on Organization of the Executive Branch of the Government, *Management of the Executive Branch* (1949), p. 37.

that the bill is presented to us by the White House concedes the power.

The question before us in the bill is not whether we have the power. The question is how far it will serve the interests of the country for us to exercise it by restricting the flexibility of action of the Department of Defense in adapting our forces to the rapidly changing conditions of our time.

This is an issue of statesmanship, of restraint in the exercise of undoubted power.[12]

Each of the several other administrative plans that had been presented since 1945 to reorganize and unify the armed services in accord with the imperative demands of modern warfare had struggled against the same legislative straitjacket and in the main been frustrated by it. The story of the 1958 reorganization bill and its background is reviewed below, because it constitutes a graphic case study of the issue of statutory prescription versus executive discretion.

The Defense Reorganization Act of 1958

World War II demonstrated the imperative need for unified military operations in modern warfare. Proposals were put forward at the end of the war for a unification of the three armed services, but these were resisted by the historic services. Finally in 1947, with the strong support of President Truman, a partial unification was effected by an act creating the National Military Establishment, headed by a Secretary of Defense. The unification, however, was more in name than in fact. Each of the three services continued to operate as formerly, and interservice rivalries continued unabated. In 1949 the powers of the Secretary were increased slightly and the overhead department was designated the Department of Defense.

Further steps taken in 1953 after President Eisenhower assumed office were still not sufficient to effect a real unification or achieve the economies and centralized departmental planning that had been hoped for. Critics in Congress blamed the President for this, but the reorganization authority granted to him and the Secretary of Defense was inadequate, largely because Congress had not relinquished its prescriptive control over the combat missions and the internal or-

[12] *Congressional Record*, Vol. 104, Pt. 11, 85th Cong., 2d sess. (July 18, 1958), p. 14259.

ganization of the three services. Moreover, the concept of each of the services as an operational entity still had strong congressional support, especially from the Armed Services Committees.

By 1958 the increasing emphasis on weaponry research and development and the successful launching of missiles and satellites had pushed farther into obsolescence the very basis on which the three services had been formed. In a special message to Congress on April 13, 1958, President Eisenhower spelled out the imperative need for unification:

> . . . Separate ground, sea, and air warfare is gone forever. If ever again we should be involved in war, we will fight it in all elements, with all services, as one single concentrated effort. Peacetime preparatory and organizational activity must conform to this fact. Strategic and tactical planning must be completely unified, combat forces organized into unified commands, each equipped with the most efficient weapons system that science can develop, singly led and prepared to fight as one, regardless of service. . . . I cannot overemphasize my conviction that our country's security requirements must not be subordinated to outmoded or single-service concepts of war.[13]

He also urged the repeal of "statutory barriers that weaken executive action," and stressed that "we must free ourselves of emotional attachments to service systems of an era that is no more."

The recommendations for reorganization, which had been agreed to by the Secretary of each of the three services and by the Joint Chiefs of Staff, were sweeping. As outlined in the message and sent more formally to Congress shortly afterwards, the plan included proposals that would:

1. Strengthen the authority of the Secretary of Defense by giving him powers to reorganize the services, reassign combatant missions, and transfer funds between the services.

2. Organize the combatant forces into truly unified operational commands under a direct line of control from the Commander in Chief through the Secretary of Defense and the Joint Chiefs of Staff to the operational commanders.

3. Strengthen the staff assigned to the Joint Chiefs by removing the limit of 210 persons, so that the new operational as well as planning functions could be performed.

[13] House Document No. 366, 85th Cong., 2d sess. (1958), p. 4.

4. Retain the three military departments as administrative, training, and supply agencies, with the function of supporting but not directing military operations; repeal the statutory provision that they must be "separately administered."

5. Create a new position of Director of Defense Research and Engineering to have charge of and to coordinate such activities throughout the Defense Department.

Congressional reaction to the plan was in the main sharply critical. The chairman of the House Armed Services Committee, Carl Vinson of Georgia, announced that Congress would not give the President a "blank check." Even the President's staunchest supporters said that the plan would have to be "watered down" considerably before Congress would accept it.

Especially strong opposition was roused by the proposal that the Secretary of Defense should have authority to reassign combatant roles and missions and to transfer funds between the services. The funds feature was, in fact, dropped before the administration's draft bill was submitted, but this did not materially lessen resistance to the idea of allowing any agent except Congress to assign combatant missions. Were the Secretary to be so empowered, opponents pointed out, he could, at his pleasure, strip the Marine Corps of its mission—traditionally the focus of congressional concern and very detailed prescription—take away missile development from the Army or naval aviation from the Navy, and indeed virtually abolish any of the services. When Pentagon spokesmen insisted that the department had no intention of making such drastic changes, a member of the House Armed Services Committee declared that Congress "must legislate in the dread that the worst man imaginable might sometime in the future be Secretary of Defense."

Opponents of the President's plan charged that it would make the Secretary a czar—with a 40-billion-dollar blank check—whereupon a group of Republicans supporting the plan countercharged that the only real czar of the military establishment was the chairman of the House Armed Services Committee, Carl Vinson. Opposition and support, however, were by no means on party lines; from both sides of the aisle it was variously charged that the administration bill if passed would downgrade the secretaries of the three services by taking them out of the chain of command and crippling their authority to administer their departments, swallow up the traditional services, create a single chief of staff surrounded by a Prussian type of general staff, and heinously impair the constitutional powers of Congress. On the other hand, Democrat Clarence Cannon, chairman of the House Appropriations Committee, came out for the administration bill, saying, "It is high time we put an end to this insane bickering between the services and eliminate billions of wastage, and begin to develop sufficient military strength to keep us out of war." And Republican Kenneth Keating of New York admonished fellow members thus: "The real question . . . is simply whether we can sufficiently modernize our defenses to meet the challenges . . . not which Member will see his pet branch top dog."[14]

The bill reported by the House Armed Services Committee on May 22 (and, which, with a minor exception, was passed by the House on June 12 by a roll call vote of 402-1) included three provisions to which the President strongly objected.

1. That, as a policy, the military functions should be exercised through the respective secretaries of the three services. Eisenhower labeled this "a legalized bottleneck," which would effectively block establishment of the chain of command from the Secretary of Defense and the Joint Chiefs of Staff to the unified combatant forces—a key feature of the President's plan. The provision was dropped in the final conference report.

2. That any suggestion for a change in the missions of the armed services must be laid before Congress for sixty days, if the Secretary of any one of the services or any member of the Joint Chiefs of Staff objected to the change. During this period the change could be set aside by a concurrent resolution of Congress; thus the legislative veto, which previously had been applied to presidential reorganization plans, would be extended to departmental reorganization plans.[15] The President assailed this as an "everyone's out of step but me" measure, which would give one military man, without regard to the views of his colleagues, "the astonishing authority" to hold up defense improvements for many months, and perhaps to block them altogether. The House Armed Services Committee defended the re-

[14] Cannon as quoted in the *New York Times,* May 7, 1958; Keating as quoted in *Congressional Quarterly Weekly Report,* June 13, 1958, p. 767.
[15] Congressional control through the legislative veto is discussed in Chapter 8.

quirement on the ground that it was the "constitutional obligation" of Congress to determine the roles and missions of the several armed services. The Senate bill dropped the provision, but substituted a version of the legislative veto that was much more sweeping. The conference report adopted this version, and thus the act as passed requires that *all* executive reorganization orders transferring functions previously assigned by law shall be laid before Congress and be subject to disapproval, not by concurrent resolution, but by a resolution adopted by either House.

3. That the Secretary of each service or any member of the Joint Chiefs of Staff would be authorized to present to Congress, on his own initiative but after notifying the Secretary of Defense, "any recommendations relating to the Department of Defense that he may deem proper." The President declared that the provision would lead to "legalized insubordination," but Congress refused to withdraw it. In this regard, it was significant that during the Senate hearings the Chief of Naval Operations and the Commandant of the Marine Corps testified in opposition to certain provisions of the administration bill; at one time Senator Russell of Georgia adjourned the hearings until a commitment was made that there would be no reprisals by the department against officers opposing the President's plan.

The final bill as cleared on July 24 for the President's signature, gave the President much of the legislation he had asked for, but considerably watered-down. Congress had retained the important power to pass upon any substantial change in the roles and missions of the services. At the request of the governors of the states, the National Guard Bureau was given status by law and thus removed from the reorganizing power of the Secretary. Other provisions safeguarded against any possible move to curtail or terminate the missions of the Marine Corps and the Naval Air Force. Although the Secretary was given the power—subject to the legislative veto—to consolidate and reassign functions, he was not authorized to abolish bureaus or offices or to create new ones to receive combined activities. (The effect of this was seen in 1959 when legislation was required to create a new Bureau of Weapons in the Navy Department to take over the functions previously exercised by the Bureau of Ordnance and the Bureau of Aeronautics. No one opposed the merger, which was a sensible response to technological change, but the necessity for securing legislation probably delayed it by several years.) The 210-person limit for the staff of the Joint Chiefs was removed, as requested by the President, but a new limit of 400 was imposed, and the members were prohibited from operating as an over-all general staff and from exercising executive authority.

On the whole, little real authority had been delegated to the Secretary to reorganize and further unify his department. The debate over this essential point had, however, been heated. A considerable number of both representatives and senators shared Symington's vigorously stated opinion, among them a member of the House Armed Services Committee who declared that it was "the duty of Congress to set up the over-all defense policy, but . . . we are not qualified to pass on the details of administration," a power that he realized most of the members seemed to be "jealous of and want to retain."

IT IS OF INTEREST to note that in July 1958 Great Britain also was completing a reorganization and streamlining of its armed forces. In January 1957 the Minister of Defence had been asked by the Prime Minister to undertake the task of reshaping the military services, in accordance with strategic needs and the country's economic capacity, and was given authority "to make decisions on matters of general defence policy affecting the size, shape, organization, and equipment of the armed forces." No legislation was required. During the following months various changes were made, especially in the overhead organization. A new post of Chief of Defence Staff was created to serve as chief adviser to the Minister (the establishment of a similar position in the U. S. Defense Department was prohibited by the 1958 Act), and the added authority temporarily granted to the Minister in January 1957 was made permanent.[16] Parliament took no direct part in the reorganization, but the changes made were subject to subsequent vigorous criticism and debate in the House of Commons. Such executive revisions are also always subject, in the unlikely event that the opposition could muster a majority against the government, to being reversed by legislation. The effect of a legislative reversal of the government, of course, would be to vote it out of office, a procedure which is legally possible, but which has not occurred for many years.

[16] New York Times, July 16, 1958.

The British government has the power to revise the executive organization from time to time to meet changed conditions and requirements without the necessity of securing legislative approval, but it must act responsibly. New departments and agencies are customarily created by statute. If the government were to put into effect organizational changes that are strongly opposed in Parliament and the country, it would face a vigorous attack upon such changes by the opposition party in Parliament, as well as by its own backbenchers in party conference.

Creation of New Agencies

When a new program is to be provided for by law, Congress must decide whether it should be administered by an existing department or by a new agency organized expressly for it. Unless a program is closely related to the functions of a department, the tendency has been to favor the creation of a new agency, but there has been considerable variation in the pattern.

Obviously, a new organization is likely to undertake the task with more zeal than an old-line department, even though such difficulties as the initial formation and staffing period must be faced. After a new activity is well established, however, it may be advisable to assign it to one of the departments, so that it may be coordinated with related programs and be brought under more effective executive control. The multiplication of "independent" agencies often results in duplication or overlapping of functions and greatly increases the difficulties of coordination, direction, and control by the President.

When Congress creates a new agency outside of the regular executive departments it must decide upon the form of its organization, particularly whether it is to be headed by a single administrator or a commission. Various factors enter into the decision. If the agency is assigned primarily administrative functions which require a large staff, and especially if vigorous executive leadership is required, as in the Federal Aviation Agency and the National Aeronautics and Space Administration, which were created in 1958, a single administrator is usually provided. If, however, important regulatory, rule-making, or quasi-judicial functions are assigned to an agency, the commission form of organization is usually provided. Although the use of boards and commissions for administration has been generally condemned by authorities in public administration, Congress has not infrequently chosen this form of organization, especially when the new activity involves important policy determinations, as in the Social Security Act of 1935 and the Atomic Energy Act of 1946.[17]

On January 1, 1961, there were fifty-five independent federal agencies outside of the executive departments, not including the Board of Commissioners of the District of Columbia.[18] Of this number, ten agencies which were temporary, advisory, investigative, or relatively unimportant may be omitted from consideration. Of the remaining forty-five, twelve were headed by a single administrator and thirty-three were headed by a board or commission. Several had both a governing board and an administrator, while one or two had an administrator with an advisory board or council. The twelve agencies headed by a single administrator included large operating organizations such as the Veterans Administration, General Services Administration, Federal Aviation Agency, National Aeronautics and Space Administration, and the Housing and Home Finance Agency, as well as agencies with relatively small staffs—e.g., the U. S. Information Agency, Farm Credit Administration, and the Saint Lawrence Seaway Development Corporation.

The agencies headed by commissions included leading regulatory bodies: Interstate Commerce Commission, Federal Power Commission, Federal Communications Commission, Securities and Exchange Commission, Federal Trade Commission, Civil Aeronautics Board, and National Labor Relations Board. A number of other commissions, such as the Indian Claims Commission, Foreign Claims Settlement Commission, Renegotiation Board, and the Subversive Activities Control Board, were concerned with adjudicating claims or with other quasi-judicial activities, and the U. S. Tariff Commission with investigatory duties. Nine agencies could be classified as government corporations, eight of them headed by boards. Several agencies headed by commissions, including the Atomic Energy Commission,

---

[17] One of the most cogent criticisms of the use of commissions for administration was made by Alexander Hamilton, quoted in Leonard D. White, *The Federalists* (1948), p. 91.

[18] See *Organization of Federal Executive Departments and Agencies,* Committee Report No. 21, Senate Committee on Government Operations, 87th Cong., 1st sess. (March 1961), p. 54.

TVA, Civil Service Commission, and the Railroad Retirement Board, had important administrative activities and their staffs ranged in size from 2,177 to 14,855 employees.

The adoption of the commission form of organization is sometimes dictated by political considerations and may be used to gain acceptance of a new program by influential groups. One consideration which doubtless influences the decision of Congress is that commissions are less amenable than a single administrator to presidential direction and, as a rule, more amenable to congressional control. In a few instances the commission form of organization has been abandoned in favor of a single headship—as in the administrations of the social security and farm credit programs. The federal government, it may be noted, has made much less use of administrative boards and commissions than most of the states. In the main, new government activities have been assigned to one of the regular executive departments instead of to independent agencies.

The Regulatory Agencies

The organization and supervision of the independent regulatory commissions, which not only exercise regulatory functions over segments of the economy, but also administer subsidies and provide important services to the regulated industries, present a special problem. Because of their quasi-legislative and quasi-judicial functions, Congress has placed them outside the regular executive departments and thus removed them to some extent from executive supervision, but their promotion and service activities need to be coordinated with other government activities and programs and hence be subject to executive direction.

The contention is sometimes advanced that these commissions are not a part of the Executive branch, but are instead "arms" of Congress. They are, in fact, responsible in varying degrees to both the President and Congress. As President Kennedy stated in a special message to Congress on April 13, 1961, both branches have important responsibilities in the oversight of regulatory commissions. The President's constitutional duty to see that the laws are faithfully executed applies to laws administered by these commissions as well as to laws administered by executive departments. "The relationship of the [regulatory] agencies to the Congress, generally speaking," stated Dean Landis, a former member of two of the regulatory commissions, in a special report to President-Elect Kennedy in 1960, "is that of any statutory branch of the executive to the Congress, with certain exceptions."[19] The President appoints the members of the commissions, subject to confirmation by the Senate, and may remove them for cause as defined by law; he passes upon their budgets, though Congress may revise his estimates; and the legislative proposals of the commissions are customarily cleared through the Bureau of the Budget. The President also makes recommendations to Congress concerning policies and legislation relating to the work of the commissions.

In recent years there has been increasing dissatisfaction both in and out of Congress concerning the activities of these agencies, and the Senate and House have each instituted investigations of them. Criticism has been directed at the decline in their personnel standards, especially since World War II, at their excessive delays, and at their issuance of regulations that hamper the operations of the regulated industries. It has also been charged that the commissions have in some instances come under the domination of the regulated industries and, in other instances, have been improperly influenced by members of Congress and of the President's staff.

Pointing to the "enormous" scope of the agencies' authority and the impact of their activities on the economy, Dean Landis called in his report for a reappraisal of their functions and activities. The report also recommended that the chairmen of the several commissions be given greater responsibility; that the President be equipped with the means to exercise greater supervision over their policies by the appointment of several assistants in the Executive Office of the President to (1) coordinate policies in the fields of transportation, communication, and energy, and (2) create an office for the oversight of regulatory agencies.

President Kennedy did not act on the latter recommendation, but did submit five reorganization plans to Congress in 1961 to strengthen the authority of the chairmen of the regulatory commissions. The plans that applied to the Civil Aeronautics Board and the Federal Trade Commission became effective. The three others were vetoed

[19] *Report on Regulatory Agencies to the President-Elect* (December 1960), p. 33.

by Congress, but legislation to accomplish the same purpose was enacted for the Federal Communications Commission. A similar bill
relating to the Securities and Exchange Commission passed the Senate and was to be acted on by the House at the next session.

The provision of needed executive and legislative controls over
the policies and administration of the regulatory commissions presents serious difficulties. Although Congress has become increasingly
critical of the activities of these agencies in recent years, it has been
unable to exercise effective supervision, yet has been reluctant to increase the supervisory authority of the President. This reluctance
has been due largely to the failure of Congress to recognize that the
two branches each have important responsibilities for the oversight
of these agencies and that their respective controls are complementary rather than antagonistic. The respective roles need to be clari-
fied and mutually agreed upon if the regulatory agencies are to be
effectively supervised.

Prescription of Executive Relationships

The relationships between one agency and another, between officers within an agency, and between the President and any part of
the chain of executive command are an important aspect of the internal structure and organization of the administrative establishment.
Here, too, Congress often exercises control by statutory prescription.
A bureau chief, for example, is sometimes granted specific authorities
independent of the department secretary; similarly, officers of an administrative agency may through various means be given a degree of
independence from presidential supervision. However, the effect intended is not always achieved, as the record shows.

By a rider to the Executive Pay Act of 1956, Congress provided
that members of the Civil Service Commission should serve six
years, with overlapping terms, whereas service previously had been
at the pleasure of the President. The act also reduced the authority
of the Commission chairman, whose office had been closely associated
with the Executive Office of the President. The new provisions were
clearly aimed at making the Commission less subject to presidential

control; nevertheless, it has to date continued to operate as a subordinate agency of the President rather than as an independent body.[20]

A bill of 1959 (S. 144) permitted the Rural Electrification Administrator to approve or disapprove REA loans without being subject to the direction of the Secretary of Agriculture. President Eisenhower vetoed the measure, stating that if enacted it would "mark a major retreat from sound administrative practice and policy . . . no subordinate should have authority independent of that of his superior."[21] There are, however, numerous statutes that do grant such authority to subordinate officers, the effect of which is to weaken the authority and supervision of the department head.

An interesting example of "relationship by legislation" was included in the Mutual Security Act of 1959. One of its provisions (73 Stat. 253) created an Inspector General and Comptroller of the International Cooperation Administration, who was to be responsible, not to the ICA, but to the Under Secretary of State concerned with foreign aid. The new officer was assigned the functions previously performed by the Evaluations Officer of ICA and also given broad powers to conduct audits and evaluate foreign aid programs, investigate improper activities, establish systems for internal audits, controls, and financial reporting, and advise the Under Secretary concerning the fiscal and budgetary aspects of annual programs.

The purpose of the measure, as stated in the House report on the bill, was "to give a single individual with the necessary supporting personnel, a sufficiently high place in the executive hierarchy, sufficient independence from control by operating officials, together with sufficient authority and money to assure that he will be able to detect shortcomings in the mutual security program and to make recommendations for correction that cannot be disregarded by those administering the program and to suspend particular operations pending a decision by the Under Secretary."[22]

Although the new officer was made responsible to a State Department official, the sponsors of the provision obviously expected him to act as a congressional agent, checking the administration of foreign

[20] The matter will be discussed further in Chapter 7, "Congress and the Civil Service."

[21] *Congressional Quarterly Almanac,* Vol. 15 (1959), p. 314.

[22] House Report No. 440, 86th Cong., 1st sess. (1959), pp. 54-55.

aid and reporting to the committees concerned any shortcomings that he discovered. During Senate debate on the bill, a member said: "For the first time we shall have an inspector general who will be able to look into difficulties which occur in various parts of the world, and will have the right to discharge and report."[23] An amendment specified that the officer's reports would be available to the General Accounting Office and to Congress, but President Eisenhower in signing the bill stated that this provision would not affect the constitutional right of the Executive to withhold documents.[24]

As a congressional agent the Inspector General proved disappointing. The man appointed to the post, John Murphy, had formerly been the ICA comptroller. In his appearance before the House Foreign Affairs Committee the following year, he testified that he regarded himself as an executive officer and that his reports would be subject to privilege.[25] Thus frustrated, Congress placed a limitation of $1 million—only about half of the budget request—on the annual expenditures of the office

Statutory provisions often require an agency or its executive officer to consult with other departments and agencies or with an advisory committee provided for by law. The prescriptions for such consultation and joint participation have

> . . . run the gamut, permitting the exchange of information, providing formally prescribed sources of advice, compelling agencies to consult, to consult and consider, to consult prior to taking specific action, hinging action on receipt of prior enabling report or request, requiring prior consultation and factfinding, requiring clearance or approval from a source external to the agency, and finally, compelling action in conformance with the request of another agency.[26]

Again, such provisions are usually aimed at furthering specific legislative policies or at gaining acceptance for a program. That they may vary in their effectiveness for the purpose intended is shown in the two examples that follow.

[23] *Congressional Record*, Vol. 105, Pt. 11, 86th Cong., 1st sess. (July 22, 1959), p. 13976.
[24] White House Press Release, July 24, 1959.
[25] *Hearings on the Mutual Security Act of 1960*, 86th Cong., 2d sess. (June 1960), p. 330.
[26] Cornelius P. Cotter and J. Malcolm Smith, "Administrative Responsibility: Congressional Prescription of Interagency Relationships," *Western Political Quarterly*, Vol. 10 (1957), p. 782.

In the Atomic Energy Act of 1946, Congress provided for a Military Liaison Committee, largely to placate the advocates of military administration of the program. The Atomic Energy Commission was expressly charged to keep the committee fully informed on all developments; the committee could appeal to various higher authorities and eventually to the President if it found itself in disagreement with AEC policy. However, although the House and Senate members of the Joint Committee on Atomic Enery envisaged a very active role for the liaison group, the arrangement never worked well. The AEC has worked closely with the military departments, but the Liaison Committee has apparently played no important part in assisting the relationship.[27] The experience is only one of the many which could be cited to demonstrate that interdepartmental relations usually cannot be formalized and channeled through a single agency, and that machinery and procedures set up by statutory prescription may prove to be unsuitable in practice.

Statutory resolution of civilian-military relationships was also a leading issue in the creation of the Federal Aviation Agency in 1958, but in this case the provisions made by Congress allowed for some desirable administrative leeway. Severe criticism following a number of disastrous mid-air crashes had forced reconsideration of the existing dual regulation—civilian and military—of air traffic and use of airspace. The only feasible solution was to create a single agency to control the movement of all airplanes—military, commercial, and private.

Early in the consideration of the bill it was decided that the new agency should be under civilian control, but the leading spokesman for commercial aviation urged the inclusion of military aviation representatives in the administrative structure, as essential to the agency's successful operation.[28] As a result, the Federal Aviation Act prescribed in some detail how the military departments should participate. The President was authorized to appoint a military officer as Deputy Administrator, if the Administrator was not a former military officer. The Administrator was authorized to enter into agreement with

[27] Morgan Thomas, *Atomic Energy and Congress* (1956), *passim.*
[28] See statement of W. A. Patterson, President United Air Lines, in *Hearings on Federal Aviation Agency Act,* Senate Interstate and Foreign Commerce Committee, 85th Cong., 2d sess. (1958), pp. 68-69.

the military services for the detail of personnel to his agency, with the stipulation that such personnel should not be subject to direction or control by the military department while on such detail; he was to report within six months to the appropriate committees of Congress the agreements entered into with the military services, Thus, although the relationship was directed by statute, the actual working arrangements were left to agency discretion.

A common provision for interagency consultation requires the head of an agency to consult with another agency prior to taking certain specified actions, and in some cases the agency consulted is granted authority to initiate the action or to veto it, thus dividing executive responsibility. Such provisions are usually adopted to placate a special-interest group which looks upon the consulted agency as its advocate and guardian. Thus, the Price Control Extension Act of 1946 required the Office of Price Administration to secure the approval of the Secretary of Agriculture to prices of certain agricultural products (60 Stat. 664). So too, the apprehensions of a special-interest group can often be relieved by the statutory creation of an advisory committee with which an agency is required to consult before it adopts policies that affect the group. Provisions are also written into law that specifically authorize executive officers to consult with various public and private organizations and officials—a requirement which would appear to be wholly unnecessary and possibly mischievous.[29]

The wisdom of prescribing interagency consultation, cooperation, and joint decision-making by law is, in most cases, dubious. Cooperation can ordinarily be better achieved without legislative mandate; a forced marriage is seldom a happy one. Effective coordination of related activities in different departments or units is a primary function of executive leadership, but it requires flexibility; thus it is ordinarily impeded rather than facilitated by rigid statutory prescriptions. To require that the executive decisions of an agency be approved by another agency not charged with administration of the decisions only serves to divide responsibility—usually with deleterious consequences.

[29] For illustrations of such legislative provisions, see Cotter and Smith, *op. cit.*, p. 769.

Procedural Legislation

A large part of the voluminous *United States Code* consists of legislation prescribing in varying detail the work methods and procedures to be followed by the executive departments and agencies. Certain titles codify the statutes applicable to the procedures of the administrative establishment in general, on such subjects as contracts, public buildings, personnel transactions—pay, allowances, travel, etc.—public lands, purchasing practices, supply, printing, and conduct of legal business. But the greatest amount of highly detailed prescription is found in the titles that deal with specific departments and the conduct of their activities.

Chapter 557 of the *Code*, which prescribes the rations of Navy personnel, provides an example of the kind and amount of detail often prescribed by law. The daily ration is classified under 14 items, among them 8 ounces of dry bread or 14 ounces of flour, 12 ounces of meat, 1 and 6/10 ounces of butter, 1 and 2/10 eggs, and 2/5 gill of oil. Another example is the annual authorization, for most agencies, of the number of automobiles that may be purchased; included are various regulations, restrictions, and exceptions as to size, weight, cost, use, and so on. This highly detailed statutory control is required by a statute enacted in 1914, which prohibited the "purchase of any motor propelled or horse drawn passenger carrying vehicle" without specific statutory authority, and thus has necessitated specific legislation and revisions for each agency from year to year.

To attempt a summary of the vast body of procedural statutes would be futile. Instead, the following brief discussion examines some of the factors that have led Congress to apply so much detailed legislation to departmental operations, and what its effects have been.

Procedural legislation is often adopted to correct or to safeguard against faulty practices, unwise or improper executive actions, waste of public funds, incompetence, and various other abuses of administrative discretion that have come to the attention of congressional committees. The reports of such abuses may be valid; they may also be highly exaggerated or based on rumor rather than careful consideration of facts. In either case, the legislation designed to correct the abuses restricts administrative discretion and usually hampers good administration. Thus Congress has enacted detailed regulations and restrictions on such matters as the letting of contracts, publications, the use of the mails, travel, automobiles, the purchase and use of supplies, various aspects of personnel administration, and the day-to-day operating details of numerous programs. In many instances such legislative restrictions continue in effect long after the need for them has passed.[30] Congress has the responsibility to inquire into the conduct of the work of the departments and to enact needed legislative safeguards and standards, but excessive legislative prescription of operating details and restrictions on administrative choice of methods is not an effective remedy.

In the continuous struggle between the legislative and executive branches under our constitutional system of checks and balances, Congress is reluctant to make broad delegations of authority to executive officers and regards legislation which fails to prescribe in considerable detail how programs are to be carried out as an abdication of its constitutional function. Yet in recent years the complexity and technical nature of many government programs have made detailed legislative prescription difficult, if not impossible; thus it has been increasingly necessary to delegate broad powers to administrators. Nevertheless, Congress still tends to write administrative minutiae into law whenever it can, not essentially because it fears that officers may decide such matters unwisely, but rather to sustain the appearance (if not the reality) of being in control.

Once the pattern of detailed procedural legislation is adopted, its continuance and expansion are almost inevitable. This was remarked on by Woodrow Wilson in 1885:

> Every statute may be said to have a long lineage of statutes behind it; and whether that lineage be honorable or of ill repute is . . . a question as to each individual statute. . . . Every statute in its turn has a numerous progeny, and only time and opportunity can decide whether its offspring will bring it honor or shame. Once

[30] A further discussion of the effects of legislation prescribing operating procedures and placing restrictions and limitations on the departments will be found in Chapter 7, especially the section "Personnel Restriction by Riders."

begin the dance of legislation, and you must struggle through its mazes as best you can to its breathless end—if any end there be.[31]

With the modern expansion of government programs, the "mazes" have likewise increased. Provisions that legislators unfamiliar with departmental operations had thought would be simple and salutary to execute often turn out to be cumbersome and unnecessarily expensive. Frequent revisions and additions are then necessary to correct not only the unwise provisions but also the administrative difficulties that often result from them.

To assure conformity with even the most simple procedural provision, a department or agency must often devise and issue interpretations and instructions; new regulations must be drawn up and issued, and controls must be established through reports and other elaborate checks. The Comptroller General also issues rulings which interpret and apply the legislation to agency actions and expenditures —and which often prevent the agency from using the methods it had already determined to be the most suitable.[32]

Conclusions

It is the constitutional function of Congress to enact legislation which authorizes the programs and activities of the executive departments and agencies, determines their broad objectives and policies, establishes the major framework of executive organization, and, to the extent "necessary and proper," prescribes in detail the executive organization and procedures. Congress is equally concerned with the Executive to assure that the policies and programs it has enacted into law are effectively carried out, and for this reason has in the past ordinarily avoided detailed legislative prescriptions which would hamper efficient administration. In recent decades, however, there there has been evident a strong tendency in Congress to write into statute many decisions that are essentially executive in character, the effect of which has been to deprive executive officers of needed discretion and to defeat effective executive responsibility. (The ten-

[31] Woodrow Wilson, *Congressional Government* (1913 ed.), p. 297.
[32] The rulings of the Comptroller General are discussed in Chapter 6.

dency as seen in personnel legislation is discussed in detail in Chapter 7.)

The determination of the internal structure of executive organizations is an essential element of management. Executive officers cannot be held responsible for results unless they are granted a reasonable discretion to organize and to reorganize the administrative units under their direction and to assign their functions. Changes in the internal organization of agencies must, as a rule, be preceded by careful study and analysis, and be put into effect at a time and in a manner that will gain staff acceptance and cooperation. To be efficient and effective, government organization must be kept dynamic, capable of performing new tasks, adapting to new techniques, and utilizing the abilities of employees.

Never before have the tasks of government been as important to society as they are today. Flexibility—a primary requisite of sound organization—is not possible if the details of organization are prescribed by statute. The increasing size and complexity of government activities and the rapid changes due to the exploding technology make it difficult, if not impossible, for Congress to act promptly in making needed revisions of the internal organization and procedures of departments. Although it is the constitutional prerogative of Congress to prescribe subordinate officers and the internal organization of departments as well as to provide for their major officers, ordinarily this should be left to the discretion of the executive officers in charge.

Detailed legislation prescribing the work methods and procedures of the departments deprives executive officers of needed discretion in planning administrative operations and in executing the functions assigned to them by law; it imposes rigid and often unsuitable procedures; it makes it difficult for departments to revise work methods to keep abreast of technical developments and changing tasks; it results in a bureaucratic administration whose primary concern is precedent and regularity instead of efficiency and service; it discourages initiative, imagination, and the willingness of executive officers to adopt innovations and to take risks in administration—qualities highly prized in private administration.

Moreover, the enactment of highly detailed procedural legislation is self-defeating. Instead of bringing about improvements and safeguarding against abuses, such legislation is often harmful to administration, in ways not anticipated. Once undertaken, it continues to place a heavy burden on Congress and its committees by necessitating corrective legislation, thus distracting them from their more important function of considering major policies and programs.

The choice of work methods and procedures used by the departments is clearly a function of management and, with rare exception, should be determined by the executive officers in charge. Not only are they better qualified than a legislative body to decide upon operating procedures because of their daily contact with administration, but they are able to elicit the participation of the staff in developing improved procedure, which is essential to employee morale and motivation. Unless executive officers are permitted wide latitude in the choice of work procedures they cannot be held responsible for operating results.

WHEN THE METHODS OF legislative control and oversight of executive organization and activity in the United States are compared to those practiced in countries with parliamentary forms of government, and especially in Great Britain, two differences emerge that in part explain why Congress relies to such an extent on the method of highly detailed regulation by statute.

The British Parliament can rely on the Treasury, with its regulatory powers and long tradition of watching over administration, to issue essential rules to the departments and to require that further controls be adopted when needed. There is no comparable central control agency in the Executive branch of the United States Government on which Congress can depend for similar oversight functions. The Bureau of the Budget has recently tended to expand its role in this direction, but Congress so far has not looked on the expansion with favor.

When executive department heads are also leading participators in the legislative process, as they are in the British Parliament, detailed statutory prescription of departmental activity is rarely found. The legislature ordinarily upholds the principle of ministerial responsibility for administrative operations, and the ministers themselves

can unite to oppose bills that they regard as encroaching on their functions. Similar interaction between Congress and the Executive
branch is inhibited by our constitutional concept of separated powers, despite the increasingly large areas of functional overlap in practice, and Congress, of course, does not possess that ultimate control
available to parliaments—the power to turn an administration out of
office.

These differences in methods of governance, however, do not
justify the excessive use by Congress of a type of control that hampers
administration and reduces its efficiency. There have always been
available to Congress several other very effective means of control,
each of which has been substantially strengthened and expanded
in recent years. The most pervasive of these—the power of the purse
—is discussed in the three chapters that follow.

3

Congress and the Budget

IN ALL DEMOCRATIC COUNTRIES the power of the purse is the cornerstone of legislative control of administration. The Congress of the United States, however, far outdoes the legislatures of other democracies in subjecting executive budgets to detailed, strict review and extensive revision and in relating financial control continuously and pervasively to the policies, programs, and activities of executive agencies. This predominance had its origin in the sweeping fiscal powers and responsibilities vested exclusively in Congress by the Constitution, but it has been greatly augmented by later developments in legislative practice—notably among them, the standing committee system.

Congress exercises control over the finances of the federal government through its authority to levy taxes and duties; to borrow money and regulate the public debt; to coin money and regulate its value; to make specific appropriation by law for all expenditures, including those to provide for the "general welfare," before money can be drawn from the Treasury; to provide for an audit of public accounts. Of these several functions, it is the appropriations process that has been the most effective as a means of legislative control of the administrative establishment.[1] The present-day aspect of the process, however, is a comparatively recent event in a long chain of developments, most of which evolved in the midst of controversy—not only between the Executive branch and Congress but also between opposing factions

---

[1] The audit process, potentially an even more effective control but, so far, not thoroughly employed as such by Congress, is discussed in Chapter 6.

within Congress. A major part of the controversy, off and on through the years, centered around the concept of a unified national budget system, but such a system was not created by law until June 10, 1921, almost exactly 132 years after the First Congress began considering ways and means for the new government in the summer of 1789.

Fairly early in congressional history the constitutional responsibility of legalizing appropriations began to be handled in part through committees, but they were a far cry from the powerful and very hard-working House and Senate Appropriations Committees of recent years, which, acting through subcommittees, not only systematically and minutely enquire into the administration of policies and programs when they review the itemized budget requests of all executive agencies, but also exercise continuing surveillance over agency activities throughout the year. The status of these modern committees and the functions of the present-day appropriations process, in relation to congressional control of administration through the budget —which is the main subject for discussion in this chapter and the two chapters that follow—can be better understood in the light of earlier developments. Therefore, this chapter reviews in brief (1) developments during the years from 1789 to 1921 as Congress faced its twin problems of financing and overseeing the administrative activities of government, (2) the movement resulting in and the passage of the Budget and Accounting Act of 1921, and (3) the budget system since 1921. Chapter 4 is concerned with the appropriations process and the methods of control it provides Congress, Chapter 5 with the reforms that have been variously proposed to improve the present budget system.

Early History: 1789-1865

The respective fiscal roles of Congress and the Executive branch emerged as a leading subject for controversy in the spring and summer of 1789, during the House debates on the organization of the Treasury Department and, especially, on the role and responsibility of its executive.[2] The debates were still not resolved when, on July 24,

[2] See James Hart, *The American Presidency in Action, 1789* (1948), pp. 214-239, for a detailed discussion of the debates.

the House appointed a Select Committee on Ways and Means, composed of one member from each state and with anti-Federalist Elbridge Gerry of Massachusetts as chairman, to consider and report an estimate of supplies for the remainder of the year.[3]

The appointment of Gerry as chairman reflected one of the main issues of the controversy. Throughout the debates he warned against allowing any of the prospective department heads to assume the aspect of ministers of state; he also strongly advocated heading the Treasury Department with a board of three commissioners instead of a single executive officer—who might, through patronage and ministerial ambitions infringe on the legislative power of the purse. For the time being, the viewpoint Gerry represented did not prevail. Not only did the Treasury bill as passed on September 2 create a single officer, one of whose duties was to "prepare and report estimates of the public revenue, and the public expenditures," but two weeks later the Ways and Means Committee was discharged and its task turned over to Alexander Hamilton, who had just taken office as Secretary of the Treasury. His report, ready within four days, recommended that funds be voted under a few generalized heads; Congress accepted the recommendations, and the "Act making Appropriations for the Service of the present year" was passed on September 29, only eight days after the report was submitted.

[3] This initiative on the part of the House rather than the Senate was, of course, undirected by the Constitution, which specified only that "all bills for revenue" must originate in the House and that the Senate would "propose or concur with amendments" on them. A motion to have appropriation bills originate solely in the House had been defeated in the Constitutional Convention, the matter having been one of the central points at issue in the great controversy over the basis of representation in the two houses of Congress. However, No. 58 of *The Federalist* (by Madison) gave firm construction to the basic constitutional intention of keeping the spending and revenue functions closely related: "The House of Representatives cannot only refuse, but they alone can propose, the supplies requisite for the support of government. They, in a word, hold the purse—that powerful instrument . . . for obtaining a redress of every grievance and for carrying into effect every just and salutary measure." The House in 1789, by creating a body to prepare estimates, apparently chose to put this construction into practice.

Within a few years appropriations were being included in revenue bills, and therefore their origination in the House became a firmly established custom that persisted even when the two kinds of bills were later on separated. In 1856 the Senate tried its hand at originating two appropriation bills, which the House tabled. In 1881 the rights of the Senate in this regard came up for debate, but the question was not resolved. The Senate's prerogative of amendment, however, has been a powerful instrument and has kept the House from assuming complete ascendancy over the funding process.

For the next several years Congress looked to Hamilton to examine and revise estimates and to advise on appropriations. Not all members were content with this; one of his opponents in the Senate complained that "nothing was done without him," and a member of the House remarked that the House would soon " 'not be the Representative of their constituents but of the Secretary.' "[4] Nevertheless, Congress continued to enact the recommended appropriations without referring them to a committee for review, but the Secretary's ascendancy was fast becoming a central point of the increasing controversy and friction between the Federalists and the Republicans.[5]

When Swiss-born Albert Gallatin came to Congress as Senator from Pennsylvania in 1793, he lost no time in showing his Republican tendencies by leading an attack on the fiscal policies of the Administration; the Federalists in turn, recognizing a dangerous opponent, brought up the charge that he had not fulfilled the constitutional requirement of nine years' citizenship for senatorial office—a charge eventually upheld by the Senate's vote, strictly on party lines, 14 to 12 against him.[6] But the Federalists were only briefly rid of Gallatin as a thorn in the flesh. In 1795, Pennsylvania returned him to Congress as a member of the House of Representatives.

Had the Hamiltonian practices been maintained, a financial system similar to that of the British government might possibly have developed, but the Republican preference for strict congressional control of the purse strings was soon to prevail. In 1795, with Hamilton's resignation from the Treasury and a Republican majority in the House, a Ways and Means Committee was again established to make recommendations on taxes and appropriations—the proposal being introduced by Gallatin, who was also appointed as one of the fourteen committee members. Five days after the committee's institution, Secretary of the Treasury Oliver Wolcott submitted his estimates of appropriations for 1796 to it for review.

The Republicans in the House also intended to have their way about another aspect of the main controversy. Since 1790 the method employed in the first few appropriation acts—voting lump sums under

[4] Wilfred E. Binkley, *President and Congress* (1947), p. 36, citing respectively *Journal of William Maclay*, p. 385, and *Annals*, 1st Cong., 2d sess., p. 1449.
[5] See Leonard D. White, *The Federalists* (1948), Chap. 26.
[6] See Raymond Walters, Jr., *Albert Gallatin* (1957), Chap. 5.

a few major heads, according to Hamilton's advice—had been under increasing fire from the Madisonians, who wanted detailed itemization, and the issue had become central when the Federalists first lost their House majority. By the spring of 1798, Republican views had so much prevailed that Secretary Wolcott complained in a letter to Hamilton:

> The management of the Treasury becomes more and more difficult. The Legislature will not pass laws in gross. Their appropriations are minute; Gallatin, to whom they yield, is evidently intending to break down this department, by charging it with an impracticable detail.[7]

As the letter was being written, the House was passing a military appropriations bill, its items specified in distinct detail. The strongly Federalist Senate, however, refused to agree to the itemization and amended the bill so as to consolidate appropriations. The House later accepted the amendments, and for a time the House Republicans, once more in the minority, pressed their case against Treasury practices less vigorously.

The respite was only temporary. On entering the Presidency in 1801, Jefferson made Gallatin his Secretary of the Treasury. It was on Gallatin's advice that he urged in his annual message to Congress (December 1801) that appropriations should be in "specific sums to every specific purpose susceptible to definition," that transfers of funds from one purpose to another be prohibited and contingency funds reduced. Hamilton at once took up the cudgels in a series of published letters signed "Julius Crassus." In Number XI of the series he described the plight of administration under such a system.

> The exigencies of the public service are often so variable that a public agent would often find himself full-handed for one purpose, empty-handed for another, and if forbidden to make a transfer, not only the service would suffer, but an opportunity, with very strong temptation, would be given, to traffic with public money for private gain; while the business of government would be stagnated by the injudicious and absurd impediments of an overdriven caution.[8]

The views of Hamilton and Gallatin to some extent differed only

---

[7] Lucius Wilmerding, Jr., *The Spending Power* (1943), p. 46.
[8] *Ibid.*, p. 53.

in degree. Gallatin himself had warned in 1796 that "it is impossible for the Legislature to foresee, in all its details, the necessary applications of moneys and a reasonable discretion should be allowed to the proper executive department."[9] As Secretary of the Treasury, Gallatin continued to stress itemization by Congress, as one way of attaining the strict accountability of expenditure he believed in. Now, however, being an administrator and not a congressman, he also favored strict accounting to the Treasury through legislation and cooperation between himself and Congress in considering estimates, but his philosophy of finance was always directed at achieving a unified budgetary system, with outgo responsibly related to income.[10]

By 1802, however, excessive itemization of appropriations had brought on a multitude of deficiency requests from the departments. At this point Congress looked at its own organization. Ways and Means, which had been renewed annually since its reinstitution in the House in 1795, was made a standing committee, its jurisdiction to include revenue and appropriation bills, general oversight of the public debt, and examination of the departments as to expenditures and the economy of their management.[11] When a similar committee was created somewhat later in the Senate, Congress was launched on its way toward paramount authority over government finance.

But at this stage imposition of authority still did not guarantee compliance. How to insure (1) that executive officers would spend funds only for the purposes intended when voted and (2) that deficiency requests would not be made remained a central problem that appeared to defy solution. In 1814 the House created a Committee on Public Expenditure, in order to relieve burdened Ways and Means of its watchdog function over the departments; the hoped-for control did not result, however, and the committee was heard of only sporadically, although it survived until 1880.[12] As the decades passed, the problem was central to the often chaotic struggle between Congress and the executive agencies. Congress constantly sought to impose control through increasingly splintered appropriations and increasingly

[9] *Ibid.*, p. 38.

[10] Walters, *op. cit.*, pp. 147-148, 262.

[11] See *Hinds' Precedents of the House of Representatives* (1907), Vol. 4, Sec. 4020.

[12] See Daniel T. Selko, *The Federal Financial System* (1940), p. 91.

rigid and complicated legislation; the departments just as constantly made use of the two loopholes most available to them—transfer of funds and subsequent requests for deficiency appropriations—a strategy that in effect violated the appropriations laws but which was soon so much the rule that Congress was forced to allow it. Over several decades the pendulum swung back and forth confusingly between relaxation and re-enforcement of the laws. But whatever was done, Congress could not seem to avoid the action it most abhorred —voting deficiency funds; in the words of one member, the departments "can make these deficiencies, and Congress can refuse to allow them; but after they are made it is very hard to refuse to allow them."[13]

The problems of government finance before the Civil War were, of course, very different from those to be encountered in later years. Total expenditures as late as the period 1846-1853 averaged less than $50 million annually.[14] Revenue from customs duties alone sometimes yielded adequate revenues for the needs of the still comparatively small government and at times even produced embarrassing surpluses.

By 1860 the House Ways and Means Committee had become the most powerful body in Congress. Its tight control over finance often led it to reject expenditures proposed by other members of Congress and appropriations authorized by other committees; enjoying a special status under the rules, it was able to dominate House proceedings, and its chairman was second only to the Speaker in influence. Any suggestions that its work should be divided and a separate committee for appropriations be created were strongly resisted not only by its members but also usually by the House leadership.

The conduct of the Civil War rapidly placed unexampled burdens on Congress. The work of the Ways and Means Committee was especially increased; near the war's end, the demand for a committee concerned only with appropriations could no longer be denied. Opponents of division still contended that one committee "should raise and spend the revenue . . . to make ends meet," but Thaddeus Ste-

[13] See Wilmerding, op. cit., passim, for a detailed review of the long struggle; the quotation is from p. 136.
[14] Henry Jones Ford, The Cost of Our National Government (1910) p. 121.

vens, Ways and Means chairman, now appeared indifferent to such arguments. On March 2, 1865, the new committee was instituted, with Stevens as its chairman; its prime duty was to review the estimates and report the general appropriation bills. At the same time, jurisdiction over currency bills was given to a new Committee on Banking and Currency.[15] In 1867 the Senate also divided up the work of its Finance Committee and created a Committee on Appropriations.

Chaos and Loopholes: 1865-1909

Within a short time the House Appropriations Committee had made itself thoroughly unpopular. Members of other committees and House members in general were jealous of its power, as a privileged committee, to bring its bills to the floor in precedence over other business at any time. They were also frustrated by its resistance to their attempts to increase funds for agencies they favored and for projects in their own districts. In 1876 the committee's work and power were further augmented by a rules change which allowed substantive riders to be attached to appropriation bills, provided the riders reduced expenditures. Thus, in effect, the committee's tasks included general policy matters, as well as finance. Although not all of its members welcomed the new authority, the committee as a whole was soon being accused of dictating both general legislation and appropriations.[16]

The obvious overload of work provided a rationale for which the jealous had long been seeking. Revolt first took effective form in 1877, when the Committee on Commerce was given complete jurisdiction over the rivers and harbors bill—that chief reservoir of "pork-barrel" legislation—which formerly had been prepared by Commerce but was always referred to Appropriations to report. In the rules revision of 1880, management of appropriations for agriculture and forestry was given to the legislative Committee on Agriculture and Forestry; in 1885 the dispersal movement was in full swing, with jurisdiction over

[15] See D. S. Alexander, *History and Procedure of the House of Representatives* (1916), pp. 234-236.
[16] For further details of the events described briefly here and in the three following paragraphs, see Leonard D. White, *The Republican Era: 1869-1901* (1958), pp. 64-65; Alexander, *op. cit.*, pp. 238-253; Selko, *op. cit.*, Chap. 4.

the bills for foreign affairs, the Army and Military Academy, the Navy, post offices and postroads, and Indian affairs being transferred to the five legislative committees concerned. The Appropriations Committee was left with only six of the fourteen annual funding bills. Thus there were eight committees that received estimates and reported bills, each acting independently of the others. The Senate soon adopted a similar arrangement.

This dispersion of responsibility led almost at once to confusion and greatly increased expenditure, as a number of legislators had urgently warned that it would. Most of the departments received part of their funds through the respective legislative committees and part through the Appropriations Committee, but a few of them were still wholly under the latter's jurisdiction, as were all of the independent agencies. There was no consistency to the pattern of scrutinizing and reporting estimates; the Appropriations Committee by and large was aiming at control and economy, while most of the legislative committees, "having intimate and for the most part cordial relations each with a particular department, launched out into an unrestrained competition for appropriations, the one striving to surpass the other in securing greater recognition and more money for its special charge."[17] Prior to 1878 most agencies submitted their estimates directly to Congress; an act of that year required the estimates to be submitted *through* the Secretary of the Treasury, who was authorized to compile but not to revise them.[18] The finishing touch to this fiscal crazy quilt was the ruling that all deficiency requests were still to be referred to the Committee on Appropriations.

Thus the concept of close and responsible budgetary control which Hamilton and Gallatin, each in his individual way, had urged now seemed almost completely lost sight of. With many of the department heads and bureau chiefs sharing in the general irresponsibility of this spending heyday, the rapid growth of federal expenditure during the next decade became a national scandal. The congressional floodgates were open, and funds flowed out unabated for such projects as improvements for rivers and harbors that carried little traffic, and superfluous post offices for tiny villages. Omnibus public works bills were logrolled through House and Senate with zest, each member being

[17] Wilmerding, *op. cit.*, p. 143.
[18] Selko, *op. cit.*, pp. 81-82.

bound to cooperate if he hoped to achieve the projects he wanted for his own constituency. In 1889, James Bryce commented on the situation:

> More money is wasted in this way than what the parsimony of the appropriations committee can save. Each of the other standing committees, including the committee on pensions, a source of infinite waste, proposes grants of money, not knowing or heeding what is being proposed by other committees, and guided by the executive no further than the members choose. . . .
>
> Under the system of congressional finance here described America wastes millions annually. But her wealth is so great, her revenue so elastic, that she is not sensible of the loss. She has the glorious privilege of youth, the privilege of committing errors without suffering from their consequences.[19]

Movement for a National Budget System

During the period from Grant to McKinley the administrative operations of the government became increasingly more numerous, complex, and financially demanding. Yet the chaotic dispersion of responsibility in Congress for the process of funding their needs continued to be matched by the lack of any centralized authority in the Executive branch to propose, examine, and revise department estimates. The chief of each bureau prepared his own estimates, often padding them in the expectation of cuts by Congress, then passed them on to the department head, who in turn, usually without revision and entirely without interdepartmental reference, sent them to the Treasury Department. The Secretary of the Treasury transmitted them unchanged to Congress.

The President's part in the process was especially remote. He "had little, if anything, to do with the level or content of the estimates, with the amount or objects of congressional appropriation, or with the actual funds annually made available. . . . [The] process . . . began with the bureaus, continued with the Appropriations Committee or Committees, and ended with Congress. The President was not a party."[20] He was also not a party to the tailoring of expenditure to revenue. The

[19] Bryce, The American Commonwealth (1922 ed.), Vol. 1, pp. 180, 184.
[20] White, The Republican Era, pp. 97, 99.

estimates of expenditure were prepared without reference to the estimates of income for the fiscal year. When, as the law required, the Secretary of the Treasury submitted the two sets of estimates together to Congress, proposed expenditures were frequently found to be far in excess of expected revenues. The responsibility of cutting outgo to match income then devolved on the House Appropriations Committee.[21]

In consequence, financial control—one of the strongest means of influencing the work, plans, and policies of the executive departments and agencies—was exerted, not by the Chief Executive, but by Congress. Yet the great number of deficiency appropriations which Congress was compelled each year to vote and the obvious fragmentation of legislative oversight policy demonstrated that its control was not only inefficient but also far from complete.

That some form of budget control was a pressing need had been recognized intermittently for a number of years both by various members of Congress and by officers in the Executive branch. But not until a pile-up of Treasury deficits in 1909 excited special alarm did Congress take action to mitigate the existing chaos in some degree. The Sundry Civil Appropriations Act approved March 4, 1909, contained the following provision (Section 7):

> Immediately upon the receipt of the regular annual estimates of appropriations needed for the various branches of the Government it shall be the duty of the Secretary of the Treasury to estimate as nearly as may be the revenues of the Government for the ensuing fiscal year, and if the estimates for appropriations, including the estimated amount necessary to meet all continuing and permanent appropriations, shall exceed the estimated revenues the Secretary of the Treasury shall transmit the estimates to Congress as heretofore required by law and at once transmit a detailed statement of all said estimates to the President, to the end that he may, in giving Congress information of the state of the Union and in recommending to their consideration such measures as he may judge necessary, advise the Congress how in his judgment the estimated appropriations could with least injury to the public service be reduced so as to bring the appropriations within the estimated revenues, or, if such reduction be not in his judgment practicable without undue injury to the public service, that he may recommend to Congress such loans or new taxes as may be necessary to cover the deficiency.[22]

[21] See Ford, *op. cit.*, pp. 127-128.
[22] 35 Stat. 1027.

The intention of Congress in approving Section 7 was most certainly not to enhance presidential authority or to deprive itself of any jot of its jealousy guarded financial power. Rather, the clause was probably an attempt to deflect the mounting public criticism of governmental extravagance away from Congress and toward the Executive branch, where Congress had been insisting the responsibility for extravagance belonged.[23] Nevertheless, although the authority thus backhandedly afforded the President was so circumscribed and unimplemented as to be almost no authority at all, in the light of later events the law represented a distinct and significant step on the road to a unified budgetary system.[24]

President Taft did not use the authority as directed, but undertook instead to reduce the estimates *before* they were submitted. Having no staff of his own qualified to do the job, he directed the members of his Cabinet to scrutinize the estimates of their bureau chiefs with great care. The effort resulted in substantial reductions, but, despite the President's urging that the full amounts requested be appropriated, Congress proceeded to cut the estimates as usual, except those for favored activities. As a consequence, the departments were faced with serious financial difficulties and once again had to appeal to Congress for deficiency appropriations to carry on essential activities.

The experience confirmed Secretary of the Treasury Franklin MacVeagh in his opinion that no permanent reform could be effected without legislation, a trained budget staff, and the general support of Congress. In his annual reports for 1909, 1910, and 1911 he stressed the need for a responsible, unified budget system in which Congress and the Executive branch would cooperate fully, and urged that Congress provide for its establishment.

Because of the continued, and increasing, public demand for economy in government, President Taft was able to secure an appropriation from Congress in 1910 to employ "accountants and experts from official and private life to . . . inquire into the methods of transacting the public business of the Government . . . with the view of inaugurating new, or changing old, methods . . . so as to attain greater efficiency and economy."[25] On March 8, 1911, the Commission on Economy and Efficiency was established by the President to conduct studies

[23] See Ford, *op. cit.*, p. 109.
[24] See W. F. Willoughby, *The Problem of a National Budget* (1918), Chap. 8.
[25] 36 Stat. 703.

of organization and administration, especially in relation to the financial system. Taking the position that no real improvement in the administration of financial affairs was possible until a budget system was adopted, the Commission set to work on a thoroughgoing report that would present the need for such a system.[26]

In his message transmitting the report to Congress on June 27, 1912, President Taft severely criticized the existing practices in detail, then summarized as follows:

> So long as the method at present prescribed obtains, neither the Congress nor the country can have laid before it a definite understandable program of business, or of governmental work to be financed; nor can it have a well-defined, clearly expressed financial program to be followed; nor can either the Congress or the Executive get before the country the proposals of each in such manner as to locate responsibility for plans submitted or for results. . . .
>
> The purpose of the report . . . is to suggest a method whereby the President, as the constitutional head of the administration, may lay before the Congress, and the Congress may consider and act on, a definite business and financial program; . . . to provide each Member of Congress, as well as each citizen who is interested, with such data pertaining to each subject of interest that it may be considered in relation to each question of policy which should be gone into before an appropriation for expenditures is made; . . . in short, to suggest a plan whereby the President and the Congress may cooperate—the one in laying before Congress and the country a clearly expressed administrative program to be acted on, the other in laying before the President a definite enactment to be acted on by him.[27]

The report, submitted on the eve of Taft's campaign for re-election, was never acted on by Congress, but the importance of the Commission's work was widely acknowledged. The movement for a coordinated budget system accelerated rapidly. A number of leading national journals featured articles that criticized the existing financial system of the government, especially the congressional practice of dealing with appropriations, and urged legislation to provide a national budgetary system. In October 1912, when the United States Chamber of Commerce conducted a poll of its member organizations,

[26] *The Need for a National Budget System,* House Document No. 854, 62d Cong., 2d sess. (1912).
[27] *Ibid.,* p. 4.

out of a total 583 votes cast, all but 10 were in favor of a national budget law; in 1917 the Chamber reaffirmed its advocacy in a strong resolution passed at its annual meeting. In the presidential election of 1916 both the Democratic and Republican platforms included a budget system plank. In 1918, Representative (soon Senator) Medill McCormick of Illinois submitted a comprehensive plan to the House for a national budget system, pointing out as he explained the plan how limited, under the existing system, congressional control of expenditure actually was.

The Budget and Accounting Act of 1921

In 1919 a Select Committee on the Budget was created by the House of Representatives to consider the problems of the existing financial system and to propose legislation for a national budget system. Beginning on September 22, the committee, headed by James W. Good of Iowa, chairman of the House Appropriations Committee, conducted intensive hearings for two weeks.[28] Statements were taken from thirty-seven distinguished witnesses, among them former President Taft, several members of the 1911-1913 Commission on Economy and Efficiency, Secretary of the Treasury Carter Glass, and former Secretary of War Henry L. Stimson.[29]

From the outset the committee was in general agreed that a national budget system had become a necessity. The discussion therefore was focused on such questions as what kind of budget agency would best serve the need and whether the budget should be prepared

[28] Chairman Good had asked William F. Willoughby, director of the Institute for Government Research (in 1927 to become a division of the newly chartered Brookings Institution) to help the Select Committee draft a budget bill. The Institute and Willoughby had been playing a vital role in urging the establishment of a national budget system. During 1917 and 1918, the Institute had published five studies that were to serve as valuable sources of material to Congress in drafting the bill that was finally passed as the Budget and Accounting Act of 1921. Willoughby's recommendations, made both in his book, *The Problem of a National Budget,* and in his testimony before the Select Committee and the Senate committee concerned, were adopted with scarcely any modification. And after the act was signed into law, President Harding called on the Institute to take a major technical role in bringing the new budget system into operation.

[29] *National Budget System:* Hearings before the Select Committee of the House on the Budget, 66th Cong., 1st sess. (1919).

by the President or by the Secretary of the Treasury under his direction. The committee favored the establishment of an independent auditing and controlling officer who would be responsible to Congress, believing that such an office would greatly strengthen Congress's control over finance and serve as a counterbalance to the proposed Bureau of the Budget, which was expected to strengthen the President's hand. The committee wanted an auditing officer who would also examine departmental administration and report his findings and recommendations to the appropriations committees, thus aiding them in their work. Witnesses Taft, Glass, and Stimson urged that the power of Congress to increase the budget as submitted by the President be strictly limited, but the proposal found no favor with the committee. A further recommendation by Taft and Stimson that Cabinet members be permitted to speak on the floor of each house in defense of their budgets also received little support.

At the conclusion of the hearings the Select Committee reported out the Good bill, which provided for an executive budget under the President, assisted by the Bureau of the Budget. It also established the General Accounting Office, headed by a Comptroller General, who would be responsible to Congress. In the report that accompanied the bill, the basic defects of the existing practice were summarized as follows:

> Expenditures are not considered in connection with revenues; . . .
> Congress does not require of the President any carefully thought-out financial and work program representing what provision in his opinion should be made for meeting the financial needs of the Government; . . . the estimates of expenditure needs now submitted to Congress represent only the desires of the individual departments, establishments, and bureaus . . . [without any] superior revision with a view to bringing them into harmony with each other . . . or of making them, as a whole, conform to the needs of the Nation as represented by the Treasury and prospective revenues.[30]

On October 21, after a debate of several days in which no opposition was raised against an executive budget, the House passed

[30] *National Budget System*, House Report No. 362, to Accompany H.R. 9783, 66th Cong., 1st sess. (1919), p. 4.

the Good bill, 285 to 3, and sent it to the Senate. Preoccupied with the Versailles Treaty, the Senate failed to consider the bill before the end of the session. President Wilson's message to Congress on December 2, 1919, urged the enactment of a budget law which would fix the responsibility for preparing the budget on the Executive. Stressing the need for a single, comprehensive plan of expenditure related to the nation's income, Wilson stated:

> The budget so prepared should be submitted to and approved or amended by a single committee of each House of Congress, and no single appropriation should be made by the Congress, except such as may have been included in the budget prepared by the executive or added by the particular committee of Congress charged with the budget legislation.[31]

In the spring of 1920 the Senate referred the House bill to its Select Committee on the Budget, of which Senator Medill McCormick was chairman. The committee struck out of the House bill all provisions after the enacting clause and substituted the provisions of McCormick's own bill, which made the Secretary of the Treasury rather than the President responsible for preparing the budget. The Senate passed the measure in this form unanimously. In the compromise bill finally reported by the conference committee, the responsibility for preparing the budget was placed on the President, but the Bureau of the Budget, though created to assist the President and responsible to him, was located in the Treasury. The Comptroller General, head of the new General Accounting Office, would be removable only by concurrent resolution of Congress.

President Wilson vetoed the bill, maintaining that the removal provision infringed upon the President's constitutional powers. No further action was taken by Congress until the spring of 1921, when the bill was modified to provide for the removal of the Comptroller General by a joint resolution, which requires the signature of the President. In this form it was signed into law by President Harding on June 10, to become known as the Budget and Accounting Act of 1921.[32]

[31] *Congressional Record*, Vol. 59, Pt. 1, 66th Cong., 2d sess. (Dec. 2, 1919), p. 29.
[32] 42 Stat. 20.

The act did not include any change in the organization and procedure of Congress itself in passing on appropriation bills, but the assumption had been made that each chamber would revise its committee system by changing its rules. The House, in fact, had adopted a resolution in June 1920 providing for the assignment of all appropriation bills to a single committee. Representative Good's report accompanying the resolution stated that the change was essential to complete the budgetary reform and would enable Congress to pass upon the budget "in one measure," with a "full and comprehensive discussion . . . of the big problem of Government finance. Members of Congress can see at a glance the entire picture." Good further ventured the opinion that the use of a single appropriation bill would have a restraining influence on Congress in passing legislation authorizing new activities.[33] The Senate amended its rules in March 1922 to create a single Appropriations Committee, and made a few other procedural changes in its handling of appropriation bills.

The Budget System After 1921

The re-establishment of a single appropriations committee in each house failed to bring about a "full and comprehensive discussion . . . of the big problem of Government finance," nor did it lead to the use of a single appropriation bill or consideration of the budget as a whole. The department estimates were still passed upon through numerous appropriation bills, each considered by a separate subcommittee and voted at different times, with the result that Congress continued its old practice of passing upon the budget piecemeal. The President's budget, which was presented as an over-all financial plan, was taken apart and assigned to various subcommittees, each of which considered only the part assigned to it. Although the chairmen of the full committees exercised some influence, in the main each subcommittee functioned as a separate body, subject to little coordinating control. The full committees gave only perfunctory review to sub-

---

[33] *National Budget System:* House Report No. 373 to Accompany House Resolution No. 324, 66th Cong., 1st sess. (1919), p. 10.

committee reports and recommendations and rarely altered them.

Nevertheless, the new budget system worked remarkably well during its first decade. Even though Congress persisted in fragmenting the over-all financial plan, the very fact that such a plan was presented enabled the process to be handled more intelligently. Furthermore, the President's estimates were ordinarily accepted as the maximum amounts which the appropriations committees would consider, and relatively few changes were made. In the first four years after the system went into effect the average annual reductions by Congress were only about $10 million, less than one half of 1 per cent of budgets which totaled over $2.5 billion.[34] On the other hand, the ever-present congressional pressures for spending were held in effective check by the sanction accorded the executive budget. During most of the 1920's the President and the Bureau of the Budget demanded strict economy of the departments, and the appropriations committees refused to entertain the departments' pleas for restoration of cuts made by the President in their estimates. This was a period of substantial annual surpluses, which were used to reduce the national debt. The budget for fiscal 1930, for example (which was still typical of the 1920's even though the calendar year marked the beginning of the great depression), totaled $3.3 billion, and there was an unexpended surplus of $738 million to apply to national debt reduction.

The decade from 1931 through 1940 witnessed an unprecedented peacetime increase in expenditures, accompanied by substantial annual deficits. Expenditures rose from slightly under $4 billion in fiscal year 1931 to more than $9 billion in 1940, as Congress voted large sums of money at President Roosevelt's request for emergency relief and various forms of work relief in attempts to cope with the continuing problem of unemployment. Although deficit financing and the mounting national debt were viewed by many with alarm, neither Congress nor the President was willing to curtail expenditure as long as the high rate of unemployment continued. In 1939 and 1940 the rate diminished somewhat, but full employment was not substantially achieved until our entry into World War II—at which time military spending had already begun to soar.

[34] W. F. Willoughby, *The National Budget System* (1927), p. 145.

Growth of the Federal Budget[35]

The combined expenditures of the six years of the World War II period (1941-1946) amounted to over $380 billion; combined deficits were $211 billion.[36] In the emergencies of wartime, neither the Bureau of the Budget nor the appropriations subcommittees were able to give the customary careful scrutiny to budget estimates, and congressional control over expenditures was necessarily relaxed. Public demands for economy ceased to be heard, being replaced by demands for the maximum war effort.

The end of the war brought renewed public pressure for economy in government and for the exercise of tighter controls, by both Congress and the administration, over public spending. In 1947 federal expenditures were $39 billion—compared to well over $60 billion in 1946—and in 1948 decreased to $33 billion. From then on, despite perennial economy drives, they rose, at first slowly but steadily, then sharply. Total budget expenditures for 1959 amounted to $80.7 billion, or 21 per cent of the national income; receipts were $68.3 billion, leaving a record peacetime deficit of $12.4 billion.

As of 1961, there seemed little prospect for any reversal of the long-term secular trend for the budget to increase. From 1930 through 1959, income exceeded outgo in only five fiscal years—1947, 1948, 1951, 1956, and 1957—and only in 1948 was the surplus fairly substantial. As of 1962, an annual budget in excess of $90 billion would be taken for granted, and unless international tensions were relaxed it was anticipated that the figure could soon reach $100 billion.

The tremendous growth in peacetime expenditures since the end of World War II may be attributed in large part to the necessities of the cold war and the increased involvement of this country in international affairs. A defense budget of approximately $50 billion annually, or almost half the total budget, is accepted today as the minimum needed for reasonable national security. Defense and related operations have become so vast and extensive that to exercise essential

[35] Unless otherwise specified, the figures in this section are taken from the pertinent annual issues of *Budget of the United States* and *Federal Budget in Brief* and relate to fiscal years.
[36] Lewis H. Kimmel, *Federal Budget and Fiscal Policy, 1789-1958* (1959), p. 320.

executive and legislative control is an almost unmanageable task. For fiscal 1963 atomic energy activities alone were budgeted at $2.88 billion—nearly equal to the total budget of the government thirty years earlier; space research at $2.4 billion; and foreign aid at slightly over $4 billion.

The increase in nonmilitary expenditures has also been great and illustrates, perhaps even better than emergency spending does, the immense range and complexity of modern government operations. The Department of Agriculture, for example, originally consisted of the Forest Service and a handful of bureaus concerned with agricultural education and research and the administration of a few regulatory acts; in 1889, when its head officer was elevated to Cabinet status, its annual budget was about $2 million. From then on, activities steadily multiplied, but up to 1929 annual expenditures had not exceeded $145 million. After 1933, when the department undertook new action programs to rescue a depressed agriculture, its budget increased to over $1 billion annually; by the end of the depression such programs had become a fixed and major part of the department's activity and policy. Increases in expenditures after World War II reached a peak in the $6.7 billion budgeted for 1959.

The increase in activities and expenditures for federal public health programs has also been striking. In 1929, $9.5 million was budgeted for public health use; in 1959 the figure was $704 million; the 1961 estimate was $971 million.

Even these few statistics make it obvious that the task of examining and passing upon the budget has become vastly more difficult than it was during the ten years after the national budget system was instituted, when members of the appropriations subcommittees with several years of service could consider themselves sufficiently well-informed about the operations and administration of the departments to examine their estimates in great detail. Today, a thorough personal knowledge of all the greatly enlarged, complex, and often far-flung operations undertaken by most of the departments is almost impossible to acquire. Largely because this is so, the subcommittees have in recent years tended to devote less attention to the details of administration and specific items of expenditure and more to questions of departmental policy and program.

The change is a desirable one—and would be even more so if, as a consequence of it, Congress devoted a greater degree of attention to over-all budgetary policy and its impact on the economy. In the 1920's, when government expenditures required less than 5 per cent of a national income rarely as high as $80 billion, the President, in preparing the budget, and the congressional committees, in reviewing it, were primarily concerned with the allocation of scarce resources among competing programs and the relation of total expenditures to total revenue. But when expenditures require, as they did in 1959, over 20 per cent of a national income of $399.6 billion, it is vitally important for the government to consider the resulting impact on the domestic and international economy. The budget, including revenues as well as expenditures, has become the most important single means whereby the government may promote economic growth, stability, and maximum employment.

Yet certain features of both the budget system per se and the procedures of Congress in dealing with it often impede not only the adoption of a wise and consistent fiscal policy but also the timely adjustment of budgeted revenues and expenditures from year to year to meet changing economic trends. For example, a substantial part of the expenditures for any year are relatively uncontrollable, since they represent fixed charges, prior obligations, or statutory commitments. The difficulty of making opportune fiscal decisions is further increased by the long lapse of time, due in part to cumbersome legislative procedures, between the preparation of plans and estimates and the eventual expenditure. For ordinary continuing activities the lag is usually from one to two years; for new or enlarged programs, especially those concerned with public works and military armament, it may be as much as five years. (These difficulties in procedure and their consequences are discussed further in the two following chapters.)

The change in the purpose and philosophy of federal expenditures since the end of the 1920's has been as notable as the vast increase in amount. Yet the methods whereby Congress exercises control over departmental estimates have changed only slightly from those employed in the 1920's when administrative programs and activities were simpler in purpose and extent and annual expenditures never totaled more than $2 to $3 billion. Theoretically, the Committee on Appropriations in each house is the point at which Congress coordinates its control of national budget policy and where, if at any place, the changing purpose of expenditures must be reckoned with and adapted to. However, neither committee performs successfully as a coordinator. The House committee especially, although in some respects "slowly adjusting to the realities of a shrinking globe," appears to have developed "neither a philosophy nor methods" to deal with the extensive budgets of recent years, and is still "a committee in flux, heavily burdened with the legacy of the past."[37]

Thus the hope voiced by Representative James Good in 1920 that the pending budgetary reform, combined with the change of House rules to create a single Appropriations Committee, would enable Congress to undertake each year a "full and comprehensive discussion . . . of the big problem of government finance" is still far from realized. Among the legacies of the past that burden the money committees and Congress as a whole are the parochial pressures which an individual congressman believes he must heed if he is to win reelection and which are thus responsible for part of the inconsistency often seen in fiscal legislation. However, the major impediments to effective, consistent consideration and determination of broad fiscal policies by Congress reside in the structure and methods of the appropriations process itself, which we will now examine.

[37] Holbert N. Carroll, *The House of Representatives and Foreign Affairs* (1958), pp. 141, 142.

4

The Appropriations Process[1]

THE PIECEMEAL PROCEDURE used by Congress in passing on the President's budget provides no occasion for a "great debate" on fiscal policies which would inform and educate the public and fully establish the President's responsibility for his financial program. Each of the twenty or more appropriation bills acted on annually is considered at a different time and independently of the others and of the budget as a whole. There is no time when Congress debates and votes on the whole Budget or considers the comparative needs of the major programs, the relationship of proposed expenditures to estimated revenues, and the effects of the contemplated budget on the national economy and on international affairs.

In no other area of legislation does Congress rely so greatly on the committee system. Each house usually accepts the recommendations of its Appropriations Committee on the bills submitted by the respective subcommittees, the House with some debate but of a kind that leaves much to be desired from the standpoint of policy discussion, the Senate ordinarily with little or none. If a challenge does arise, it is rarely serious—and nearly always resisted successfully by the involved subcommittee. Those representatives and senators who are not members of the Appropriations Committees, and even those who are but who have not served on a specific subcommittee whose bill is

[1] See Arthur W. Macmahon, "Congressional Oversight of Administration: The Power of the Purse," *Political Science Quarterly*, Vol. 58 (1943), pp. 161-190, 380-414; Elias Z. Huzar, *The Purse and the Sword* (1950), *passim;* Holbert N. Carroll, *The House of Representatives and Foreign Affairs* (1958), Chaps. 8, 9; Arthur Smithies, *The Budgetary Process in the United States* (1955), Chaps. 6-9; Robert Ash Wallace, *Congressional Control of Federal Spending* (1960).

being reported, seldom have sufficient knowledge to challenge the subcommittee's detailed revisions of a highly complex estimate or its judgment on departmental activities and programs.

The difficulty of acquiring information on the vastly complicated details of modern budgets is often acknowledged by members of Congress. In 1952, for example, Carl Vinson, chairman of the House Armed Services Committee, in urging acceptance of the Defense appropriation bill as reported by the Appropriations Committee said:

> They [the subcommittee] deserve the support of every member of this House because they are in a far better position to know the needs and necessities of national defense than you and I, who have not given . . . [the bill] the complete and detailed study it should have.[2]

This atmosphere of acceptance, however, stops at the doors of the House and Senate respectively; neither house automatically accepts the action of the other. When the House has voted a revision of an estimate as recommended by a subcommittee, the revision is usually appealed by the department to the corresponding Senate subcommittee, and more often than not the reduction will be in large part restored. The resulting differences in the bill are compromised in conference, usually at about the midway point, but on occasion the conferees of one house or the other refuse to yield and thus force acceptance of their previous action.

The Committees on Appropriations

> It is not much of an exaggeration to state that the money committees of House and Senate constitute a third house of Congress. All of the policies arising from the diverse committees of Congress in response to the pressures they feel are filtered again through the appropriations committees.[3]

In both House and Senate, assignment to these powerful committees ranks high in member preference, despite the heavy burden of work entailed. Several terms of service in Congress are the customary

[2] *Congressional Record*, Vol. 98, Pt. 3, 82d Cong., 2d sess. (April 7, 1952), p. 3641.
[3] See Carroll, *op. cit.*, Chap. 8, for discussion of Appropriations Committee organization; the quotation is from p. 142.

prerequisite to the assignment: as of 1959, the fifty members of the House committee had an average of 3.38 years service prior to assignment, members of the Senate group, 5.26 years. Currently, however, each house has been making it a practice to appoint a few freshmen members. Once assigned, a member rarely leaves the committee, and thus the average length of continuous service is notable: in 1959 the House group average was 8.74 years—Democrats, 10.20 years, Republicans, 6.55. Representative John Taber of New York, ranking miniority member, had then been on the committee for 36 years, Chairman Clarence Cannon of Missouri, 30 years, and twenty-two others, at least 10 years. On the Senate committee, continuous service averaged 7.44 years. Carl Hayden of Arizona led with 32 years, followed by Richard B. Russell of Georgia with 26 and Styles Bridges of New Hampshire with 22; more than a third of the others had served 10 years or more. A member from a safe congressional seat eventually rises to the influential position of chairman of a subcommittee or its ranking minority member.

Each committee member ordinarily serves on at least two of the subcommittees—which numbered, as of 1960, fourteen in the House and eleven in the Senate—through which the full committee actually operates. For the Senate committee the average of such assignments is about five per member; all but two of the subcommittees have a membership of twelve or more. Six of the groups also each have three ex-officio members from the corresponding legislative committee—its chairman and the ranking members from each party. In the House, new committee members are often given only one assignment, while seniors customarily have three; the membership on most of the groups is from five to ten.

There is no doubt that the two appropriations committees constitute the principal agency of Congress in the exercise of legislative control over the executive departments, but the basic realities of the "power of the purse" reside at the subcommittee level. As noted in Chapter 3, each subcommittee is ordinarily subject to little direction or coordinating control by the full committee, although subcommittee chairmen and ranking miniority members do consult with the respective leaders of the full committee before marking up a bill, and some coordination is achieved thereby, especially in the House. The vastly detailed bill and the accompanying many-paged report are as a rule accepted by the full committee without change, after perhaps only one hour of consideration—and often then goes to the floor on the same day, where the subcommittee is customarily in charge of the debate. Thus:

> It is not the Congress, not the House or Senate, not even the appropriations committee as a whole that should be thought of as abstractions, set against administration. The reality is a handful of men from particular states or districts, working with a particular committee clerk on a multitude of details.[4]

This parochial aspect of the committees is also seen in the degree to which their members seek assignments to subcommittees that pass upon appropriations of concern to their constituents. Members from agricultural districts, for instance, want to be assigned to the subcommittee which deals with appropriations for the Department of Agriculture and related activities; similarly, those who represent areas to which flood control irrigation, military construction projects, and so on are important seek assignment to the respective subcommittees concerned. Certain subcommittees, however, including State, Justice and Judiciary, Foreign Operations, Commerce, and Treasury, pass upon few items of local concern.

The subcommittee assignments in the House are made by the Appropriations Committee chairman and the ranking minority party member for their respective parties. For a number of years after the institution of the budget system, chairmen followed the practice of not assigning a member to a subcommittee that passed upon items of special interest to his district, but after 1937 the practice lapsed.[5] A study of the House Appropriations Committee made in 1953 reported that "all eleven individuals who served on the [Agriculture] subcommittee during the 78th, 79th, and 80th Congresses represented districts with predominance of agriculture. . . . Of the 22 Appropriations Committee members who served on the Interior Department Subcommittee in the years examined, the vast majority represented districts with special concern with matters handled by the Depart-

[4] Macmahon, *op. cit.*, p. 181.
[5] See *ibid.*, p. 178.

ment."[6] In the 86th Congress, however, one member from a non-agricultural district—New York City—was appointed to the Agriculture subcommittee, evidently to represent consumers' interests.

In the Senate the assignments are dictated largely by member preference and seniority, with the result that almost the entire membership of the subcommittees which pass upon appropriations of local concern consists of those who have a personal stake in the decisions. The Department of Agriculture subcommittee in the 86th Congress, for example, included senators from Georgia, Virginia, Florida, Oklahoma, Mississippi, Nebraska, North and South Dakota, Idaho, Arizona, and Connecticut; of these, only Connecticut has a substantial urban population. The members of the Interior Department subcommittee came from Arizona, New Mexico, Wyoming, California, Nevada, Idaho, North and South Dakota, West Virginia, Texas, Georgia, Arkansas, and Tennessee—all states with special interest in the work of the department—and almost all of these states were also represented on the Public Works subcommittee.

The pros and cons of this practice are difficult to evaluate, for the personal stake of a member in the activities of departments whose funds he decides upon involves many intangible factors. Further, there are certainly advantages for a department if the members of the subcommittee dealing with it are acquainted with and vitally interested in its programs. Nevertheless, the practice undoubtedly often leads to budgetary decisions that favor local rather than national considerations.

The Staffs

The Appropriations Committee of each house has long had the advantage of an expert staff especially notable for its stability in point of its members' continued service, despite party shifts. On the House committee staff, a fifteen-year average length of service for the professional members is not unusual; the Senate average is only slightly less. The position of clerk (the unpretentious title of the staff head) of the House committee was filled from 1884 to 1944 by only two men —James C. Courts and his successor Marcellus C. Sheild. As of 1961,

[6] Robert S. Friedman, "Policy Formation in the Appropriation Process, with Special Emphasis on the House Appropriations Committee" (doctoral dissertation, University of Illinois, 1953), p. 278.

the Senate committee's veteran clerk Everard H. Smith had served for twenty-two years, after formerly establishing a record as assistant clerk.

In the earliest days staff members were selected largely on the basis of personal or party patronage considerations, but having been appointed, they acquired expertness in the work of the committee and were retained by succeeding chairmen. More recently, selection has been primarily based on qualifications, and those chosen are usually persons with budgeting or administrative experience in the departments. Clarence Cannon, chairman of the House Appropriations Committee, states that he has never "appointed anybody recommended politically" to him, "because the positions are too important to be made subject to patronage. Many of . . . [the staff] have been trained by the Bureau of the Budget. No joint committee can secure more experienced experts at any price."[7]

Prior to 1940, the staffs were small in size, particularly in relation to the work load; neither of them consisted of more than six to eight professionals and a very few clerical workers. Since then there has been a substantial increase. In 1960 the regular full-time staff of the House committee consisted of forty-nine employees, of whom twenty could be classified as professional, and the Senate committee had a total of thirty-one employees, of whom twenty-two were professional. In the decade 1949-1959 annual expenditures of the House Appropriations Committee increased from $237,940 to $878,895. The salaries paid to professional staff are relatively high by government standards: in 1960 senior staff members were receiving an annual $16,000 to $17,000.

Each committee also maintains a small investigative staff, and the House committee borrows a substantial number of temporary investigators, on a reimbursal basis, from the departments and the FBI when their services are needed. In addition, the General Accounting Office makes available members of its staff on request to assist the committees, as it is required to do by law. The investigation reports are used by the subcommittees in considering the estimates of specific departments and agencies.

The use of a temporary staff for investigations has been strongly

[7] *Hearings on H.R. 7888 and S. 913,* House Committee on Rules, 82d Cong., 2d sess. (1952), p. 38.

defended by Chairman Cannon, who has pointed out that the practice enabled the committee to secure the services of persons with special qualifications for particular investigations. Some years ago he described the disadvantages of maintaining a large, permanent investigative staff as follows:

> What happens when you put men permanently on the staff? They get lazy. They develop friendships with the departments. If you get misfits it is hard to fire them. They develop a camaraderie with the members of the committees and get their salaries raised. Everybody downtown knows them. When they enter the door the word is passed through the building, "Here comes that fellow from the committee." When there is no investigation they sit around cooling their heels and their time and their salary is wasted.[8]

The House Appropriations Committee has developed a carefully considered procedure for conducting investigations. All assignments are made in writing and must be approved by both the chairman and the ranking minority member of the subcommittee and of the whole committee—a requirement designed to prevent investigations from being used for partisan purposes. Since the early 1950's the committee has received an annual appropriation of $500,000 for investigations, and in the last several years has spent approximately this amount.

The investigation reports are used by the subcommittees in considering the budgets of the departments or agencies concerned. Earlier, they were seldom printed, but recently the more important reports and the department replies have been included in the published hearings. Thus the material is available to all members of the two appropriations committees and to members of Congress and the public.

A special type of temporary investigative staff was utilized by the House committee during the 80th Congress and again during the 83rd, when the Republican party controlled the House. Chairman John Taber secured the loan of accountants and businessmen (about forty for the 80th Congress, and some seventy-five for the 83rd) from leading corporations, taxpayers' associations, Chambers of Commerce, and accounting firms. Acting as consultants and investigators, usually without salary and with the assistance of personnel borrowed from the General Accounting Office, they were assigned to conduct surveys of the programs and activities of various departments and to recommend

---

[8] Quoted by Douglas Cater, "The Power of the Purse and the Congressman," *Reporter,* Dec. 11, 1951, p. 26.

budgetary reductions. The existing evidence concerning the effectiveness of these consultants is somewhat conflicting. Some members of the Appropriations Committee regarded their work as highly valuable; others doubted that outsiders unfamiliar with government procedures, the legislative background of government programs, and the complexities of the budget process had been able to acquire enough knowledge, in the brief time available, to give useful advice.[9]

Larger staffs to assist the work of the appropriations committees have been frequently urged both in and outside of Congress. The subcommittees with the largest workloads usually have two or more staff assistants, but a number of the others in each house have only one. Advocates of larger staffs point to the huge appropriations passed on by the subcommittees and maintain that a good deal more professional assistance is needed to study the department budgets in greater detail for evidence of inefficiency, waste, inflated estimates, and poor administration. The Joint Committee on the Organization of Congress stated in its 1946 report that "Congress has not adequately equipped itself to resist the pressures of departments and agencies in behalf of larger expenditures," and recommended that the staff of each Appropriations Committee be augmented so as to provide four full-time assistants for each subcommittee.[10] However, although the Congressional Reorganization Act of 1946 later authorized the committees to employ as many staff assistants as were required, the regular staffs have still been kept relatively small. In the House, Chairman Cannon has strongly opposed creating a large permanent staff, maintaining that in time it would tend to increase its power and jurisdiction until it became a "Frankenstein which could not be controlled or dislodged and could be used for partisan purposes."[11]

The Subcommittees in Action

In their laborious task of reviewing the huge federal budget, the appropriation subcommittees, especially those of the House, place great reliance on the formal hearings at which department and bu-

[9] See Chapter 9 for a more detailed discussion of congressional investigations.
[10] Senate Report No. 1011, 79th Cong., 2d sess. (March 1946), pp. 19 and 20.
[11] *Congressional Record*, Vol. 89, Pt. 1, 78th Cong., 1st sess. (Feb. 11, 1943), p. 887.

reau officials explain and defend their budgets and programs. Beginning sometimes even before the opening of the congressional session, the hearings are held almost daily, often in both morning and afternoon, and for a major bill concerning one of the larger departments may extend for several weeks. Special sessions are also held—more often in the Senate than the House—to permit members of Congress and other interested persons and groups to testify, but the bulk of testimony is presented by the agencies concerned. The great detail of the budget examination is indicated by the length of the printed hearings, which are made available to other members of Congress before the bill is finally reported. For a House hearing on one of the larger departments, the printed version, which is usually heavily edited and also excludes off-the-record testimony, will often exceed 2,000 pages. The Senate transcripts are somewhat less voluminous.

House hearings are generally well attended by the subcommittee members concerned, but for the Senate hearings attendance is frequently sparse—no more than two or three members may be present of a total membership of ten to fifteen. The poor attendance is doubtless due in part to conflicts with other meetings, since Senate members customarily serve on several other committees, and on numerous subcommittees. The result is that decisions on the budget estimates are delegated to the chairman of a Senate subcommittee to a larger extent than happens in the House.[12]

The Senate hearings are often open to the public, and when important estimates are under consideration the audience may be quite numerous. House subcommittee sessions as a rule are closed—even to other members of Congress and members of the other appropriations subcommittees—and much of the testimony is off the record. The House committee has traditionally shrouded its operations in mystery; chairmen and the staffs of other committees "confess that the Committee on Appropriations is the most difficult duchy to penetrate."[13]

The hearings are based on the department budget documents as re-

---

[12] For the ten sessions held in 1958 by the Senate subcommittee on the Interior Department, for example, the average attendance was 2.5. Senator Hayden of Arizona, the chairman, attended all sessions and at four of them was the only member present. Senator Dworshak of Idaho attended six sessions, Senator Young of North Dakota four, one other member two, three members one; four members attended no sessions.

[13] Carroll, op. cit., p. 143.

viewed and revised under the direction of the Bureau of the Budget and the President; thus the witnesses are usually defending a revised version of their original estimates. The departments also provide the subcommittees with voluminous mimeographed explanatory notes, commonly known as "justification books," which describe programs, activities, and administrative organization and include statistical data on operations, previous expenditures, and the budget estimates. Subcommittee members often complain that the justification books contain far too much detail, and the present trend seems to be a reduction in length.

At the opening of the hearings the department head, accompanied by his principal assistants and the department budget officer, makes a general presentation concerning the programs, objectives, policies, and major features of the budget, and answers questions. In the House the sessions with a department head tend to be merely a formality of little value. In the Senate, however, subcommittee members, having the advantage of knowing what action the House has taken on the department's budget, often make this stage of the hearings the occasion to discuss major issues. Nevertheless, in both houses the major portion of the hearings is devoted to interrogation of bureau officers and their assistants, who are highly informed on the programs and expenditure details.

In the first ten years or so after the Act of 1921 was passed, the subcommittees were disinclined to go behind the President's budget decisions, but in recent years members have often been outspokenly critical of cuts made under the direction of the Budget Bureau and the President, and have been likely to ask witnesses from favored agencies to supply the original estimates and defend them against the reductions imposed. The practice obviously places a witness in a difficult position, especially if he himself does not agree with the President's actions or does not fully understand the reason for them.

The interrogation of witnesses tends to be unsystematic and repetitious, partly because it is common practice for each subcommittee member to have his turn at questioning. Depending on the interests of each member and his degree of acquaintance with the agency's work, one group of questions may be searching and relate to vital issues of policy or administration, another may wander off into a trivial but detailed backwater. Not many members have sufficient firsthand knowledge of the complex programs and activities to inquire into specific operating details. In the general atmosphere of impromptu cross-examination, questions dealing with important policy issues are frequently not followed up.

> Often a broad answer blunts a leading question that is not pressed home. [A former Representative asked of the Chief of Staff], "General, . . . have you made any study of the elimination of branches in the Army?" The answer was, "Yes, sir"; and with that the matter was dropped. The interrogation shifted to the average age of enlisted men.[14]

Such exchanges, which are frequently found in the printed records, suggest that the hearings are subject to serious limitations as the basis for the determination of funds to be allocated to each department and program. The poor attendance at the sessions of the Senate subcommittees is perhaps an indication that senators, at least, consider their other committee assignments more important. Members often complain that they must approve large expenditures with too little examination because they feel insufficiently informed about the work of the departments to conduct properly searching inquiries.

However, subcommittee members need not be experts in the work of the departments to conduct the kind of inquiry which would enable them to apply intelligent judgment to money questions. The major decisions they make—or should make—relate to issues of both policy and politics, and it is an essential principle of democratic government that the final determination of such decisions shall be made by the elected representatives of the people rather than by experts and appointed administrators. When the hearings are concerned primarily with the programs and policies of the departments, as they have been increasingly in recent years, instead of with small expenditure details as formerly, the subcommittees are better able to make intelligent decisions about the plans and budget requests of the departments.

[14] Macmahon, *op. cit.*, p. 384.

Methods of Control

In passing on the department budgets the subcommittees, as the operating units of the appropriations committees, currently exercise three distinct but closely related types of control: (1) they determine the amount of funds to be allocated to each major program or activity of each department; (2) they pass upon the administrative policies of the departments in the execution of programs assigned to them; (3) they investigate the administration of the departments and exercise continuous oversight over departmental activities, and apply such controls as they determine are needed.

Allocation of Funds

The first function of the appropriations committees is to allocate available funds among the competing programs and activities of the government and to determine the level at which each program shall be conducted. The organization and procedures of the subcommittees are reasonably well designed to reach decisions concerning the needs of each department and of each program and activity within departments, but no provision is made for comparing the program needs of one department with those of other departments, as well as with the total funds available. This is the major weakness of the present method by which Congress appropriates funds, and, although various proposals have been made to correct it (see Chapter 5), so far no workable solution has been found.

It is widely assumed that the appropriations committees' prime function is to examine the budgets of the departments and make substantial reductions wherever possible, and that they would be derelict in their duty if the reductions were not proposed.[15] This is first of all obviously an oversimplification of their responsibilities, for the committees do a great deal more than determine the amount of money to be appropriated to each department, as will be discussed below. Further, it is not always desirable that reductions be made. Legisla-

[15] See Paul H. Douglas, *Economy in the National Government* (1952), especially Chap. 10.

tive review of the budget is important, but indiscriminate reduction of the budget by the legislative body is an invitation to the departments to inflate their requests in anticipation of cuts. This, indeed, was the basic fault of the system prior to 1921, which it was expected that the budget system would correct.

If a legislature substantially revises the budget, obviously the chief executive and his administration cannot be held responsible for the fiscal management of the government and the integrity of the budget. In Great Britain, where responsibility for finance is placed inescapably on the government in office, all votes on supply are treated as votes of confidence, and although Parliament debates the budget at great length, it makes no changes whatever. It is contended that if Parliament were to revise the supply estimates, the ministers could not be held responsible.

Under the United States' form of government it is the prerogative of the legislature to revise the executive budget; it may increase as well as decrease individual items, or it may strike out items altogether and add new ones. If sound budgetary practice is followed, however, the legislature would normally make relatively few changes in the budget as submitted by the chief executive. In New York State, for example, when the governor and the legislature are of the same party, it is unusual for the legislature to make any changes in the governor's budget. The same is true of some other states. After the budget has been prepared and revised under the direction of the President, substantial revision should ordinarily be unnecessary, especially if it has been prepared, as is usually true, with close attention to legislative policies. Changes that are made by Congress when the budget is under consideration, it should be recognized, are often dictated by a few influential members who occupy key positions on the finance committees, and may not necessarily reflect the considered judgment of the assembly. The changes are often increases for the benefit of particular groups or sections rather than reductions in the interest of economy.

The statistics published by Congress at the end of each session, showing the changes it has made in the President's budget, do not reflect the changes accurately. A total reduction of $1 billion or more is sometimes indicated, but many of the specific reductions are "paper cuts" that do not affect actual expenditures. For example, a "paper cut" occurs when a subcommittee recommends less than the amount required to meet a definite obligation, or when it approves the spending plans of an agency but cuts its appropriations, advising it to return at the beginning of the next session for a supplemental appropriation. That the total appropriations picture can be misleading was pointed out by the House Appropriations Committee in 1957:

> It may come as a surprise to many to know that while the last session of Congress was *reducing* the President's request for "appropriations" in appropriation bills by $257 million, it was at the same time, in other than appropriations bills, *increasing* the President's request for other types of obligating and spending authority by $1,736 million.[16]

The difficulty of determining with accuracy the extent to which Congress reduces or increases the President's budget is due largely to the complexity of the process, to the different types of appropriations in which funds are voted, and to the confusing terminology—which includes such words as authorization, obligation, appropriation, contract authorization, and expenditure. The amount appropriated for each fiscal year does not indicate even approximately what the actual expenditures will be. An appropriation authorizes a department to incur obligations to spend, but the spending may be spread over several years. Therefore, a large part of the expenditures in each fiscal year is based on appropriations of earlier years, and reductions voted by Congress often have little effect on expenditures during the fiscal year to which they apply. Further, Congress annually votes huge supplementary and deficiency appropriations, usually totaling several billion dollars, and reductions voted earlier are often restored. Thus the same items may appear twice in the President's budget requests— first in the regular budget and later in the requests for supplemental and deficiency appropriations—but only once in appropriations.

During the fifteen years from 1946 through 1960, Congress appropriated less than the President requested in each year. In all but two years the reduction exceeded $1 billion; in eight of the years it exceeded $2 billion, and in three it exceeded $5 billion.[17] For the fiscal years 1955-1960 (see tabulation below), a comparison of the total estimates submitted by the President and of all appropriations—regular, supplemental, permanent, and indefinite—indicates that Congress

---

[16] *Administration Plan to Improve Congressional Control of the Budget,* House Report No. 62, 85th Cong., 1st sess. (1957), p. 9. (Emphasis in original.)

[17] *Appropriations, Budget Estimates,* etc., Senate Document No. 61, 86th Cong., 1st sess. (1959), p. 644.

annually voted an average of $2.2 billion less than the President requested.[18]

	Estimates	Appropriations	Reductions
1955	$60.8 billion	$58.0 billion	−$2.6 billion
1956	66.0	63.9	− 2.1
1957	73.3	73.0	− 0.3
1958	78.1	73.1	− 5.0
1959	81.7	81.1	− 0.6
1960	83.5	81.6	− 1.9

Actual expenditures during the period, however, exceeded the *original* budget estimates by an average of $2.8 billion annually. Congress often appears to be reducing the President's budget estimates by appropriating less than he requests, while taking other actions that increase expenditures. In 1955, for example, it reduced President Eisenhower's requests for public works, but voted $47 million to start 107 new projects not included in the budget, the eventual cost of which will exceed $1.5 billion.[19] It often passes a measure—such as a salary increase for federal employees—which requires additional expenditures, but does not vote the necessary funds, which then must be provided in subsequent appropriations.

There are periods when the leadership of Congress, and especially that of the appropriations committees, is more economy-minded than the President; at other times the effective drives in Congress are for greater expenditures, while the President acts as a restraining force. In general, the appropriations subcommittees, particularly in the House, strive to reduce department requests, but programs that have strong congressional support are often increased. A striking example of such increases is seen in the following comparison of the budget estimates and appropriations for the National Institutes of Health, during fiscal years 1955-1961:

	Estimate	Appropriation	Increase
1955	$ 71.1 million	$ 81.2 million	$ 10.1 million
1956	89.1	97.6	8.5
1957	126.5	184.4	57.9
1958	190.1	211.2	21.1
1959	211.2	307.7	96.5
1960	294.3	400.0	105.7
1961	400.0	560.0	160.0

[18] Figures from *The Budget for 1961*, Hearings Before the House Committee on Appropriations, 86th Cong., 2d sess. (1960), p. 98.

[19] See testimony of Percival F. Brundage, Director of the Bureau of the Budget, before the House Judiciary Committee in hearings on the item veto, May 27, 1957, p. 22.

When account is taken of the actions of not only the appropriations committees but also other committees and individual senators and representatives, the over-all effect of Congress on the federal budget through the years is unquestionably for *greater* rather than *less* expenditures. In part, this happens because responsibility for finance in Congress is divided among many committees, subcommittees, and individuals, while the responsibility of the President is direct and inescapable. Other committees of Congress often press for expansions of the programs which come under their jurisdiction and recommend legislation committing the government to greater expenditures. Individual members urge economy in general but seek additional expenditures which will benefit their own constituents. Although both the President and Congress are under public pressures for expanded government programs, the effective pressures on each are not the same; as a result, the President often urges programs that Congress rejects or reduces, while Congress authorizes expenditures which the President opposes. These differences in point of view are a fundamental feature of our constitutional system.

The possibility that substantial reductions can be made either by the President or by the Congress is far less than is commonly supposed, since (as noted in Chapter 3) a large part of the budget consists of fixed obligations and other expenditures that are relatively uncontrollable from year to year. For example, interest payments on the public debt, veterans' pensions and benefits, payments into retirement funds, grants to the states under statutory requirements, and farm price supports, all of which are relatively uncontrollable, were estimated at $26.9 billion for 1960.

Many other expenditures are only slightly more controllable. There is, for instance, relatively little that Congress can do about postal expenditures, as a member of the House Appropriations Committee stated recently; too, given the present international situation, substantial reductions in defense expenditures are out of the question. Numerous other activities are carried on under legislation which commits the government to a prescribed level of expenditure, leaving the President and the Congress little discretion. A leading official of the Bureau of the Budget has estimated that short of a radical change in the international or domestic situation the budget is subject to not more than a 5 per cent increase or similar decrease by the President and Congress. It is at the legislative stage, when new and expanded programs and commitments are being considered, that more effective controls are urgently needed, for it is at this stage that responsibility for financial decisions in Congress is splintered among its numerous committees and subcommittees.

The several appropriations subcommittees of the two Houses follow no uniform or consistent policy; some are economy-minded and recommend substantial reductions, others follow the opposite course and recommend increases. Programs that are of benefit to organized groups or to particular areas, such as farm price supports, public works, veterans' pensions and services, subsidies to aviation, merchant marine, and other industries are seldom cut by Congress. Agencies with strong congressional support, among them the FBI, are assured of securing their requests; activities such as the Public Health Service and its medical research that are highly favored by leading members usually have their budgets increased. On the other hand, activities that lack clientele support or are opposed by organized groups often suffer severe cuts. In 1959, for example, the House Civil Service Committee was able to block a small appropriation for the President's Career Executive Commission.[20] During World War II the National Resources Planning Board and the Fair Employment Practices Commission, neither of which had been authorized by legislation, were terminated by the refusal of Congress to vote funds for their continuation. Public power projects are usually opposed by private utilities, and the Farm Bureau Federation has successfully opposed certain farm programs.

Local interests are often paramount in subcommittee budget decisions. When cuts are made, departments are often directed by the appropriations subcommittee not to close any field offices, especially in districts represented on the committee; on the other hand, when economies are necessitated by cuts, departments are sometimes accused of arranging for them in an area that will cause protests to be made to members of the appropriations committees. In 1957, Postmaster General Arthur Summerfield, by threatening to curtail postal services to avoid a deficit, was able to force the committees to reverse their previous action and to vote supplemental funds. The shortage was due largely to the fact that Congress had voted salary increases without voting additional funds.[21]

[20] See Chapter 7, section on "The Career Executive Development Program."
[21] For examples of the effects of local and constituency interest on appropriations, see Friedman, op. cit., Chap. 2. David C. Knapp, the author of another study

THE APPROPRIATIONS PROCESS

A subcommittee's attitude toward a specific program and its relations with departmental officials and bureau chiefs can greatly influence its action on a department budget. A chairman who opposes a program such as foreign aid, whether on principle or for other reasons, is able to impose drastic reductions that represent his personal views rather than the views of a majority of Congress. On the other hand, he and the other members of the subcommittee may overemphasize the importance of a program in which they are keenly interested and become its leading advocates. Relations between subcommittee members and department officials are usually cordial and marked by mutual respect and confidence, but in exceptional cases personal feuds have led to indiscriminate slashes in appropriations.

When considering reductions in departmental administrative expenditures, the subcommittees usually have difficulty in determining whether an agency is being administered with efficiency and economy and whether a reduction of expenditures would impair essential services. Reliable and objective criteria of administrative costs are seldom available, and judgments based upon impressions are apt to be erroneous. Actually, reductions that can be made in administrative expenditures are relatively small in comparison with total costs, and in the past have often proved to be false economy, weakening the administration by forcing the discharge of experienced employees and a rapid turnover of personnel. Nevertheless, reductions are often made in the belief that the estimates have been padded to some extent, and that cuts will force more economical operation; if a subcommittee thinks also that the administration is inefficient or unduly expensive, the reductions will be substantial. Although a department may point to economies it has achieved through improved procedures and management, hoping thereby to avoid reductions, the subcommittees are not always impressed and at times vote further reductions—a gesture which tends to discourage such efforts by the departments.

To a large extent the decisions of the subcommittees are based, as they should be, on the personal judgment of their members, espe-

---

of the appropriations process, reports that he was informed by the chairman of the House Agriculture Appropriations Subcommittee that all increases of local services voted by the committee, as far as the chairman could remember, were at the repeated requests of members. See Knapp, "Agricultural Policy Formation and the Appropriations Process" (doctoral dissertation, University of Chicago, 1953), p. 69.

cially the senior and leading members, derived from firsthand observations and evaluations of the programs in the field. Some members devote a considerable amount of time between sessions to inspecting all aspects of the work of the department whose budgets they pass upon, and nearly all members keep in close touch with the activities that are specifically in their own areas of interest. It is unfortunate that the pressure of other duties does not allow more time for inspection trips, which would yield valuable insights into the work of the departments.

Many of the decisions reflect the judgment of one member, or only a few members, or even the clerk. In some instances individual members are assigned to investigate certain parts of the budget, a practice which has considerable merit. At times a subcommittee uses the "meat-ax" approach, making reductions in round figures without determining where they are to be applied, a practice which is generally condemned as arbitrary but which does have the merit of giving a department's executive officers discretion in determining where reductions may be taken with the least impairment of program.

Control of Administrative Policies

In passing on the department budgets the appropriations committees are as concerned with department policies and administration as with the allocation of funds. Legislative policies are not complete when legislation is enacted, but arise continuously as it is put into effect. The complexities of modern government programs make it necessary for Congress to grant wide authority and discretion to executive officers, which it would be reluctant to do without some means of ascertaining whether executive officers are exercising this authority wisely. The task of checking falls partly on the legislative committees, but to an even greater extent on the appropriations subcommittees, which annually review the departments' activities and future plans and, having the powerful sanction of passing on the budget, are able to exercise continuous direction and supervision of department policies and administration. The subcommittees, of course, operate within the framework of legislative policies determined by statute, but within this framework play a highly influential role.

In many instances the Appropriations Committee of the House has sought to impose policies on a department that are contrary to those favored by the corresponding legislative committee, and executives of the department are thus subject to conflicting instructions without any clear legislative policy to guide their actions. There are often wide differences in the attitudes of the two committees toward particular programs. The appropriations committees of both houses are often accused of encroaching upon the jurisdiction of the legislative committees. However, in the Senate the difficulty is largely avoided because of the overlapping membership of the legislative and appropriations committees. In addition, the rules of the Senate provide that three members of a legislative committee shall serve as ex officio members of the corresponding appropriations subcommittee.

The hearings of the appropriations subcommittees and their reports contain many examples of policy decisions and directives. Though policy decisions are often written into the appropriation acts, it is usually not necessary to do so since the subcommittees can issue verbal instructions to department officers, secure commitments from them as to future actions, or write policy directives in the reports, all of which actions have about the same effect as law. The questions asked of department witnesses during a hearing are strong indications of the subcommittee's wishes about policies and thus have an important effect on department administration and future plans. The determination of the amount of funds allocated to each program is in itself an important policy decision.

An illustration of the role of the committees in passing on policies is afforded by the 1943 controversy over the Agriculture Department's decision to use soil conservation payments—previously used to limit production—to stimulate production of certain critical crops that were in short supply. The American Farm Bureau Federation strongly opposed the plan when it was announced, favoring the use of price increases as an incentive to greater production. The House Agriculture Appropriations Subcommittee called special hearings on the plan, and department officials were taken severely to task for failing to consult with it before taking the action. A few days after the hearings the subcommittee announced that the plan would not be permitted to go into effect. "With one decisive stroke, the House subcommittee killed a plan to develop a subsidy program within an accepted policy framework."[22] During the later House debate on the appropriation for the agricultural conservation program (ACP), Chairman Clarence Can-

[22] David C. Knapp, "Congressional Control of Agricultural Conservation Policy: A Case Study of the Appropriations Process," *Political Science Quarterly*, Vol. 71 (June 1956), p. 262.

non declared: "We are determining . . . this afternoon the policy of the Government on subsidies. . . . We are deciding it for many years to come."[23] Knapp reports that between 1940 and 1950, "Congress relied in large part upon the appropriations process for reviewing the operation and policies of the ACP," and that the nine basic changes in policy during this period were all made through appropriations legislation.

Another policy controversy between the Department of Agriculture and the House Agriculture Appropriations Subcommittee during President Eisenhower's second term concerned the sale of surplus agricultural stocks in the world market. The subcommittee repeatedly urged the department to sell larger quantities abroad to reduce the embarrassingly large surplus stocks, but the Secretary refrained from dumping quantities that would break the world price and impair U. S. relations with other countries. In its desire to reduce the surpluses of agricultural products, the subcommittee disregarded the effect of the policy on our foreign relations, but the Secretary of Agriculture was under obligation to consult the State Department and to follow a course that would be consistent with declared foreign policy.

When the same party is in control of the Presidency and the Congress, the appropriations committees have a strong voice in determining administrative policies which are of concern to them; however, a determined department with the support of the President may successfully resist committee dictation. During the last six years of the Eisenhower administration, when Congress was controlled by the Democrats, the Department of Agriculture frequently and successfully resisted attempts by the House subcommittee to dictate agriculture policies. Nevertheless, a department as a rule feels responsible to the committee for its policies and administration, and follows its wishes in most matters. Failure to do so may lead to reductions in appropriations.

Committee Oversight of Administration

If an appropriations subcommittee believes that the administration of an agency is faulty there are several steps it may take. It may ventilate its criticisms in its report, which it often does, and call on the

[23] *Ibid.*, p. 263.

agency to improve its administration; it may cut the appropriation, hoping thereby to force the agency to improve; it may attempt to curb abuses by writing restrictions and limitations into the appropriation act; it may issue instructions or directives to the agency, either verbally or in its report; and it may call attention to the problem and require the agency to conduct an inquiry and report its findings, recommendations, and the corrective actions that it has taken.

A subcommittee expects not only to be kept informed of department operations but also to be consulted *before* important decisions are made. In the controversy cited above concerning soil conservation payments, members of the House Agriculture Appropriations Subcommittee were especially incensed because the Secretary of Agriculture had publicly announced the new subsidy plan without consulting them in advance. In the regular hearings on the agriculture appropriations bill, Mr. Cannon told department officials pointedly, "We were right here to be consulted. You could have called us on the phone and we would have been glad to have welcomed you at any time on thirty minutes' notice."[24] An agency may also be instructed to consult with the subcommittee in advance on certain specific actions. In 1954 the Forest Service, for example, was told by a minority member of the agriculture subcommittee to consult with the subcommittee before disposing of or exchanging lands within or near the national forests; the member stated his concern that otherwise sales might not be handled properly. In its report the subcommittee also made clear that it expected to be consulted before forest research was undertaken in any country except Canada.[25]

Criticism of any activity by members of a subcommittee during the budget hearings is a signal to a department to secure committee clearance of the expenditures for such activity thereafter. In 1945 the chief of the Soil Conservation Service was criticized by the chairman of the House Agriculture Appropriations Subcommittee for making a trip to Africa, under the auspices of the Office of War Information, to explain the values of soil conservation. The chairman feared that such activities would increase competition from abroad with American agriculture. Thereafter the agency meticulously cleared all foreign travel with the

[24] *Ibid.*, p. 262.
[25] House Report No. 1510, 83d Cong., 2d sess. (1954), p. 7.

committee, even a pleasure trip of an employee to Mexico at his own expense.[26]

Through such consultations a subcommittee chairman keeps in close touch with the activities of the department and is able to enter an objection to any proposed action which he disapproves. He plays a role not unlike that of an executive officer in charge, though the decisions of the latter are based on rather different considerations. In the majority of cases the proposed action of the department is approved, provided a suitable explanation is made, but the fact that it is subject to the veto of the subcommittee (actually the chairman, in most cases) may materially influence the decision of the department.

It is not uncommon for the departments to be given specific instructions by the subcommittees or by individual members concerning administrative actions to be taken. In 1946 the Census Bureau was directed by its House appropriations subcommittee, on the suggestion of Representative John J. Rooney of Brooklyn, to move the Foreign Trade Office from Washington to New York and combine it with the New York branch office. The bureau opposed the move, and two weeks later was able to secure instructions in its deficiency appropriation that the office be located in Washington. Mr. Rooney was not a member of the deficiency subcommittee.[27] Another interesting case involved Senator Richard Russell of Georgia. Having discovered that the agricultural conservation program payment to his state was less than the payment to some other states of comparable size, the Senator suggested during the agriculture appropriation hearings in 1945 that a new formula be adopted which would provide a "fairer distribution of funds." Within a year a new formula under which Georgia benefited was put into effect, with the approval of the subcommittee in each house. However, states whose funds were reduced by the new formula objected, and the plan was abandoned the following year.[28]

The Appropriation Acts

Congress annually acts on some twenty regular appropriation bills, several supplemental and deficiency appropriations, a number of indefinite appropriations which are paid out of earmarked revenues,

[26] See Friedman, op. cit., p. 167.
[27] Ibid., pp. 153-158.
[28] See Knapp, Political Science Quarterly, pp. 269-270.

and special appropriations under various statutes. In addition, there are permanent appropriations—for such charges as interest on the public debt—reappropriations, contract authorizations (which require subsequent appropriations), and authorizations in substantive legislation for loans or expenditures to be paid out of designated funds without appropriations (so-called back door financing). Funds may be voted as available for a designated period, or they may be available until expended (no-year appropriations).

An appropriation does not actually set aside a certain sum of money which may be expended during the coming fiscal year, but is an authorization to a department to incur obligations to spend and to pay for their obligations. Unobligated balances, as well as funds that have been obligated but not spent, may be carried over to subsequent fiscal years if so authorized. This feature of the process has been strongly criticized because it has resulted in huge carryovers of spending authority. (A proposal which would avoid carryovers by placing the budget and appropriations on the basis of "annual accrued expenditures" instead of the authority to obligate is discussed in Chapter 5.)

That issue which has been a perennial question in congressional control of finance since the beginning of the government—the use of itemized versus lump sum appropriations—is still perennial, and up until World War II the appropriation structure continued to lack consistent and logical form in this regard. Funds might be voted in relatively small amounts to cover highly detailed expenditures, or they might be voted as lump sums for huge programs. Since the mid-1940's, however, Congress has in the main materially reduced the number of items and thus simplified the appropriation structure. Between 1941 and 1959 the number of items in the appropriation for the Department of Agriculture was reduced from 137 to 43; for the Post Office Department, from 61 to 5; for the Treasury Department, from 61 to 16; and for the Bureau of Indian Affairs, from 183 to 9.[29] Many former items of only a few thousand dollars have been dropped, and the former practice of allocating funds to individual field offices has been largely abandoned.

The actual change in the structure, however, is not as great as it may appear, for a number of the lump sum items include sub-items, which have the same effect as separate items, and the acts often ear-

---

[29] Figures computed by the author from the relevant appropriation acts.

mark certain of the funds for specific activities. In addition, the committee reports may include specific instructions as to how funds may be used and how reductions are to be applied. Moreover, even when appropriations are in lump sums the departments do not have a free hand in expenditures, since they are expected to conform closely to the detailed budget estimates they presented. Any substantial variance from the estimates must be for a very good reason, and is ordinarily cleared in advance with the subcommittees. Nevertheless, the reduction in the number of items has been an improvement, for it gives the departments increased flexibility and enables the subcommittees to devote more attention to program plans and objectives instead of relatively small expenditure items.

Some members of the subcommittees have been unhappy about the change, gradual though it has been, still fearing that lump sum appropriations will weaken congressional control. In 1958 the Department of Agriculture sought to combine the three separate authorizations for farm loans—farm ownership, farm operations, and soil and water conservation projects. The chairman of the House appropriations subcommittee objected that such a measure would permit the department to use all of the authorized funds for one type of loan. Another member said that it would "take away from Congress, and from the seven of us here present, the right to cinch down any specific appropriation for a certain purpose." The desired change was not allowed.[30]

An appropriation act is written in technical, legal, and lengthily involved language and contains a vast body of statutory authorizations, provisions, and restrictions. The following types of provisions are typically included: statements of the activities or objects for which each item may be spent; allocations to or limitations on expenditures for sub-items; restrictions and limitations, such as the limit on the number of automobiles that may be purchased and the maximum price that may be paid per car; prohibitions of the use of funds for certain activities; authorizations of expenditures for activities not specifically authorized by legislation; exemptions from certain other statutory provisions; directions concerning administration; and substantive legislation. The 32 regular and special acts for fiscal 1960 required 248 pages of fine print, totaling approximately 100,000 words.

[30] Hearings Before the House Agriculture Appropriations Subcommittee, 85th Cong., 2d sess. (1958), Pt. I, p. 38.

The item for the Agricultural Conservation Program in the 1960 appropriations furnishes a good example of typical provisions.[31] In addition to making available for the program the sum of $241,500,000, the item authorized the use of ("not to exceed") $6,000 for exhibits at fairs within the United States; limited administrative expenses to $26,832,950, but exempted aerial photographs from this limitation; limited the amount that could be transferred to the administration account under Section 392 of the Agriculture Adjustment Act of 1938; prohibited the use of any funds for regional or state information employees, but this was not to preclude answering inquiries of, or supplying information to, individual farmers at the county level; authorized the use of funds for the administration of the 1960 soil conservation program and limited the payment to an individual participant in the program to $2,500; prohibited any change in the soil program in any county which would restrict eligibility requirements below those of 1957 and 1958, unless recommended by the county committee and approved by the state committee; prohibited any reduction in the allocation of funds to any county below the 1958 level; authorized the use of ("not to exceed") 5 per cent of the allocation to any county for the use of the services of the Soil Conservation Service for technical assistance; authorized the use of ("not to exceed") 1 per cent of each county allocation for technical services of any other public agency; allocated $2,500,000 for technical services in formulating and carrying out conservation practices and $1,000,000 for conservation practices related to flood prevention in approved watersheds; authorized the purchase of seed, fertilizers, trees, and other services with the approval of the Secretary of Agriculture; prohibited the use of funds for the salary or travel of any person convicted of violation of the Hatch Act or the Code provision prohibiting the use of public funds to influence any member of Congress for or against legislation.[32]

Such provisions make it clear that the appropriations committees are concerned with a great deal more than the allocation of funds to the various and competing programs. Describing the language of some appropriation items as a "jungle of detailed provisions," the first Hoover Commission recommended that a comprehensive survey be made, looking toward a long overdue simplification of appropri-

[31] 73 Stat. 171.
[32] Since the passage of the Hatch Act, this last prohibition is more or less standard.

ation structure, language, and procedure.[33] The distinguished former clerk of the House Appropriations Committee, Marcellus C. Sheild, had earlier urged simplification of the form of appropriation bills, stating that it would "greatly facilitate the consideration and understanding of them by Congress and the public. Most of them are a mass of detail which has grown like Topsy . . . and there is no systematic plan or central theme pervading all of them."[34]

It is generally recognized that the numerous restrictions, limitations, and prohibitions included in the appropriation acts create serious difficulties for administrators, often in ways not anticipated by Congress. Not so commonly recognized is that such restrictions also make the task of the appropriations subcommittees more difficult, especially since they tend to be continued from year to year long after the need for them has passed. During the debate on the Agriculture appropriation bill for fiscal 1948, Representative Everett Dirksen of Illinois spoke on the "thousand and one different provisions" such bills contained and deplored the "labyrinthian wilderness of restrictions" which made the task of the subcommittee difficult.[35]

A maximum limit is often placed on administrative expenditures, usually in fixed amounts, but at times as a percentage of total expenditures. A few appropriation acts continue to place limitations on the number of persons who may be assigned to personnel work.[36] Special limitations are also commonly placed on expenditures for informational activities, printing, travel, attendance of employees at professional meetings, employment of consultants, and various activities which are regarded as suspect by the appropriations subcommittees. Since the early 1940's most appropriation acts have carried a standard provision prohibiting the employment of any person who belongs to an organization that asserts the right to strike against the government, or that advocates the overthrow of the government by force or violence. For certain departments, notably Defense, an act may include numerous special restrictions applicable only to that department.

[33] Commission on Organization of the Executive Branch of the Government, *Budget and Accounting* (1949), pp. 12-13.

[34] "Improvement of the Federal Budget Function from the Congressional Viewpoint" (a paper delivered by Sheild before the Washington Chapter of the Society for the Advancement of Management, April 22, 1947).

[35] *Congressional Record*, Vol. 93, Pt. 5, 80th Cong., 1st sess. (May 27, 1947), pp 5877, 5878.

[36] Personnel riders are discussed in Chapter 7.

Among the appropriation restrictions are many that have been adopted by Congress to correct reported administrative abuses or waste of public funds; once written into law, they tend to remain year after year, coalescing into an outdated and unnecessary accretion. In recent years a number of these have finally been dropped—but others continue to be added. A department is usually hesitant to recommend that previous restrictions be dropped unless they cause serious difficulties and added expense, preferring to get along with them rather than risk the displeasure of the subcommittee. In many cases a way can be found to circumvent the restriction, but often at added expense.

Although some method of control over departmental expenditures is essential, there are a number of valid objections to the use of appropriation restrictions for this purpose. When rigid and arbitrary rulings are applied to widely varying situations, their effect is at best problematical, and in some situations they may prove to be unworkable or damaging to administration. Even those restrictions which appear, on the surface, simple and salutary may later be found complicated and difficult to apply, necessitating elaborate controls and records and the issuance of innumerable directives and interpretations to field officers. In any case, every restriction leads to increased central supervision and control—and thus usually to added expense—and makes delegation to field officers more difficult.[37]

It may be noted that the British Parliament and the parliaments of other western European countries make little use of appropriation restrictions and limitations, looking instead to the finance department to exercise needed controls over the other departments and to issue needed regulations concerning expenditures. (This is also true of the legislatures in some of our American states.) In Great Britain the Public Accounts Committee of Parliament often calls on the Treasury to exercise tighter controls over the departments when it discovers evidence of waste or imprudent management, and each department is itself expected to issue needed regulations and maintain needed controls over subordinate units.

Internal administrative controls exercised by executive officers and staff agencies in day-to-day operations are preferable to legislative re-

[37] In 1949 the Comptroller General issued a *Study of Restrictions on Expenditure of Appropriated Funds*, in which the major types of restrictions then in use were summarized, and a number of recommendations were made for their discontinuance or modification.

strictions and limitations in appropriation acts, which often create more problems than they solve. Internal controls may be adapted to meet changing conditions and requirements; they can also be carried on as a continuous part of normal administrative technique in a wide variety of forms, including not only rules and regulations, but also manuals, instructions, consultations, the requirement of advance approval, and so on. Each legislative committee of Congress that exercises oversight of a department could well provide a check on internal controls and insist that they be adequate without imposing excessive centralization. Arthur Macmahon has pointed out that "fitful legislative intervention is no substitute for controls within administration. The most valuable contribution of legislative oversight is to galvanize the disciplines of administration itself."[38]

Authorizations to a department to carry on certain activities and to make certain expenditures that have not been specifically authorized by direct substantive legislation sometimes make up a large part of an appropriation act. This legislation, usually highly technical, is sought by the department itself to avoid disallowances of expenditures by the Comptroller General. Thus the Agriculture Department's program for the eradication of Bang's disease in cattle was carried on for more than fifty years under the sole authorization of its appropriation acts. The rules of both houses prohibit substantive legislation in appropriation acts, but a good deal of it is in essence enacted in this manner. The legislative committees, however, strongly object to the practice except on minor details.

A significant debate in this regard occurred in 1947, when the agriculture appropriation bill was reported under a rule barring points of order. The bill repealed important provisions in the AAA act of 1938, reduced the authorization for the school lunch program, and made other important legislative changes. Representative Clifford Hope of Kansas, chairman of the legislative Committee on Agriculture, opposed the rule, saying that the bill contained at least six "important matters of legislation which should be considered by the Committee on Agriculture . . . every time we adopt a rule of this kind we undermine all the legislative committees and take a step toward making the Committee on Appropriations a big super committee." Another member declared: "If you adopt this rule . . . you are simply vesting

[38] Macmahon, *op. cit.*, pp. 413-414.

in the Subcommittee on Appropriations for Agriculture, down in a little closed room somewhere, the power to determine the agricultural policy for the Congress . . . without the people who are interested having any opportunity at all to be heard and present their case."[39]

Committee Reports

The reports accompanying the appropriation bills carry almost as much sanction as the bill itself and provide the means whereby the subcommittees exercise various controls over the departments. Consisting primarily of explanations of changes that have been made in the executive budget, they may also include criticisms of the departments, directions concerning future policies and administration, instructions as to where increases and reductions are to be applied, and instructions to the departments to inquire into certain problems and report their findings and recommendations. Occasionally discussion and evaluation of the programs for which funds are appropriated will be included, but this is exceptional.[40]

A report is ordinarily prepared by the clerk of the subcommittee under the direction of the chairman. Before its submission to the parent house it must be approved by both the subcommittee and the full committee. Approval by the subcommittee is not always unanimous but it is rare for a minority report to be submitted, since members who do not agree with the majority may reserve the right to oppose the report on the floor. The full committee seldom makes changes in a report.

The Bill in the House

The rules and procedures under which an appropriation bill is considered in the House strengthen a subcommittee's efforts to secure its adoption. Being privileged, the bill can be called up at any time upon the Speaker's recognition of the subcommittee chairman concerned, without the necessity of securing a special rule, although a rule is sometimes secured as protection against points of order. Little

[39] *Congressional Record*, Vol. 93, Pt. 5, 80th Cong., 1st sess. (May 27, 1947), pp. 5874-5875.
[40] See, for example, the reports accompanying the appropriations for the National Institutes of Health, which ordinarily review in considerable detail the research being conducted.

or no time is allowed to interested citizen groups, the department officials, or even other members of Congress to study the bill and to make their views known before the debate takes place. To prevent opposition forces from mustering strength to challenge the committee on the House floor, the House Appropriations Committee follows the practice of not releasing its bills and committee reports until just before they are taken up. As a result, the debate is concerned with detailed items in the bills rather than fiscal policy and fails to inform the country about the issues involved. If more time were allowed for study and discussion of the bills and the committee reports, the issues could be ventilated in the press and a much more informed debate would be possible.

In considering a bill the House resolves itself into the Committee of the Whole. Democrats and Republicans are allotted equal time for debate, with the subcommittee chairman and ranking minority member in charge. Before the general debate is opened, the major features of the bill are discussed by the chairman and other members of the subcommittee. Much of the debate that follows is irrelevant, since those members who are allotted time to speak are permitted by the rules to take up any subject they desire. This part of the general debate is regarded by leading members of the Appropriations Committee as practically worthless.

The bill is then taken up section by section under the five-minute rule. At this stage amendments are offered from the floor, and the debate becomes relevant. Amendment proposals are generally of two types: (1) those offered by individual members to increase certain items of special interest to them, often relating to activities in their own districts or of interest to their constituents, and (2) those offered by economy-minded members to reduce various items.

The subcommittee members strongly oppose both types of amendments, fearing that once an amendment offered on the floor is adopted, the floodgate will be opened for others. When the pressure by other members of the House is very strong to increase a particular item, the subcommittee often brings in its own amendment for the increase, thus avoiding a defeat on the floor. There may have been substantial disagreements within the subcommittee while the bill was being marked up, but, once these have been compromised, all members of the group join in resisting any proposal that would disturb the agreement reached. Only very rarely is a group of other House members able to marshal enough support to overturn the subcommittee.

When the bill is reported out of the Committee of the Whole to the House, any member may force a second vote on any amendment adopted in the Committee of the Whole, but amendments that were voted down previously cannot be brought up again. Motions may be made at this stage to refer the bill back to the Appropriations Committee with instructions to make specified revisions, but they are invariably voted down, and only serve to provide a record vote.

Members of the subcommittees often assert that partisanship has played no part in their deliberations. However this may be, when roll call votes are taken in the House "party voting" is the rule rather than the exception. An analysis made by Robert S. Friedman of forty-four roll call votes on appropriation bills over a period of years indicates a remarkably high degree of party cohesion. The Democrats showed substantial party allegiance (90 per cent voting together) in thirty-one instances, and the Republicans in thirty-five. The average party allegiance for the Democrats was 91.61 per cent, for the Republicans, 93.43 per cent. Twenty-two votes, or 50 per cent, were classified as "party votes," which is very much higher than the average for other legislation.[41] There is also a high degree of party cohesion in the votes in Committee of the Whole, especially when the opposition party is endeavoring to make a record for economy.

The Bill in the Senate

The Senate's role in appropriations is very largely delegated to its Appropriations Committee. Many items that have been reduced by the House are customarily increased by the Senate committee, which also not uncommonly proposes increases over the President's requests. The bills as reported by the committee are usually approved quickly and without contest by the whole Senate and sent to conference, where the differences between the House and the Senate will be compromised. Occasionally, however, an important policy issue stimulates major debate. And if an amendment is offered from the floor to increase individual items it is usually given sympathetic consideration and may be voted as a courtesy to the senator involved.

[41] Friedman, *op. cit.* (see footnote 6, above), p. 297.

The total changes made in the President's budget by Congress in 1958 and 1959 (for fiscal 1959 and 1960) are fairly typical of the actions of the two houses:[42]

	1958	1959
Total estimates of President	$71.5 billion	$74.1 billion
Reported by House Committee	70.0	71.2
Reduction	1.5	2.9
Voted by House	70.1	71.3
Reported by Senate Committee	73.8	73.9
Increase over House	3.7	2.6
Voted by Senate	74.1	73.9
Final appropriation	72.7	73.0

The Conference Committee

The conference committee wields a great power over the final decisions on appropriation bills. In probably no other legislative area does the conference process play such an influential role, for ordinarily there are many differences to be compromised. As we have seen, both chambers anticipate its action—the House voting more drastic reductions than it would otherwise do and the Senate voting liberal increases over the House votes—each knowing that the final determination will be made later. This practice gives the subcommittees even greater power, since their ranking members invariably compose the conference committee. Amendments that have been adopted by either house over subcommittee opposition can be, and often are, stricken in conference.

In compromising the differences in the amounts voted by the two houses the conference committee usually agrees upon a midway figure in round numbers, but if one side refuses to yield to this extent it may force the acceptance of another figure. Often each side will yield on certain items. There is always great pressure to reach agreement promptly, since appropriation bills are usually passed near the end of the fiscal year when new funding is needed. In addition, Congress is anxious to complete its work and adjourn. Thus, the situation is usually conducive to hasty action rather than careful deliberation.

[42] Compiled from summaries placed in the *Congressional Record* by the chairman of the House Appropriations Committee.

Conclusions

The appropriations process of Congress is well designed to enable the appropriations subcommittees to perform the tasks which they undertake. Coming from safe districts as a rule, the members serve for long periods on the same subcommittees and thus the senior members are usually well informed about the activities of the departments whose budgets they review. In addition, the subcommittees, especially in the House, are assisted by experienced and well-qualified staffs. For the kind of review which they make of department budgets, the appropriations subcommittees ordinarily make a thorough examination and arrive at intelligent decisions. Yet the increasing size and technical nature of government activities make the task increasingly difficult for members who have many other calls upon their time. No longer can they have the intimate firsthand knowledge of department activities that was possible a generation ago when the government was much smaller and the pressures upon members of Congress were much less than they are today.

The subcommittees also exercise oversight of the activities of the departments and agencies whose budgets they review. This is one of their most important functions. It duplicates to some extent the oversight exercised by the legislative committees, but is usually more continuous and effective. Although the departments are thus subject to several overseers, each committee normally exercises the function in a limited and selective way and the duplication is therefore not great.

There are, it must be noted, serious weaknesses in the appropriations process of Congress. The manner of selection and assignment of members to the subcommittees is especially subject to criticism because the members tend to be proponents of the programs whose budgets they review. The internal disciplines of Congress are not sufficiently strong to prevent the overloading of the appropriations subcommittees with members from states and districts vitally affected by the programs that they are assigned to review.

The appropriations process and the authorization of programs are subject to strong pressures from within and without Congress in behalf of spending programs. The counter pressures that exist are usually much less potent, for congressional organization in effect invites and facilitates the spending pressures by its dispersal of decision-making among many largely autonomous committees and subcommittees. This wide dispersion is the glaring weakness of the methods Congress employs to consider finance: when responsibility for fiscal policy is distributed among so many power centers it is all but destroyed. It is thus not surprising that sectional and special interests often prevail over the interests of the country as a whole; on the contrary, it is remarkable that Congress is able to act as responsibly as it does.

As noted briefly at the beginning of this chapter, the procedures of the present appropriations process seriously disable Congress in considering the budget as a whole and in deciding on expenditures in relation to available revenue, to their impact on the national economy, and to the obligation of the country in international affairs. There is no vantage point from which Congress can take a comprehensive view of government finance, nor is there an occasion for a central "great debate" on fiscal policy. The ten or more appropriations subcommittees in each house consider expenditures at different times and largely independently of each other, and the numerous appropriation bills they annually report to Congress are also considered separately and at different times. Neither house, as a rule, discusses the bills in an effective manner. The House hurries a bill into debate before the public and even other members of Congress become aware of what the issues are; the Senate debate, coming late in the session, is more often than not perfunctory. From beginning to end of the process, minimum attention is paid to the budget as a whole.

As a consequence, the administration is not held definitely responsible for its fiscal policies and the public is not informed. Congress, in its turn, not having weighed the relative needs of each program in relation to other programs and to the general financial position of the government, lacks a sound basis for allocating available resources in a manner that best serves the national interest. Such an allocation is undoubtedly the most important function of a legislative body in passing on finance, but Congress is unable to discharge it rationally and effectively.

Several other factors in the institutional pattern contribute heavily to this inability. For example, the legislation that authorizes expenditure programs, which in many respects is more important in terms of the budget than appropriations legislation, is dispersed for consideration among practically all committees of Congress and can seldom be viewed as a comprehensive whole. Again, the revenue budget is considered apart from the expenditure budget. This separation of the two aspects of the federal government's total budget is defended on the grounds that the double task is too great to be assigned to a single committee; nevertheless it prevents Congress from considering the two aspects in their proper and vital relationship.

As long as responsibility for financial decisions is so widely dispersed, Congress will inevitably continue to concern itself with the details of financial measures rather than fiscal policies, and the country necessarily will continue to look to the President rather than to Congress for leadership in fiscal affairs. Various proposals for reforms to enable Congress to exercise more effective control over federal finance are reviewed in the following chapter, but it may be questioned whether procedural reforms alone can substantially alter the institutionalized pattern of congressional action on the budget.

5

Proposals for Budget Control Reform

WHEN CONGRESS REVIEWED and voted on the proposed budget expenditures submitted by President Kennedy for fiscal year 1963 (preliminary actual, $92.6 billion), its procedures were essentially the same as those employed for fiscal 1922, when the new national budget system became effective and expenditures were $3.3 billion. Both in and out of government there has been increasing criticism of the methods and organization of congressional budgetary control and recognition that they must be overhauled if Congress is to cope effectively with the vast financial affairs of the present-day government. In the Executive branch, budget administration has undergone continuous revision and improvement over the years, but, so far, the fiscal procedures of Congress have resisted major change, although numerous proposals for revising them continue to be introduced in every session.

Much of the criticism of the present budget system is roused by the annual deficits that have become the rule rather than the exception and by the consequent continuing increase of the national debt, despite the rising prices and high level of business activity prevailing since the end of World War II. The pressures for increased federal expenditures appear to have become stronger than the demand for economy. Like many other legislative bodies, Congress has found it easier to vote new programs than to raise the taxes to pay for them.

While it is no longer considered necessary or desirable to balance the budget annually, it is generally accepted today that the budget should be managed so as to promote economic stability and growth, and to mitigate the effects of economic recessions and periods of inflation. However, as noted earlier, the extent to which the budget can be adjusted to meet current economic trends and needs is seriously limited by certain factors of the system—among them the fixed charges and relatively uncontrollable expenditures which make up a large part of each annual budget and the long time lag between the preparation of estimates and the actual expenditures. The increased funds voted by Congress during the recession of 1958, for example, did not result in increased expenditures until the economy had already begun to turn upward in 1959 and the problem, according to some authorities, then was one of controlling threatened inflation.

It is also difficult to adjust tax rates to meet cyclical changes in economic conditions, especially to increase them when needed to curb inflationary trends. The Executive branch may be hesitant to make specific proposals promptly. And Congress, too, may be reluctant to vote tax increases, though it has demonstrated that it can respond quickly enough to urgent reasons cogently presented. During boom periods when government revenue is high and the budget is balanced, there is always a strong demand for tax reduction, in preference to debt reduction, though the effect of tax reductions may be inflationary; in periods of recession, when deficits occur, the legislature is reluctant to lower tax rates and thereby increase the deficits. As a result, the tax structure in this country tends to be rigid and subject to relatively little adjustment to meet changing economic requirements. In contrast, the British government is ordinarily able to revise the tax rates promptly whenever changes are needed to cope with economic conditions.

The Grounds for Criticism

Major criticism has been directed at the present budgetary procedures of Congress on the following grounds:

1. Congress never adequately considers expenditures in relation to revenues and the impact of the budget on the economy.

2. The budget is passed piecemeal, and each of the numerous sep-

arate appropriation bills and revenue measures is acted upon independently of any other.

3. The responsibility for passing on the executive budget is divided among ten or more appropriations subcommittees in each house, which function largely as independent bodies with little supervision by the respective appropriation committees.

4. The lack of adequate controls over legislation authorizing government activities often commits the government to future expenditures without sufficient consideration of the financial implications and greatly reduces the controllability of the budget.

5. The budget review conducted by the appropriations subcommittees gives too much attention to expenditure details and too little attention to policies and programs.

6. The extensive length of the annual budget and appropriations cycle handicaps planning for future programs and necessitates substantial revisions of the budget after it is submitted.

7. The present method of budgetary review does not enable Congress to take effective steps in promoting efficiency and economy in administration.

8. Local interests and pressure groups exert an undue influence on authorizing legislation and appropriations.

9. The large carryover of spending authority weakens congressional control.

10. "Back door" spending authority adds another piecemeal action on the budget, increasing the difficulties of rational action on the budget as a whole.

11. Appropriation acts include a "jungle" of detailed restrictions and limitations which hinder efficient administration.

12. The annual enactment of huge deficiency and supplemental appropriations defeats sound budgetary administration.

13. Neither House nor Senate Appropriations Committee has a staff large enough to conduct a thorough examination of department estimates and administration.

14. If the national budget system is to function effectively, a cooperative working relationship is needed between the financial committees of Congress and the Bureau of the Budget. This has not developed.

Numerous suggestions for reform and revision of congressional budgetary procedures have been made in recent years by the Executive branch, by informed groups outside of government, and by members of Congress. Among the most important have been proposals to establish a so-called "legislative budget"; to consolidate the many appropriation acts into a single act; to give the President an item veto; to place the budget on an annual accrued expenditures basis; to establish a congressional budget staff. The history of these proposals for change, which in some cases includes their temporary implementation, and of others is reviewed briefly below.[1]

The "Legislative Budget"

The Legislative Reorganization Act of 1946 created a joint committee on the budget, drawn from the committee on appropriations and the committee on revenues in each house—a measure often advocated as a reform of budgetary procedure. The new committee would meet early in the session and "after study and consultation, giving due consideration to the budget recommendations of the President, report to . . . [the] respective Houses a legislative budget for the ensuing fiscal year, including the estimated over-all Federal receipts and expenditures." The report, due by February 15, was to contain a recommendation for the "maximum amount to be appropriated," and would be accompanied by a concurrent resolution adopting this budget and fixing the appropriations ceiling.[2]

In 1947 the joint committee could agree on an appropriations ceiling only after prolonged debate, whereupon the House and Senate disagreed on the resolution and the conference committee did not resolve the difference. In 1948 agreement was more prompt, but there was complaint in both Senate and House that the concurrent resolu-

[1] For further discussion of criticism and reform of congressional organization and procedures, see Arthur Smithies, *The Budgetary Process in the United States* (1955), Chap. 9; George B. Galloway, *The Reform of the Federal Budget* (mimeo, 1950); Jesse Burkhead, *Government Budgeting* (1956), Chap. 12; Elias Huzar, *The Purse and the Sword* (1950), Chap. 7; and Robert A. Wallace, *Congressional Control of Federal Spending* (1960), Chaps. 10-12.
[2] 60 Stat. 832.

tion was too general to be of help to the financial committees. During the House debate on the resolution the legislative budget provision was termed "not of any great value" and "unworkable," mainly because it attempted to establish a ceiling too early in the session and before the department budgets had been examined by the appropriations committees.[3] By 1949 it was obvious that the plan was not accomplishing its purpose, and the joint committee has not functioned since then.

Revival of the plan has been urged but with a smaller committee (in 1947 its membership was 102—the full roster of the four financial committees), which would submit its report later in the session after the appropriations committees had examined department budgets. It seems unlikely, however, that a plan of this type can succeed, so long as the House of Representatives, jealously guarding its special role in finance, continues to be unwilling to delegate any effective control over its decisions to a joint committee that might be dominated by members of "the other body."

Although the objectives of the "legislative budget" plan were laudable, the procedure adopted proved to be impracticable, given the lack of change in other procedures. It is doubtful that Congress can ever effectively consider the budget as a whole, and hence have a basis for considering broad fiscal policies. Its committee organization and procedures are reasonably well geared for the job of examining the spending plans of the departments in detail—but not for any real consideration of fiscal policy. It seems clear that Congress and the country must look to the President for an over-all fiscal program. His responsibility to the country as a whole forces him to consider the budget as a whole, the financial condition of the government, the available revenues, and economic considerations, whereas the responsibility of members of Congress to their individual constituencies often impels them to be primarily concerned with specific programs and expenditures, rather than the fiscal position of the government. Nevertheless, improved procedures would enable the committees to give greater attention to the relative claims of competing spending programs of the several departments. The appropriations committees of

[3] *Congressional Record,* Vol. 94, Pt. 2, 80th Cong., 2d sess. (Feb. 27, 1948), pp. 1875, 1879.

some states, for example, hold the recommendations of their subcommittees until all are reported, then give serious consideration to the spending budget as a whole. The subcommittee recommendations can then be revised on the basis of total recommended appropriations in relation to total estimated revenues.

The Consolidated Appropriation Act

The use of a single or consolidated appropriation bill in place of the numerous regular appropriation bills (fourteen, as of 1961) has long been advocated in Congress, especially by Senator Harry F. Byrd and Representative Clarence Cannon. In 1950 Congress actually used a consolidated bill, a composite production of the House appropriations subcommittees, but abandoned the idea in 1951 because the leadership of both houses and a majority on the appropriations committees regarded the 1950 attempt as unsuccessful. Continuation was defeated by a 31 to 18 vote of the House Appropriations Committee.

The principal advantage of a consolidated bill is that it would enable the appropriations committees and each house to consider all regular appropriations at one time, when there is definite information concerning the total proposed appropriations in relation to estimated revenues. Economy advocates believe that such information would act as a restraint on deficit financing. Further, funds could be allocated on the basis of the relative needs of major programs throughout the government.

Opponents point to the unsatisfactory experience in 1950, when the appropriations bill did not reach the Senate until May 10 and was not finally signed into law until September 6, two months after the beginning of the fiscal year. It has also been charged that a consolidated bill would (1) not provide full information about proposed expenditures in relation to revenues, for it does not take into account supplemental and deficiency appropriations; (2) be too large and involved to be understood and debated intelligently by the members; (3) increase the likelihood of "pork-barrel" items; (4) facilitate the use of percentage or "meat-ax" reductions and other legislative riders; (5) impose excessive delays in starting department programs; and (6), unless it was accompanied by the item veto, deprive the President of his veto power.[4]

Most of these objections could be overcome if the schedules and procedures of the appropriations committees were revised; in 1950, however, no changes of this sort were made. The subcommittees carried on their examinations of the department budgets as in earlier years, and neither of the full committees attempted to review and revise the subcommittee recommendations. Each subcommittee took charge of the bill when its section was reached, and the debate followed the same pattern as in earlier years, except that it extended over a longer continuous period and disrupted other legislative business.

No advantage is gained by using a single appropriation bill unless its result is a consideration of the budget as a whole after information is at hand concerning total proposed appropriations and available revenues. This result failed to materialize in the 1950 experiment. If a consolidated bill is to be of value, the appropriations committees must undertake to review the budget as a whole and to revise the subcommittee recommendations much more thoroughly than heretofore. It would also be necessary to streamline the subcommittee examinations of the department budgets, with emphasis on programs and policies rather than administrative details and objects of expenditure.

The Item Veto

An item veto on appropriations was first provided in this country in March 1861, when the constitution of the Confederate States granted the power to President Jefferson Davis. Owing to the abnormalities of the war years, the power was apparently never exercised, but the provision was later copied in the postwar laws of Georgia (1865) and Texas (1866). Within the next few years at least nine more states had instituted the provision. In 1873, because of the increasingly common practice in Congress of attaching riders to appropriation bills, President Grant recommended in his Annual Message that an amendment authorize "the Executive to approve of so much

[4] See John Phillips, "The Hadacol of the Budget Makers," *National Tax Journal,* Vol. 4 (September 1951), pp. 255-268; see also "Individual Views of Mr. Hayden," in Senate Report No. 267, 83d Cong., 1st sess. (May 1953).

of any measure passing the two Houses of Congress as his judgment may dictate, without approving the whole." This, he bluntly added, "would protect the public against the many abuses and waste of public moneys that creep into appropriation bills."

An amendment proposing to confer the item veto power on the President was introduced in Congress on January 18, 1876 (H. R. 46, 44th Cong., 1st sess.), and in nearly every session since then some form of the proposal has been put forward. The idea has had backing from leading members of Congress and from a number of Presidents of both parties, including Hayes, Arthur, Taft, Franklin D. Roosevelt, and Eisenhower—but it has also had strong congressional opposition, largely because the power would enable the President to veto local public works projects pushed by individual members. From 1876 to 1961 over 150 item veto proposals have been introduced in Congress; only a few of these have been reported, and most of the few adversely. Hearings have from time to time been held on the subject—the latest in 1957[5]—but none of the proposals has yet been brought to a vote in either house.

Forty-one states, as of 1961, use the item veto—among them Alaska and Hawaii, whose constitutions granting the power to their governors were approved by Congress on their admission to the Union in 1959 and 1960. Congress has also granted the power to Puerto Rico, Guam, and the Virgin Islands. The experience in the states having the item veto, according to studies on the subject, appears to have been satisfactory, with substantial economies resulting in some cases. There has been little criticism of the governors' use of the power, since in the main it has been used sparingly, and principally when appropriations exceeded estimated revenues. Governor Earl Warren of California, for example, used the item veto (and the power to reduce items) extensively in 1948, when the legislature appropriated approximately $21 million in excess of estimated revenues, announcing that he would use these powers to bring the budget into balance. In other years, when the legislature kept within estimated revenues, he made little or no use of the power. Rarely has it been used to overturn legislative actions except for compelling reasons. The very fact that a governor has the item veto to use has often influenced the legislative ac-

[5] *Item Veto*, Hearing Before Subcommittee No. 3, House Committee on the Judiciary, 85th Cong., 1st sess. (May 1957).

tion on his budget, making it unnecessary for him to exercise the power. In several states governors can reduce items, a power used more extensively than the veto. It should be noted also that in many states the legislature customarily passes the appropriation act during the closing days of the session and adjourns before the governor has acted on it, thus giving him an absolute veto.[6]

Advocates of an item veto for the President differ as to whether a constitutional amendment would be required or whether legislation would suffice. Some contend that the President's constitutional veto power actually includes the item veto, basing their argument on the provision (Article I, Section 7) that not only every bill, but also "every Order, Resolution, or Vote to which the Concurrence of the Senate and the House of Representatives may be necessary . . . shall be presented to the President. . . ." for his approval or disapproval. Thus it is possible to argue that every appropriation item is a "vote," or at least could be so designated by legislation.

Those who favor the item veto point out that the President is virtually deprived of his veto power with respect to appropriation bills, which usually authorize funds for widely diverse activities. Public works appropriations, for example, often include several hundred projects, many of which the President may object to, yet he can exercise his veto power on those found objectionable only by disapproving the funds for all the projects in the bill. Most appropriation bills reach the President near the end of the session, when funds are urgently needed by the departments and a veto might have serious consequences. Thus, complete disapproval of appropriation bills has been rare; most Presidents have chosen to accept objectionable provisions rather than jeopardize essential activities.

It is presumed that the President would principally use the item veto to disapprove funds for unbudgeted public works projects added by Congress to the appropriation bills, and thus advocates of the power believe that important economies would result. In the 1957 hearings Percival F. Brundage, Director of the Bureau of the Budget, stated that had President Eisenhower had the item power in 1955 and 1956

[6] For further discussion of the state experience, see *ibid.*, Statement by Frank W. Prescott, pp. 78-92, and Prescott, "The Executive Veto in American States," *Western Political Quarterly*, Vol. 3 (March 1950), pp. 98-112. Also see M. Nelson McGeary, "The Governor's Veto in Pennsylvania," *American Political Science Review*, Vol. 41 (October 1947), pp. 941-947.

he would have vetoed unbudgeted public works whose eventual cost before their future completion was estimated to be in excess of $2 billion.[7] In both 1955 and 1956, when signing the bill, the President condemned the practice of appropriating for unbudgeted projects, especially when the necessary engineering plans and cost estimates had not been completed, nor a determination made of economic feasibility. In 1959 he disapproved the public works bill *in toto* for this reason, but Congress passed it over his veto—one of the rare occasions when an Eisenhower veto was overridden.

Opponents maintain that the item veto would weaken congressional control over finance, and, as Representative Clarence Cannon put it during the 1957 hearings, "would . . . give the Executive a club which could be held over individual Members, and even whole delegations, to coerce their cooperation on wholly unrelated legislative propositions in which the Executive was especially interested."[8] Opponents contend also that the President does not need the item veto, since he has the power to impound funds for activities that he does not approve. However, Presidents have ordinarily been unwilling to exercise this power except for the most compelling reasons, because such action is strongly resented by Congress and regarded as a defiance of its will. Consequently, the impounding power has rarely been used except when justified by new conditions arising after Congress has voted appropriations.[9]

Several bills to prohibit impounding of funds were introduced in the 85th Congress, but no action was taken. A celebrated incident involving the power occurred in 1949 when Congress, in passing the 1950 military appropriations bill, voted extra funds and contract authority for a fifty-eight-group Air Force, although President Truman had requested funds for only forty-eight groups. As had been predicted in the Senate debate, when the President signed the bill on October 29, 1949, he impounded the extra funds and stopped the use of the contract authority, totaling altogether $375 million. When

[7] *Item Veto*, Hearing Before Subcommittee No. 3, p. 22.

[8] *Ibid.*, p. 95; and see the statement of Senator Paul Douglas, *ibid.*, p. 93, for a similar opinion.

[9] Congress has authorized the Bureau of the Budget to establish reserves "to provide for contingencies or to effect savings whenever savings are made possible by or through changes in requirements, greater efficiency in operation, or other developments subsequent to the date on which such appropriation was made available." (31 U.S.C. 665)

hostilities in Korea broke out in 1950 the President requested and secured additional funds for defense. The following year the House
Appropriations Committee excoriated Truman for the 1949 impounding, but at the same time trimmed his budget for the Air Force by up-
wards of a billion dollars.

The item veto would provide the most effective available safeguard against the waste of federal funds on local public works projects that are not economically justified, or are not a federal responsibility. Since the end of World War II, Congress has annually voted
public works authorizations totaling hundreds of millions of dollars,
including many items that were not asked for by the departments
and the President. Even a country as wealthy as the United States
will be forced sooner or later to exercise more effective controls over
this type of expenditure and to curb pork-barrel practices. Congress
itself, in the face of strong pressures from individual members, has
been unable to establish the needed controls. The item veto is unpopular with many members of Congress because it would lessen the
likelihood of securing public works projects for their districts, but it is
precisely for this reason that other members of Congress favor it.

Annual Accrued Expenditure Budget

In 1955 the second Hoover Commission recommended that the executive budget and congressional appropriations be put on an "annual
accrued expenditures" basis instead of the long-used "authority to
incur obligations."[10] Appropriations for annual accrued expenditures
would apply only to the fiscal year for which they are made, with a
period allowed at the end of the year to pay outstanding bills and to
settle the accounts; the legislature would thus be enabled to control
the amount of expenditure annually. Unexpended balances at the end
of the year would revert to the Treasury. Under the present procedure of authority to obligate, expenditures during each fiscal year are
based in part on appropriations for the year, and in part on earlier
appropriations. Approximately one third of each year's appropriations

[10] Commission on Organization of the Executive Branch of the Government,
Budget and Accounting (June 1955), pp. 17-25; *Task Force Report on Budget
and Accounting* (June 1955), pp. 33-40.

is regularly carried forward to subsequent years. The authority to incur obligations may be granted for one year or for a longer period, or may remain in effect until the authority has been used (no year appropriation).

The difference between the two forms of budget is most clearly seen in long-lead-time programs—for example, public works projects (other than water resource projects) or the procurement of "military hardware," such as airplanes or ships. On the authority to obligate basis, an entire long-lead-time project is funded when the initial appropriation is made and is carried in the appropriation for that year, though the expenditures are spread over several years. (The actual funds are not set aside but made available by the Treasury as disbursement is made.) With an annual expenditure budget, only the funds needed in each fiscal year would be appropriated. However, government departments would presumably be granted authority to enter into contracts requiring expenditures over a period of years by contract authorization in the initial appropriation, or by the legislation authorizing the program.

As noted earlier, a budget system based upon authority to obligate results in huge carryovers of spending authority from year to year. From 1956 to 1961 the unexpended balance annually carried over from appropriations was approximately $40 billion dollars, most of which was in the form of outstanding obligations. In addition, balances of spending authorizations in other legislation of around $30 billion have been carried over annually.[11] It is asserted by some persons that the carryovers greatly handicap Congress and the President in controlling expenditures. It is also asserted that because of the carryovers Congress has virtually "lost" its control over expenditures—an obvious exaggeration, since Congress certainly exercises control over long-lead-time projects when it appropriates funds for them, a control which is in some respects more effective than contract authorizations and annual appropriations, for funds are voted for the entire project when it is initially authorized. Moreover, Congress may revise previously granted spending authority. The appropriations committees require the departments to furnish detailed information on the balances that are carried over, and these are taken into account when new appropriations are voted.

[11] U. S. Bureau of the Budget, *Federal Budget in Brief*, 1961, p. 43.

Those who advocate the annual accrued expenditure form of budget claim that (1) it would avoid the unpredictability resulting from the large carryovers of spending authority and thus enable Congress and the President to control the amount of expenditures each year; (2) it would provide an annual review and reconsideration of spending authority previously granted; (3) it would result in large annual savings. The last claim especially has been hotly disputed by opponents.

As a consequence of the Hoover Commission recommendation, legislation providing for this form of budget was introduced in both houses. A Senate bill to amend the Budget and Accounting Act of 1921 in this respect was passed in 1957, but was blocked in the House by the vigorous opposition of the House Appropriations Committee. In 1958 such a bill did pass the House, but only after being amended in a way that practically struck out the key position for an annual accrued expenditure budget. The act (P. L. 85-759) merely authorized the President to recommend annual accrued expenditure limitations for any appropriation accounts when he determines that a satisfactory system of accrued accounting has been established. In 1959, President Eisenhower recommended such expenditure limitations on six appropriation items involving a total of slightly over $300 million, but the House Appropriations Committee rejected them. The act terminated in April 1962, having had no effect.

Establishment of a
Congressional Budget Staff

Beginning in 1950, Senator John L. McClellan of Arkansas has introduced a bill in each session of Congress to create a congressional budget staff under the auspices of a joint committee. The primary function of the staff would be to make a detailed examination of the department budgets, comparable to that conducted by the Bureau of the Budget for the President, and to assist the appropriations committee of each house. The bill, co-sponsored by a number of senators and widely supported in the press, passed the Senate in 1952 with little or no opposition. A similar bill in the House was blocked by the Appropriations Committee, and then countered by a move that provided additional funds to ensure large increases in the staffs of both House and Senate appropriations committees. The McClellan bill has passed the Senate several times since then, but the House Appropriations Committee, chary as always of the special role of the House in financial legislation, has continued to oppose the idea.

Thus it appears unlikely that Congress will establish a joint budget staff to serve the appropriations committees. Nevertheless, the proposal merits consideration here, since it reflects a number of earlier similar proposals, all of which were intended to strengthen Congress in passing on the budget. Advocates of the measure contend that the country cannot look to the President and the departments to exercise economy, but must rely on Congress to make substantial reductions in the President's budget.[12] They also maintain that the existing staffs of the appropriations committees are not of sufficient size to examine department budget estimates and administration in the detailed manner necessary to supply the committees with the information they need.

The committees, it is contended, cannot look to the department officials who appear before them to provide the assistance and advice needed, for the officers necessarily defend the budget as presented and are biased in favor of their own activities. It is pointed out that members of the appropriations subcommittees are often handicapped in matching wits with department witnesses, who are thoroughly informed about their own programs and can draw upon large expert staffs for assistance, while the subcommittees usually have only a single clerk to aid them.

Similarly, the subcommittees cannot turn to the Bureau of the Budget for aid, for the Bureau staff is required to support the President's budget as submitted, and hence is unable to advise where further reductions could be made.[13] All of the government witnesses, it is asserted, favor government spending, while no one presents the case for the taxpayer. During hearings on the McClellan bill in 1951, Senator A. S. Mike Monroney declared that Congress needs a staff that "would follow the budget requests from the time they become a glint

---

[12] "Are we going to sit supinely by," asked Senator McClellan, "and let the schemers, wasters, and spenders saddle the Nation with ruinous inflation, economic chaos, and bankruptcy?" See *Congressional Record*, Vol. 98, Pt. 3, 82d Cong., 2d sess. (April 7, 1952), p. 3591.

[13] See Paul H. Douglas, *Economy in the National Government* (1952), pp. 63-65.

in a bureaucrat's eye until they went through the budget office, and then when the Appropriations Committee got the budget . . . [the staff] would know as much about what was in [it] as the man who made it up."[14]

Congress has to date relied on the Bureau of the Budget to make a detailed examination of the department estimates and has not considered it necessary or wise to establish a congressional staff to duplicate its work. To do so would reverse the decision made in enacting the Budget and Accounting Act of 1921, and without doubt would have far-reaching effects on the President's control of the executive departments.

A large congressional budget staff that is able to conduct a detailed examination of the department budgets and programs would in all probability greatly influence the decisions of the appropriations committees, who would come to rely heavily on its advice. Such a staff would also exert a great deal of influence and control over the departments, rivaling that of the Bureau of the Budget. This would be bad for the executive departments and it would be bad for Congress. It would create a congressional bureaucracy with great power, and one that could not be held responsible for its actions. To justify its existence, this staff would necessarily be critical of department plans and explanations, which is the privilege of persons who have no responsibility for results. It would probably come under the domination of leading committee members, and submit data and recommendations in accord with their wishes. The establishment of a congressional budget staff to duplicate the work of the Bureau of the Budget is justified only if Congress loses confidence in the Bureau and considers it necessary to have its own staff to examine the budget estimates.

That the appropriations committees need highly competent staffs to aid them in their work is beyond question. The work of each subcommittee is facilitated by a staff which works closely with it and under the direction of its chairman, and which can secure any desired additional information, prepare analyses and digests, arrange for hearings, transmit committee instructions to the department officials,

[14] *To Create a Joint Committee on the Budget,* Hearings Before the Senate Committee on Expenditures in the Executive Departments on S. 913, 82d Cong., 1st sess. (May 1951), p. 24.

prepare draft reports, and so on. The present staff of the House Appropriations Committee, which includes a small group of highly competent, experienced regulars and an investigative group that can be expanded as needed, appears to be well designed to meet the needs. A larger staff would probably create more problems than it would solve.

Other Proposed Reforms

Considering the Budget as a Whole

In 1955 the Eisenhower administration proposed a plan to improve congressional control of the budget which would have had about the same effect as a consolidated appropriation act, although the present separate appropriation acts would be retained. Under the plan all appropriation bills would be passed before a newly established deadline of June 1, but none of them would be submitted to the President at this stage. When all bills were passed, Congress would have thirty days before the start of the fiscal year to consider the budget as a whole, taking into account the relation of authorized expenditures to estimated revenues, and to make over-all revisions through the device of an amendatory appropriation bill, which would be prepared by the House Appropriations Committee for submission to both houses. The plan also provided that a summary scoresheet on the total budget and the action of Congress on earlier bills would be submitted when each appropriation bill was taken up in each house.

After conducting hearings on the plan, the House Appropriations Committee rejected it as "impracticable," "unrealistic," and displaying a "lack of understanding of the facts inherent in legislative procedures." The committee objected particularly to the amendatory appropriation bill, which would require a second round of consideration and debate, and saw no advantage in the plan over the consolidated appropriation act which Congress had abandoned after a year's trial.[15]

[15] *Administration Plan to Improve Congressional Control of the Budget,* House Report No. 216, 85th Cong., 1st sess. (March 1957).

A Separate Capital Budget

The adoption of a separate capital budget in addition to the ordinary budget has often been suggested. Capital budgets are widely used by state and local government for public works and relatively permanent structures, and are customarily financed through bonds, which are paid off during the life of the improvement. The Swedish government has used a capital or investment budget for many years, limiting it, however, to public works and capital improvements that are "productive," that is, revenue producing. In 1949 the first Hoover Commission, stating that constant confusion is caused by the mingling of current expenditure and capital outlays, recommended that the budget estimates of the departments should be divided into two categories: current operating expenditures and capital outlays.

Proponents of a separate capital budget maintain that it would make the whole budget more understandable and result in better consideration of each part. They point out that the concept of a balanced budget is not applicable to a budget which includes capital improvements as well as operating expenses. It may be noted that the federal budget also includes activities that are self-supporting, including business enterprises, credit operations, trust funds, and self-liquidating projects. Many who favor a capital budget similar to that used in Sweden believe that it would enable the federal government to embark on a much larger conservation and resource development program, while opponents fear that it would lead to indiscriminate and economically unjustified public works projects.[16]

Shorter Budget Cycle

Revision of the budget cycle has been the subject of various proposals. One of these advocates the adoption of long-term budgeting, especially with regard to public works, and a number of resolutions for this change have been introduced in Congress from time to time. The Bureau of the Budget staff regularly prepares long-term forecasts not only of public works but also of operating expenditures, but these forecasts are designed solely to facilitate analysis of annual plans and estimates and have no official status. Long-range budg-

[16] For a thorough but critical account of capital budgeting, see Jesse Burkhead, *Government Budgeting* (1956), Chap. 8.

ets would be highly desirable in certain areas, particularly where advance planning and continuity of program are needed, and long-range budget forecasting is useful in all activities.

The adoption of biennial budgets has been proposed as a way of lessening the heavy burden imposed by annual budgets on the departments and the appropriations committees. There are doubtless certain activities for which a biennial budget would be suitable, but it would not be desirable to place the entire budget on a biennial basis.

A serious difficulty in sound budget planning and administration in the United States is the long period of time between the initial planning and preparation of the estimates and the final adoption of the budget. It is significant that the British government's budget is prepared, reviewed, and put into effect within less than six months, while in this country more than a year is required for the whole cycle. The time lag necessitates substantial revisions after the budget is submitted to Congress and results in large deficiency and supplemental appropriations, which are contrary to sound budget practice. A reduction of the time lag would enable the departments to submit much more accurate estimates, take into account current operating experience (which is impossible at present), and avoid the need for large supplementary appropriations. It would also permit more accurate forecasting of economic trends. The Hoover Commission Task Force recommended in 1955 that the period of preparation of the budget and consideration by Congress be limited to one year immediately prior to the beginning of the fiscal year to which it relates, but the proposal did not meet with favor in Congress.[17]

Two factors mainly account for the long period required to prepare and adopt the budget: first, the present procedures of Congress in dealing with the budget take at least six months, and often more, to be completed; second, the budget submissions have become so elaborate that the departments and the Bureau of the Budget also need at least six months to prepare, review, and revise the budget for presentation to Congress. The over-all period of time could be reduced if the budget document and other materials submitted in support of it by the departments were streamlined and simplified. However, this would be possible only if the appropriations committees were willing

[17] Commission on the Organization of the Executive Branch of the Government, *Task Force Report on Budget and Accounting* (1955), p. 3.

to forego the detailed examination of the estimates and would give their attention primarily to program and policy issues. There has been a trend in this direction in recent years, but it is not likely that the period required for the preparation of the budget and the action on it by Congress can be materially shortened.

Tighter Control of Authorizations

A number of proposals have been made to establish tighter controls over legislation that authorizes new activities and commits the government to future expenditures, sometimes without adequate attention to the financial implications. The problem is especially acute because of Congress's practice of authorizing activities in specific detail, which limits the discretion of both Congress and the executive departments when such activities are carried out. The common practice in the states and in many other countries is to authorize activities and programs by broad legislation which does not commit a government to carry on programs at a specified level and affords the departments and the legislative body wide discretion concerning activities to be undertaken. Under such a system the level of expenditure is determined from year to year. In contrast, a large part of federal expenditure today is required by prior legislation, and there is little that the President and the appropriations committees can do under existing legislation to reduce it.

The responsibility for recommending legislation authorizing new programs is assigned to the various legislative committees, and hence is hopelessly divided. Members of these committees usually become strong supporters of the specific departments with which they deal. Often coming from districts which are special beneficiaries of the programs on which they deliberate, they also frequently develop a strong feeling of responsibility for these programs without any corresponding responsibility for the finances of the government as a whole. It is understandable that the committees exercise a powerful influence on future programs and expenditures, since Congress relies largely on their recommendations in passing on authorizations. Under this procedure it is not surprising that the effective drives in Congress are for the expansion rather than the curtailment of government programs and expenditures.

One proposal for more effective control over authorizing legislation suggests that bills concerned with new activities, when reported by legislative committees, be referred to the appropriations committee for a report on the future cost before being taken up for action. This practice is followed in some of the states and has merit. If the proposal were adopted, the appropriations committee, on receipt of a bill authorizing new programs, should ask the Bureau of the Budget for a report on the financial implications of the bill, thus providing the administration with an orderly way of expressing its view on the pending legislation. The procedure would require all congressional committees to give much greater attention to the financial implications of legislation authorizing new activities.

The authorization of public works projects constitutes a special problem. The practice of authorizing individual projects by law inevitably results in political determination on the basis of personal, party, and local pressures, and is unquestionably highly wasteful. Individual members of Congress are expected by their constituents to "bring home the bacon" in the form of local projects, which in many instances are economically unsound and provide a substantial subsidy to local property owners.[18]

A solution to the problem is offered by a precedent already established by the many state legislatures that no longer authorize *individual* public works projects—except those involving very large expenditures—and instead enact legislation which sets up policies and criteria applicable to various kinds of projects. This practice, if adopted by Congress, would relieve individual members of the local pressures to secure federal expenditures for their districts, take the "pork" issue out of election campaigns, and prevent much of the waste and uneconomic expenditure that obtain under the present system. Congressional control over public works would increase rather than decrease, for Congress would be able to establish definite standards and policies and hold the executive officers strictly accountable for observing them. Although at present such a change would doubtless incur strong opposition in Congress, sooner or later legislation of this type will be necessary to curb the mounting cost of public works.

[18] See examples cited in Douglas, *op. cit.*, pp. 89-115.

Closer Relations Between the
Appropriations Committees and the Budget Bureau

When the Budget and Accounting Act of 1921 was passed it was assumed that the Bureau of the Budget would assist the finance committees of Congress, especially the appropriations committees, and that the director of the Bureau would speak for the President and explain his budget. Section 212 of the act specifically requires the Bureau to furnish such aid and information as these committees may request. In the early days of the Bureau the director often met with the appropriations committees, but his staff was small and members were not assigned to attend the hearings of the appropriations committees and subcommittees.[19] As a consequence, the appropriations committees have seldom called on the Bureau for assistance and information about the budget, and there have been relatively few personal contacts between the committees and their staffs and the Bureau staff. The budget presentations are made entirely by the departments; no member of the Bureau is present, except as requested by the committee.

That an informal, consultative relationship between the appropriations committees and the Bureau of the Budget has not been developed is unfortunate, for it would have facilitated the work of both groups and provided the appropriations committees with information and assistance not otherwise available. Since 1958 the House committee has invited the director of the Bureau and his chief assistants to meet with it at the opening of the session to explain the basis of the President's budget, but this does not meet the information needs of the subcommittees during the later hearings with department witnesses. For example, subcommittee members often want to know the reason for a specific action of the President on a department budget. Obviously, the answer can be best supplied by a member of the Bureau staff, since department officers are seldom fully acquainted with the reasons for the President's decisions, and their explanations would tend to represent departmental views rather than the President's. During the hearings questions frequently arise about government-wide practices, the programs of other departments, the accuracy of workload and cost estimates, and similar matters; on these the testi-

---

[19] See Charles G. Dawes, *The First Year of the Budget of the United States* (1923), *passim.*

mony of a Bureau official would be of great value to the subcommittee.

One of the serious weaknesses of the present procedure, and a cause of frustration to appropriations subcommittees, is that effective means are lacking, as a rule, for dealing with alleged unsound administrative practices. The facts are often obscure and may entail problems that are complex and government-wide in scope. Close working relations with the Bureau of the Budget would enable the subcommittees to refer such matters to the Bureau for investigation and corrective action. It cannot be doubted that such day-to-day relations would greatly aid the subcommittees in their work, and enable the Bureau, as the President's agent, to explain and defend his budget.

In most states, the governor's budget director or one of his assistants customarily attends the hearings of the appropriations committees. Although this official does not ordinarily participate actively in the presentations, which are made by department officers, he is often called on by the committees to answer questions, to supply additional information, and to explain the budget actions of the governor. These day-to-day contacts greatly facilitate the work of the appropriations committees and keep the governor in close touch with the work of the legislative committees.[20]

Sound budgeting and wise management of the finances of the government require close cooperation between Congress and the Executive branch. As Rowland Egger has stated, the budget is the vehicle of the President's "most significant act of legislative leadership and most important act of collaboration. . . . If the President and the Congress are to discharge their common and overlapping policies, the formalistic aspects of the separation of powers may have to be substantially modified."[21] Under our form of government it is necessary, of

[20] In a few states the finance committees of the legislature borrow personnel from the executive budget office to serve as committee clerks during the session, with the understanding that these employees will be wholly responsible to the committee while they are on loan. This practice may be criticized as contrary to the principle of separation of powers, but it appears to have worked to the satisfaction of the legislative committees. The same practice obtains in some other countries. In France and Sweden the parliamentary committees on finance borrow personnel from the Ministry of the Treasury, and in West Germany the Director of the Budget works closely with the finance committee of the Bundestag. In Great Britain members of the Treasury staff are in constant attendance at meetings of the Public Accounts Committee of the House of Commons, and assist the Committee of Estimates.

[21] Egger, "The United States Bureau of the Budget," *Parliamentary Affairs,* Vol. 3 (1949), pp. 48-50. In a memorandum prepared for the first Hoover Commission in 1949, Professor Egger stated: "The greatest single deterrent to good budgeting

course, to preserve the independence of decision and action of each branch, but there is no reason why there should not be frequent consultation and open communication between the two branches in budgetary matters, a practice which would better enable each to arrive at its decisions. Congress and the Executive branch cannot operate in water-tight compartments, especially in financial matters. The greater the mutual understanding, confidence, and respect, the better each will be able to perform its own functions. The absence of day-to-day personal contacts breeds misunderstanding, suspicion, and distrust, and makes cooperation more difficult.

It may be objected that staff members of the Bureau of the Budget could be of little assistance to the appropriations committees, since they are under instruction to support the President's budget and hence could not recommend reductions. But what the committees really need is not advice on where to make reductions (although some members think that they do), but detailed information on department programs and activities and on the reasons for the President's budget decisions, which will enable them to decide for themselves what action to take.

It may also be objected that members of the Bureau staff would be hectored by subcommittee members. This has not been the experience in the states; on the contrary, the budget officers in attendance command the respect and confidence of the committee members because of their expert knowledge of the budget. Various other largely theoretical objections may be raised, but the experience in many of the states indicates that a close, informal working relationship on budgetary matters is highly practicable and beneficial to both branches.[22]

Questions for a Select Committee

Almost half a century has passed since 1919, when both houses of Congress established select committees to consider the adoption of a national budget system. In that period the annual expenditures

---

at the present time is a persistent and pervading failure of liaison on budgetary matters between the President and the Congress." (*The Division of Estimates of the United States Bureau of the Budget* [mimeo], p. 17.)

[22] A White House release of December 8, 1959, stated that the Bureau of the Budget desired to extend and enlarge its cooperative relations with the financial committees of Congress as a major step in improving the budget system.

of the federal government have become a vastly more complex and important factor in the national economy and in world affairs. There is great need for Congress once again to establish a select committee to conduct a broad inquiry into the budget system and to consider how the financial system of the government may better meet the needs of today—and particularly how Congress may improve its methods in determining the fiscal policies of the government and controlling public expenditures. Since the action of Congress is inextricably associated with the preparation and administration of the budget in the Executive branch, it would be highly desirable to create a joint legislative-executive committee, patterned after the Hoover Commissions and with citizen representation, to consider all aspects of the budget system. Among the numerous questions to be considered by such a committee, the following are outstanding:

1. How may the executive budget be simplified and improved? How may it be more closely related to program, accounting control, and performance?

2. Should a separate capital or investment budget be adopted and, if so, under what policies and limitations?

3. Should long-term budgeting be used for public works and permanent structures?

4. Should the budget be placed on the basis of annual accrued expenditures?

5. Should a consolidated appropriation act be adopted?

6. How may more effective controls be established over the authorization of new programs?

7. How may Congress better consider the budget as a whole, the relation of proposed expenditures to revenues and economic conditions, and the relative needs of major programs throughout the government?

8. How may the work of the finance committees be better coordinated?

9. Should the staffs of the appropriations committees be increased? Should a special congressional budget staff be created?

10. Should the President be granted the item veto?

11. How may closer, informal working relations in budgetary matters be established between the Executive branch and the Congress?

12. What control should Congress exercise over the finances of government corporations and business enterprises of the government?

6

Control Through the Audit

ONE OF THE POTENTIALLY STRONGEST MEANS of legislative control of administrative performance is provided by a regular audit of the financial transactions—and especially the expenditures—of the executive departments. If properly utilized, the audit enables the legislature to hold executive officers to a strict accounting for their use of public funds and their conduct of administration. It is important to distinguish the *legislative* audit from the procedures used *within* the administration to control expenditures on behalf of the chief executive and department heads.

The scope of a legislative audit of public accounts is ordinarily much broader than the sort of audit that is given the books of a business firm. It includes not only a scrutiny of the accounts to determine whether they are adequate and accurate, but also an examination of the legal basis for the expenditures to ascertain that public funds have been used only for purposes for which they were voted. The auditor is usually required to report to the legislature any improper expenditures or defects in the accounting system; in many instances he is also instructed to report any expenditures or administrative operations he considers to be wasteful or unduly inefficient.

Experience with auditing arrangements, in public and private organizations both here and abroad, suggests the following conditions as essential to an effective auditing system:

1. The audit must be conducted by a person or agency independ-

128

ent of the executive and responsible only to the legislature or other governing body.

2. It must be a post-audit, that is, conducted after the financial transactions have been completed; as a corollary, the auditor should not have responsibilities requiring him to take any part in decisions on transactions which he is subsequently to audit.

3. It should be comprehensive in scope, as intensive as the auditor deems necessary, and prompt, so that the results of the audit will be laid before the legislative body while they are still timely.

4. The legislative body must be suitably organized to receive, consider, and act on the audit reports.

The auditing system in the federal government, which is the subject of this chapter, deviates in important respects from the arrangements stated above, and Congress has never had fully effective use of this important means of legislative control. The weaknesses lie deep in the authorizing statutes and historical evolution of the auditing system.

Some Historical Landmarks

Soon after the establishment of the federal government, Congress began to grope for ways of assuring itself that the money it had appropriated had been properly spent. After several early experiments with committees to examine the accounts and reports of executive officers, the House of Representatives in 1814 established for this purpose a standing Committee for Public Expenditures. Two years later the House added six standing committees on expenditures in particular departments; later in the century a similar set of committees developed in the Senate. On the whole, these committees were futile and ineffective. Lacking expert assistance, their members usually found it impossible to penetrate the mass of detail in departmental accounts and reports in a way that provided satisfactory assurance of the propriety—or clear evidence of the impropriety—of expenditures. The committees remained in existence until the 1920's, with occasional bursts of investigatory activity, but gradually lapsed into disuse.[1]

[1] See Lucius Wilmerding, Jr., *The Spending Power* (1943), pp. 199-249, for a discussion of the history of these committees.

The Treasury Auditors

Until 1921, auditing was treated as an executive function. Under a succession of nineteenth century statutes, various officers of the Treasury Department audited and "settled" the accounts of the disbursing officers of the executive departments, as well as performing other central accounting functions.[2]

An accumulation of outmoded arrangements was reformed in 1894 by the Dockery Act, which provided for six Treasury auditors, each responsible for the accounts of specified departments. Decisions of the auditors could be appealed to another officer established by the act, the Comptroller of the Treasury, whose interpretations of the appropriation laws were final and binding on the departments. The Comptroller also could render advance decisions on doubtful points raised by the departments, and was generally responsible for prescribing the form in which accounts were kept and reported. Reports of the auditors and Comptroller were available to the congressional committees on expenditures.

This was an imperfect but not unworkable system. The auditors and Comptroller were officers of the Executive branch, but sufficiently separated from the departments, including the Treasury, to give them some independence in interpreting the law. However, their responsibility to the Secretary of the Treasury and the President, who at least theoretically could have removed them, was ordinarily sufficient to restrain abuses of their authority. Also, at least part of the time, the Comptroller accepted some guidance on legal interpretations from the

---

[2] "Settling" the accounts is a crucial aspect of public financial management. An account is "settled" when an auditor has inspected the record of transactions reported by a disbursing or other accountable officer and accepted it as representing transactions properly made. But if the auditor thinks an expenditure improper he "states an exception" and "disallows" a certain amount. If the accountable officer cannot correct the account to the auditor's satisfaction he is liable for any sums due the government, and must either recover the money from whoever has received it or pay it himself (personally or by recourse to his bond) before the account can be settled. The officer who settles accounts therefore has great power to interpret the law on the propriety of administrative activities or procedures and to enforce those interpretations on the operating agencies. A further crucial question is whether the auditor who settles the account always has the last word in disputes with the departments over interpretations of law or whether he is subject to guidance or his rulings subject to appeal to some other officer—and if so, who this other officer is. More on this later in the chapter.

Attorney General.[3] The principal defects of the system were that it blurred auditing with what were properly executive control functions and did not assure that Congress was receiving adequate, independent audit reports. As long as the auditors and Comptroller were executive officials there lurked a suspicion that they might not be altogether free to perform their functions independently or report all questionable practices to Congress. Also, since the auditing and reporting were done by the same officers who had determined the legality of expenditures and settled the accounts—persons who were already committed and compromised, so to speak—Congress was not getting the benefit of a completely independent review of executive transactions.

Establishment of the General Accounting Office

The next major reform came in the Budget and Accounting Act of 1921, which still remains as a cornerstone of the federal financial management system.[4] The act abolished the Treasury auditors and Comptroller and established the General Accounting Office, headed by the Comptroller General. In so doing, Congress eliminated one weakness in the previous system. The GAO was declared to be "independent of the executive departments," and the Comptroller General, although initially appointed by the President, was placed beyond executive control by being given a fifteen-year (nonrenewable) term and made removable only by a joint resolution of Congress. He was directed to submit reports on executive expenditures to Congress—and in later legislation was specifically designated "an agent of the Congress." Another error of the old system, however, that of vesting control powers in auditing officers, was not remedied. The Comptroller General received all the functions and powers previously exercised by the Treasury auditors, including not only auditing the departmental accounts but also the power to prescribe the accounting systems of the departments, interpret laws relating to expenditures, and settle accounts and claims with the power of disallowance.

Not long after the act went into effect there began to be complaints that the Comptroller General, John Raymond McCarl, was exercising

---

[3] For history and evaluation of these pre-1921 arrangements, see Harvey C. Mansfield, *The Comptroller General* (1939), pp. 23-65.

[4] 42 Stat. 20.

his powers so vigorously and construing the law so narrowly t
ministration was being hampered. Declining to accept the A
General's interpretations of the laws, McCarl made and enfor
own interpretations. By freely exercising his power of disallow
penditures, he forced the departments to come to him for adva..
cisions on doubtful points. Pre-audits (GAO audits prior to disburs-
ment) were instituted for some kinds of expenditures, and McCarl
sought to extend the practice throughout the government, further blur-
ring the distinction between the normal executive function of pre-ex-
penditure control and the audit. Fortunately, this practice was largely
abandoned by his successors.

During the McCarl regime the departments were required to send
all their vouchers and accounting records to the GAO for audit; disallowances, which usually were made long after the actual expenditures,
required lengthy correspondence before decisions were reached. Mc-
Carl's strict construction of the laws and conservative ideas about accounting practice forced cumbersome and expensive procedures on the
departments. Long delays often were caused by the necessity for getting advance decisions on the legality of proposed activities. In the
1930's, New Deal activities of which the Comptroller General was
known to disapprove seemed to be especially subject to adverse rulings.
McCarl was denounced as an irresponsible tyrant by executive officials
and in turn warmly defended by conservatives and economy advocates
on Capitol Hill.

In the mid-1920's the numerous separate congressional committees
on expenditure in the various departments had been consolidated into
a Senate and a House Committee on Expenditures in the Executive
Departments. Although the two committees at times provided sympathetic audiences for the reports of the Comptroller General, they
were neither very active nor very effective in dealing with the financial
system as a whole. The Comptroller General flooded them with detail,
but gave them little help in their broader responsibilities.

Attacks and Adjustments

Proposals to reallocate functions and curb the power of the Comptroller General were made as early as the Harding administration, renewed by President Hoover, and put forward most strongly by President Franklin D. Roosevelt pursuant to the recommendations of his

Committee on Administrative Management (the Brownlow Committee) in 1937. The essence of the 1937 proposal was to declare the functions of prescribing the accounting system, settling the accounts of disbursing officers, and rendering advance rulings on proposed expenditures to be executive functions, and return them to the Treasury Department. The Comptroller General, to be renamed the Auditor General, would be left with the strictly post-auditing function of scrutinizing completed transactions; he could report his findings to the Executive branch and to Congress, for whatever action they might choose to take, but he could not reopen completed transactions or enforce his rulings directly on the departments.[5] This attack produced resentment but no immediate reform, as Congress rallied to the defense of the Comptroller General. Meanwhile, however, McCarl had retired, and his successor, although making no immediate changes, proved a little more accommodating to the needs of the departments.[6] The urgencies of World War II also encouraged the GAO to some selective loosenings of the procedural bonds.

After the war there were new external pressures for modernization of the GAO. Under the Legislative Reorganization Act of 1046, both the House and the Senate Committee on Expenditures in the Executive Departments were reconstituted as Committees on Government Operations, with some professional staff resources and a renewed mandate to concern themselves with the administrative system as a whole as well as investigating the particulars. In 1947, a staff study for the Senate committee pointed out a number of anachronisms in the accounting system and urged the GAO, the Treasury, and the Budget Bureau to get together in an effort to clear up some of the conflicting requirements being imposed on the departments.[7]

That same year, Congress authorized the first Commission on Or-

[5] President's Committee on Administrative Management, *Report with Special Studies* (1937), pp. 20-24, 171-202. Staff work for this part of the committee report was done by Harvey C. Mansfield, who later published his own more extended critique, *The Comptroller General* (1939).

[6] McCarl retired in 1936, but President Roosevelt did not fill the post until 1939, when Fred Herbert Brown, former Senator from New Hampshire, was appointed. Brown resigned in 1940, whereupon Representative Lindsay C. Warren of North Carolina accepted the office—which had been offered him twice before—and served until 1954. Joseph Campbell, administrative vice president of Columbia University, received a recess appointment to the office in December 1954 and was confirmed by the Senate in March 1955.

[7] *Financial Management in the Federal Government*, Senate Committee on Government Operations, 86th Cong., 2d sess. (1961), pp. 37-41.

ganization of the Executive Branch of the Government, chaired by former President Herbert Hoover; further attention to the financial system was clearly in order. Catching the spirit of the times, the Comptroller General took the lead in discussions with the Secretary of the Treasury, the Director of the Budget, and their respective staffs, and in 1948 announced a continuing Joint Program for Improving Accounting. While a declared objective was development of a more modern, flexible accounting system to serve more effectively both legislative and executive management needs, nothing was said about reallocating basic functions, particularly with respect to auditing.

The Hoover Commission thought this an encouraging sign but disagreed within itself as to its adequacy. In the 1949 report of the Commission the majority recommended establishment of an Accountant General in the Treasury, to have primary responsibility for prescribing Executive branch accounting systems and procedures—but subject to the approval of the Comptroller General. The majority also urged abandonment of the practice of hauling "freight carloads of vouchers" to the GAO for audit, and recommended a spot sampling system of audit in the agency offices. Two commissioners wanted to go further and in strong minority statements essentially renewed Roosevelt's 1937 proposals to return control of accounting, settlement of accounts, and interpretations of law to the Executive branch, and convert the Comptroller General to an Auditor General with only post-audit functions.

A different minority, two congressional members of the Commission, took a precisely opposite view and denounced any tinkering whatsoever with the powers of the Comptroller General.[8] In the end, this minority prevailed; when bills to implement the Commission's recommendations were introduced in Congress, even the principal Executive branch witnesses backed away from the proposed establishment of an Accountant General in the Treasury.[9]

All this effort was not entirely fruitless, however. The recommendations of the first Hoover Commission and the Joint Program were both reflected in, and in turn facilitated by, a new legislative landmark, the

[8] Commission on Organization of the Executive Branch of the Government, *Budgeting and Accounting* (1949), pp. 35-71; see also the Task Force Report, *Fiscal Budgeting and Accounting Activities* (1949).

[9] For discussion of the 1949 recommendations and their outcomes, see *Financial Management in the Federal Government,* pp. 51-68.

Budget and Accounting Procedures Act of 1950.[10] This left intact—and in some respects extended—the basic powers given the Comptroller General by the 1921 act, but overlaid them with some policy declarations and new provisions that called for reform in accounting and auditing methods, and in effect instructed the Comptroller General to perform his functions in a manner making proper allowance for the responsibilities and managerial requirements of the Executive branch. Continuing cooperation between the GAO, the Treasury, and the Budget Bureau was ordained.[11]

Since the 1950 legislation, a number of changes have been made in the operations of the GAO, and relations between it and the departments have been greatly improved. The second Hoover Commission, reporting in 1955, applauded these developments, recommended further improvements in accounting and auditing methods, and urged that the Bureau of the Budget assume more leadership in fulfilling the Executive branch's responsibilities in this area. The Commission did not suggest any modification of the Comptroller General's powers.[12]

The product of history, then, is an auditing system whose structure violates at least two of the four principles suggested at the beginning of this chapter. The effects of these statutory weaknesses can be seen in connection with the principal present functions of the GAO.

The General Accounting Office: Functions and Issues

The present-day General Accounting Office describes itself as:

> ... a nonpolitical, nonpartisan agency in the legislative branch of the Government created by the Congress to act in its behalf in examining the manner in which Government agencies discharge their financial responsibilities with regard to public funds appropriated or otherwise made available to them by the Congress and to make recom-

[10] 64 Stat. 832. Part II of this act, which is of the most relevance here, is also cited as the Accounting and Auditing Act of 1950.

[11] Under this provision, the Joint Program launched in 1948 was continued, and subsequently renamed the Joint Financial Management Improvement Program.

[12] Commission on Organization of the Executive Branch of the Government, *Budget and Accounting* (1955); see also the Task Force Report *Budget and Accounting* (1955).

mendations looking to greater economy and efficiency in public expenditures.[13]

The GAO is an establishment of about 4,700 people, the majority of whom are accountants, auditors, lawyers, and investigators. Employees are recruited on a merit basis, following examinations given by the Civil Service Commission. GAO headquarters in Washington, where the bulk of these employees are assigned, is a large, modern building near—but not on—Capitol Hill. About 1,800 GAO employees are assigned to regional and field offices in some 20 principal U. S. cities, and a small group of about 80 scrutinize expenditures abroad from offices in Paris and Tokyo. Appropriations for the support of the GAO have currently run about $43 million annually. Most years, the GAO reports that it has collected for the government, from improper or disputed payments, sums exceeding its appropriation, not to mention even greater savings made in departmental budgets by GAO's recommendations.[14]

Control of the Accounting System

In a business firm, establishment of the accounting system is ordinarily a management function, and the role of the external auditor is to report to the directors and stockholders on the accuracy of the accounts and the adequacy of the system. In the federal government, by contrast, the auditor—the Comptroller General—has authority in his own right to prescribe the principles and control the standards of accounting in the executive agencies.

The Budget and Accounting Act of 1921 transferred to the Comptroller General some of the central bookkeeping functions previously performed by the Treasury (Sec. 304), and further instructed him to

[13] U. S. General Accounting Office, *Functions of the U. S. General Accounting Office*, Report for the Senate Committee on Government Operations, 87th Cong., 2d sess. (1962), p. 1.

[14] For fiscal 1962, the GAO reported collections of over $48 million. The total reported for fiscal years 1950-62 was $708 million. In 1962, the GAO also took credit for savings of $114 million in agency operations. See Comptroller General, *Annual Report . . . 1962*, pp. 243-255.

Without entering the question deeply, it might be observed at this point that the value of an auditor generally is not measured by sums collected or recovered. Since auditors in the business world do not have authority to disallow expenditures, collections are not attributed to them, although their work may lead indirectly to recovery of funds in serious cases of fraud or malfeasance.

"prescribe the forms, systems, and procedure for administrative appropriation and fund accounting in the several departments and establishments, and for the administrative examination of fiscal officers' accounts and claims against the United States" (Sec. 309).[15] For many years the General Accounting Office used this as authority for imposing on the departments quite rigid requirements as to the kinds of accounts to be kept, reports to be made, and procedures to be followed leading to GAO approval and issuance of the "warrants" by which certain central bookkeeping transactions were accomplished. Departments and agencies increasingly complained that the GAO's system was archaic and cumbersome; that the GAO, the Treasury, the Budget Bureau, and their own internal administrative needs imposed conflicting and overlapping accounting requirements; and that the system did not accommodate the kind of internal financial control and reporting procedures that modern accounting can provide as aids to management.

Establishment of the Joint Program in 1948 reflected agreement among the interested parties, including the Comptroller General, that reform of the accounting system was needed. Although the Hoover Commission's proposal for legislation to switch primary responsibility for the accounting system to the Executive branch was rejected, the Act of 1950 was a compromise that preserved the ultimate authority of the Comptroller General but encouraged modernization and provided for greater recognition of the role and responsibility of executive agencies in shaping their accounting systems.

A carefully worded section (111) declared it to be the policy of Congress that:

(a) The accounting of the Government provide full disclosure of the results of financial operations, adequate financial information needed in the management of operations and the formulation and execution of the Budget, and effective control over income, expenditures, funds, property, and other assets.

(b) Full consideration be given to the needs and responsibilities of both the legislative and executive branches in the establishment of accounting and reporting systems and requirements.

(c) The maintenance of accounting systems and the producing of financial reports with respect to the operations of executive agencies, including central facilities for bringing together and disclosing information on

[15] 42 Stat. 23-24.

the results of the financial operations of the Government as a whole, be the responsibility of the executive branch.

(d) Emphasis be placed on effecting orderly improvements resulting in simplified and more effective accounting, financial reporting, budgeting, and auditing requirements and procedures and on the elimination of those which involve duplication or which do not serve a purpose commensurate with the costs involved.

(e) The Comptroller General of the United States, the Secretary of the Treasury, and the Director of the Bureau of the Budget conduct a continuous program for the improvement of accounting and financial reporting in the Government.[16]

Pursuant to this declaration, the Comptroller General was instructed to consult the Secretary of the Treasury and the Director of the Budget and to prescribe the "principles, standards, and related requirements" for accounting in the agencies. The agency heads, however, were given responsibility for actually establishing and maintaining systems and procedures to provide appropriate control of funds and data for reporting, budgeting, and internal management needs. The systems so established must conform to the principles and standards set by the Comptroller General, who was instructed to review and report on them from time to time. The Comptroller General, however, was instructed to perform his functions in a manner conforming with the declaration of policy and permitting the executive agencies to fulfill their responsibilities under the act.

Since 1950, proceeding through the Joint Program, the GAO and the agencies have cooperated in gradual elimination of obsolescent methods and requirements and installation of accounting and reporting procedures that provide a more effective form for management control as well as external audit and evaluation. The GAO's current position is that basic responsibility for the particulars of any agency system rests with the agency. Its own concern is with broad principles and standards. For several years the GAO maintained a special Accounting Systems Division to work with the agencies; this activity is now assigned to a combined Accounting and Auditing Policy staff. The GAO's ultimate authority over the accounting system is exercised in several ways. Statements of "principles and standards" are issued to the agencies in manual form.[17] There is also a long-range program of

[16] 64 Stat. 834.

[17] U. S. General Accounting Office, *General Accounting Office Policy and Procedures Manual for Guidance of Federal Agencies* (5 vol., looseleaf, originally issued 1957, with occasional supplements), Title 2.

review of agency and bureau accounting systems, leading to the Comptroller General's official "approval" of systems fully meeting the GAO's standards. As of June 1962, 41 of the 128 identifiable separate accounting systems in the Executive branch had been so certified, and approval had been given to major parts of 15 other systems.[18] Both "approved" and "unapproved" systems are subject to GAO review and comment in the course of ordinary audits or special investigations.

For the long run, there remains some question whether even this degree of auditor control of the accounting system is consistent with or gives encouragement to proper exercise of what should be primarily an executive management responsibility. However, the ambiguity of the Act of 1950 has permitted a balance between executive and GAO interests that for the time being seems tolerable to both parties.

Audit, Settlement, and Legal Interpretations

The heart of the power of the Comptroller General lies in his statutory authority to audit and settle the accounts of executive officers, including the making of legal interpretations incidental thereto, with his determinations final and conclusive upon the Executive branch. About the propriety of his auditing the accounts there can be no question, for this is the essence of the function of a legislative auditor, although there is room for debate about the scope, manner, and criteria of the audit. But the combination of auditing with binding power of legal interpretation and settlement is the crux of historic controversy about the Comptroller General, and the source of much of the day to day friction between the General Accounting Office and the executive agencies.

Audit. With some limited exceptions specified by statute, the auditing authority of the GAO extends to all activities, financial transactions, and accounts of the federal government. It includes the records of contractors having contracts negotiated without advertising, their subcontractors' records, and the records of certain recipients of federal assistance in the form of loans, advances, grants, or contributions. All officers of the government are required by law to make their records available and to cooperate with the GAO. The law requires an annual audit of certain specified agencies, and the accounts submitted by accountable officers must be examined within three years if individuals

[18] Comptroller General, *Annual Report . . . 1962*, p. 50.

are to be held liable for improper expenditures (except in case of fraud or criminality). Within these broad limits, the Comptroller General has wide discretion to determine the frequency, detail, and procedures for auditing.[19]

Congress's general policy with respect to accounting and auditing, as expressed in Sec. 111 (d) of the Act of 1950, is that:

> The auditing for the Government, conducted by the Comptroller General of the United States as an agent of the Congress, be directed at determining the extent to which accounting and related financial reporting fulfill the purposes specified, financial transactions have been consummated in accordance with laws, regulations, and other legal requirements, and adequate internal financial control over operations is exercised, and afford an effective basis for the settlement of accounts of accountable officers.

Sec. 117 (a) of the act, with specific respect to auditing, makes a broad grant of authority to the Comptroller General but gives him certain guidance:

> In the determination of auditing procedures to be followed and the extent of examination of vouchers and other documents, the Comptroller General shall give due regard to generally accepted principles of auditing, including consideration of the effectiveness of accounting organizations and systems, internal audit and control, and related administrative practices of the respective agencies.

With the authorization and encouragement of this act, auditing procedures have been greatly modernized in recent years. For the first two decades of the GAO, practically all of the auditing was done at its own offices, to which agencies were required to ship all the necessary papers and documents. Beginning with some exceptions made for government corporations and emergency programs in the 1930's, and continuing increasingly since World War II, there has been a trend toward conducting the audits in the operating agency offices where the books are kept—what GAO calls "site audits" as distinguished from "centralized audits."[20]

GAO now has auditing groups on a continuing basis in the head-

---

[19] See *Functions of the U. S. General Accounting Office* (footnote 13, above) pp. 9-10.

[20] As noted, the first Hoover Commission condemned the "deluge of paper work" at the GAO, and the Act of 1950 contained some permissive language encouraging GAO to make more use of the site audit.

quarters of many agencies, and has its own field staffs examining agency operations all over the country and abroad as well. Although most of the auditing now is done on the site, some classes of expenditures, such as transportation, are still audited centrally, and a few agencies are still required to send all of their vouchers and related documents to GAO for centralized audit.

Along with the shift in location of audits has gone a broadening of the scope and purposes of auditing. The traditional GAO audit—sometimes called a "desk audit" or "voucher audit"—consisted basically of a careful scrutiny of the papers on each transaction to assure that all expenditures had been legally made and documented. This was a laborious operation, requiring a large clerical staff and inevitably leading to a great deal of bickering over detail with the operating agencies. Furthermore, it had only a limited usefulness. A congressional committee staff report noted that although it "resulted in the recovery of substantial amounts of funds improperly expended, it was only incidentally conducive to an analysis of the effectiveness and economy of the management of the agencies."[21] Since 1950, the GAO has moved toward a policy of "comprehensive audits" in which emphasis is not on the individual transactions but on the soundness of the agency's accounting and financial management system and the efficiency of its operations generally. This has made possible the gradual elimination of several thousand clerical employees at the GAO. Some agencies and classes of expenditure, however, still receive a detailed and less than comprehensive audit, and even in the comprehensive audit some individual vouchers are checked, although increasingly on a sampling basis.

These developments have significantly improved the quality and usefulness of the auditing and reduced some of the old frictions between the GAO and the departments. Difficulties still arise, however, because of the confusion of control and audit functions assigned the GAO by statute and the persistent tendency of both Congress and the GAO to extend the auditing to the point where it conflicts with executive functions. A sense of the wide sweep of the auditing operation may be gained by examining what the GAO announces as the elements of a comprehensive audit.

(1) A study of the pertinent laws and legislative history to ascertain congressional intent as to the purpose of the activities engaged in by the

[21] *Financial Management in the Federal Government* (footnote 7, above), p. 121.

agency, their intended scope, the manner in which they are to be conducted, and the extent of the agency's authority and responsibility.

(2) A review of the policies established by the agency (and to the extent applicable by the central control agencies) to determine whether they (a) conform to the intent of Congress, and (b) are designed to carry out the authorized activities in an effective and efficient manner.

(3) A review of the procedures, practices, form of organization (particularly as to the segregation of duties and responsibilities), and system of reporting, review, and inspection as well as other elements of internal control to determine whether they (a) provide reasonable assurance of control over expenditures, receipts and revenues, and assets, (b) assure the accuracy, reliability, and usefulness of financial data, including the budget statements and supporting data presented to the Bureau of the Budget and the Congress, (c) promote operational efficiency, (d) result in adherence to prescribed policies, and (e) assure compliance with the requirements of applicable laws, regulations, and decisions.

(4) A review and analysis, by activities, of receipts and revenues, expenditures, and the utilization of assets together with all related control processes as a basis for evaluating the effectiveness with which public funds are applied and properly utilized. This will include comparison of performance with budget estimates and with results of prior periods and evaluation of costs of performance in relation to accomplishments.

(5) The examination of individual transactions, the confirmation of balances with debtors, creditors, and depositaries, and the physical inspection of property to the extent necessary to determine whether (a) transactions have been consummated in accordance with applicable laws, regulations, and decisions, and have been correctly classified, (b) resources and financial transactions have been properly accounted for, and (c) control processes of the agency are functioning effectively.

(6) The exploration and full development of all important deficiencies encountered and the presentation of appropriate recommendations for corrective action by the Congress, where needed, agency heads, or the control agencies such as the Bureau of the Budget, the Civil Service Commission, and the General Services Administration. This will include the reporting of any programs undertaken or transactions completed without authority of law which were disclosed during the audit as well as the stating of exceptions against accountable officers and the making of collections resulting from illegal or otherwise improper expenditures.[22]

As the GAO notes in a subsequent section, "While the goal is an evaluation of the discharge of the agency's financial responsibilities, the scope of the comprehensive audit extends to all of an agency's opera-

[22] U. S. General Accounting Office, *General Accounting Office Policy and Procedures Manual for Guidance of Federal Agencies*, Title 3, Sec. 2020.20.

tions and activities *and to all of their aspects.*"[23] Particularly to be noticed is the declared right to compare agency policies and activities with legislative intent, to assess agency organization, and to evaluate efficiency by various means including comparing performance with budget estimates. Although it clearly is the function of legislative auditors to point out any executive actions contrary to law, it is doubtful whether this should include attempts to delve into legislative history and intent beyond a plain reading of the statutes. Executive officials in charge of programs are ordinarily in close touch with the committees that originate relevant legislation and are just as well situated as outside auditors to judge legislative intent; if they disregard legislative wishes they are also in position to be brought to account without the assistance of auditors.

It is equally doubtful whether auditors should venture into the realm of general departmental policies that do not directly involve the financial and accounting matters in which auditors are professionally competent. Similarly, it can be questioned whether independent auditors should undertake to determine whether the form of organization is suitable, or to make general evaluations of performance, efficiency, and effectiveness of administrative operations. Auditors should report wasteful practices that come to their attention, but their training does not thereby qualify them to express judgments on the over-all efficiency of operations.

An efficiency audit requires a specially qualified staff and is best conducted as an internal audit responsible to management. The Comptroller General has encouraged and assisted the departments in instituting internal audits for this and other purposes, which is commendable, but there is an important distinction between the internal audit, a tool of management, and the external audit, which is to serve the legislature. The present broad sweep of the auditing function puts a substantial burden on executive agencies to cooperate and comply with the Comptroller General's regulations. This may be in accord with the preferences of Congress, but there is room for doubt whether this approach serves Congress well or leaves an administrator with the discretion he needs if he is to be held responsible for the effectiveness of operations.

[23] *Ibid.*, Sec. 2020.30. Italics added.

Settlement. The extended scope of the auditing function would not be so controversial if the Comptroller General were only empowered to report his findings and express his doubts about administrative policies and operations to the appropriate executive officials and Congress, and leave it to them to make the necessary adjustments. The rub, however, is that he also is empowered to settle the accounts—and in the course thereof to state exceptions and disallow expenditures—of executive officers. This gives him a strong sanction for enforcing his interpretations of the law and views about sound administrative procedure on the departments. To be sure, the power of disallowance is exercised in connection with specific items of expenditure which the Comptroller General considers improper under the law; he cannot disallow all the expenditures of a billion-dollar program merely because he considers it inefficiently managed. Nevertheless, the fact that the departments must eventually settle with the GAO requires them to give great weight to its views on all questions of policy and procedure, even when they involve matters on which the department's competence and judgment ought to be superior.

As mentioned above, a proposal to transfer the power of settlement to the Executive branch was central to FDR's 1937 attack on the GAO, and has been revived at various times since. Congress and the GAO, however, have always angrily resisted and successfully repulsed such efforts. In their view, the meaning of legislative control is to have the agent of Congress in position to prevent or recover specific expenditures he believes improper; authority merely to report such events after the fact would be no control at all. The fact that this interference with particular transactions weakens executive responsibility and denies Congress a truly independent post-audit is not impressive to many legislators.

Legal Interpretations. Making decisions as to whether or not particular transactions are in accord with the law and regulations is, of course, the essence of the settlement function. There is great room for differences, however, in the manner of exercise of that function. Whether the auditor construes the law broadly or narrowly, whether he is subject to any check or guidance in his constructions, whether the burden of proof in case of disagreement is on the auditor or the spending officer, and whether there is any appeal or ultimate recourse from the determinations of the auditor—these are all questions of moment and controversy.

In the course of settling accounts and passing on expenditures and claims, the Comptroller General issues legal decisions on the propriety, under all relevant laws, of past transactions. He also is authorized by law to give advance opinions on the legality of proposed transactions when asked to do so by department heads or disbursing officers. In order to avoid the danger of a disallowance, the departments usually secure advance clearance on any new type of activity, expenditure, or procedure about which there can be any doubt. In recent years, the Comptroller General has issued over 6,000 legal decisions and reports annually, the most important of which are published in *The Decisions of the Comptroller General*, a weighty series of annual volumes.

These decisions constitute an administrative code of great scope and complexity. They involve interpretations and applications of federal statutes, treaties, state and foreign laws, and administrative regulations—not to mention the judgment of the GAO concerning sound administrative and financial practice. Many decisions relate to provisions of law designed to control administrative matters of personnel, financial management, travel, use of government property, and other details. Others, however, are concerned with Congress's intent concerning major governmental programs.[24] This formidable body of interpretations tells executive officers what they can and cannot do, limits their discretion, and circumscribes the methods, procedures, and activities which they utilize in the discharge of their functions.

Executive officials have always complained that the interpretations and decisions of the Comptroller General were unduly restrictive, a drag on effective administration. They claim that the habitual tendency of the General Accounting Office is to resolve all doubts against the administrators; that statutes granting authority to administrators are construed narrowly, while statutes stating restrictions are construed broadly; and that when the statutes are silent the GAO is reluctant to give the departments latitude to choose the most effective means of implementing the purposes of the law. The GAO's restrictions, it is claimed, manifest a negative attitude toward administration and

[24] It might be emphasized that these interpretations are by no means confined to the appropriation statutes that were the initial historic concern of the legislative auditor. In a recent year, these provided a basis for only 12 per cent of the Comptroller General's decisions. Other sources were: contracts, 30 per cent; civilian personnel, 12 per cent; military pay and allowances, 18 per cent; transportation, 17 per cent; and other matters 10 per cent. See Comptroller General, *Annual Report, . . . 1959*, p. 277.

government activity in general. These complaints are less common nowadays than in the McCarl era, but continue to be made.

While it is probably inevitable that administrators will be restive under any kind of external controls, many observers—including this author—feel that on the whole many of the executive complaints are justified. In its approach to administrative matters, the GAO does have a tendency to rule against actions or procedures unless they are expressly authorized by law or are clearly essential to the conduct of authorized programs. The GAO's restrictions often seem to go beyond the reasonable requirements of protecting the public purse, and amount to a substitution of the Comptroller General's judgment for that of the responsible administrators, even on matters about which the administrators are best situated to judge. The result is a serious limitation on administrative discretion, approaching a transgression on the constitutional authority of the Executive branch.

The GAO's usual reply is that such criticisms are nonsense, since it is merely enforcing the letter of the law and the intent of Congress; the proof is that Congress seems happy with the GAO's performance; and anyone dissatisfied with the GAO's interpretations can urge Congress to clarify or change the law.

The tendency of Congress—or at least of those portions of Congress attentive to such matters—to approve of the GAO's restrictive interpretations must be conceded. The difficulty is that this puts an almost overwhelming burden on the departments to challenge or have modified any rulings they feel to be unfair. If the Comptroller General has ruled adversely in an advance opinion, the department risks a disallowance if it proceeds. Ordinarily, a disallowance is conclusive. In rare instances a disallowance can be upset by somehow getting the case into court, but this is a risky course for the accountable officer, and even if he is vindicated the results may be applicable only to this one case and will not secure a change in the general rule.

A safer course is for the department to attempt to persuade Congress to modify the statutes to provide clear authority for what it wishes to do. But this takes time and effort. Legislative committees have crowded agendas, such problems often involve technicalities that are difficult to explain, and Congress is generally reluctant to upset the Comptroller General's rulings, particularly if the Comptroller General takes the position—as he frequently does—that the law should not be changed. In many instances the departments have secured legislation of this sort, after some delay, but they are able to make this effort only occasionally and on the most important matters. The more usual course is to acquiesce in the Comptroller General's rulings and try to find alternative, even though less effective, ways of achieving the same purposes.[25]

Completely aside from its effect on administration, the result of this situation is that Congress does not get an adequate review of what has happened in the close cases. Departments that are displeased or placed in difficult situations by the Comptroller General's rulings find it hard to get Congress to review the matter. If the Comptroller General does agree with what the department wishes to do, he becomes a party to the transaction. Where then is Congress's independent post-audit?

Statutory Exceptions. Although Congress has not been willing to take away the control functions of the Comptroller General for governmental activities in general, it has over the years exempted certain agencies and programs from his control when his decisions encountered strong criticism, or the Executive branch made an unusually strong case for greater flexibility. This has ordinarily been accomplished by providing that the determinations of the executive officers shall be conclusive, subject to review only by the courts. For example, Congress has exempted certain payments to veterans, soil conservation payments, commodity credit benefits, and certain activities of the State and Defense Departments. Interpretations of the revenue laws involved in determining customs and internal revenue assessments are not open to the Comptroller General's review, although he audits revenue accounts to check on payments into the Treasury.

An interesting exception was made in the Contract Settlement Act of 1944, which Congress passed over the Comptroller General's objections. This act was adopted in part on the recommendation of Bernard M. Baruch and John M. Hancock, two highly respected figures in the world of finance, who contended in a report to the Office of War Mobilization that conversion of industry from war to peace would be seriously impeded if all the anticipated war contract settlements were to

[25] An example of this sort of sequence occurred after the Comptroller General ruled in 1939 that departments could not provide off-the-job training for government employees unless specifically authorized by law to do so, a ruling which seriously hampered training programs of the departments during World War II. This and subsequent rulings restricting the authority of departments to conduct training programs led eventually to passage of a general government employees training act—but not until 1958. See Chapter 7 for a review of training legislation.

be subject to audit and adjustment by the Comptroller General.[26] A compromise was reached which permitted such settlements to be negotiated conclusively by executive agencies, without adjustment by the Comptroller General. The Comptroller General, however, was permitted to examine the settlements after they were made and report his findings to Congress—and to the Department of Justice if fraud was suspected.

A somewhat similar principle was used to settle a long controversy over the auditing of agencies organized in the form of government corporations, such as the TVA, the Reconstruction Finance Corporation, and the numerous corporate agencies used in government credit operations. For many years the Comptroller General had sought to apply to these agencies his full powers of audit and settlement of accounts, while the corporations resisted in the name of the administrative flexibility which had been sought in using the corporate form of organization in the first place. Finally Congress reached a settled policy in the Government Corporation Control Act of 1945, which made these agencies subject to a commercial-type audit to be conducted by the Comptroller General at the corporate offices.[27] Under this act, the Comptroller General reports to Congress on the adequacy of the accounts and any expenditures he believes to have been unauthorized by law, but he does not have the power to settle accounts and enforce his interpretations of law directly on the corporations, except as that power is elsewhere given him by separate legislation.

Reports and Services to Congress

The legislative history of the Act of 1921 indicates that the primary objective Congress sought in establishing the General Accounting Office was to provide itself with a trusted source of information about the way in which public funds were being used in the executive departments.[28] To this end, the act authorizes the Comptroller General to in-

---

[26] John D. Millett, *Government and Public Administration* (1959), p. 183.
[27] 59 Stat. 597.
[28] Rep. James W. Good, chairman of the House committee sponsoring the legislation, said: "The officers and employees of this department [*sic*] will at all times be going into the separate departments in the examination of their accounts. They will discover the very facts that Congress ought to be in possession of and can fearlessly and without fear of removal present these facts to Congress and its committees." (Quoted in *Financial Management in the Federal Government*, p. 300.)

vestigate "all matters relating to the receipt, disbursement, and application of public funds" and requires him to make an annual report to Congress on the work of the GAO, including recommendations on any financial legislation he considers necessary and any other "recommendations looking to greater economy or efficiency in public expenditures." He also is required to report from time to time on the adequacy of financial control in the departments, and "every expenditure or contract made by any department or establishment in any year in violation of law." Other special investigations and reports may be made on the request of Congress or its committees. The President and the Bureau of the Budget may also request reports and information from the Comptroller General, and the GAO on its own initiative makes many reports and recommendations on matters of lesser importance directly to particular departments.

This adds up to a formidable body of reporting. In fiscal year 1962, for example, the GAO submitted 271 reports on audits and investigations to Congress, or congressional committees, or individual members. In the same year 548 reports went directly to agency officials.[29] These reports are of different types. Audit reports on government corporations relate to the accounts of a particular fiscal year, and resemble the reports customary on commercial corporate firms. Reports on ordinary executive departments and agencies, however, do not relate to a specific period, but are the result of the GAO's intermittent audits, investigations, or special studies of departmental operations.

The Comptroller General provides a number of important services to Congress in addition to audit reports on executive agencies. Special reports on executive transactions or programs are made at the request of legislative committees, or individual members.[30] Members of the GAO staff are frequently detailed to committee staffs—most frequently those of the Government Operations and Appropriations committees—to assist with investigations or analysis of legislation on financial matters. During fiscal year 1962, 158 lawyers, accountants, auditors, or investigators were so assigned for varying periods, at a total cost of over $400,000. The GAO keeps constant watch on bills introduced in Con-

[29] Comptroller General, *Annual Report . . . 1962*, pp. 265-285.
[30] "This type of work is given a very high priority and the performance of such work, particularly for congressional committees, has become a very important part of the work of the Office." See U. S. General Accounting Office, *Functions of the General Accounting Office*, p. 23.

gress. Its 1962 *Annual Report* notes 445 reports with comments on proposed legislation to legislative committees, and 23 hearings in which staff members testified.[31] These services are prized highly by most legislators, as the record of any hearing involving the GAO will demonstrate.

There are a number of unsatisfactory aspects of the GAO's auditing and reporting system, and its relations with Congress generally. For one thing, because audit reports in most cases do not relate to the accounts for a particular time period, Congress is not provided with the information it needs to hold executive officials accountable for their use of funds. This difficulty is accentuated by the fact that audit reports are often made after a considerable time has elapsed, and the departments claim that they already are aware of the deficiencies reported, or that appropriate corrective measures are under way. It is often difficult to tell just who has detected the weakness and what the current status of the matter is.

Another problem is that the scope of the reports—which grows out of the scope of the audits themselves, as discussed above—often is so wide that they involve matters of policy and administration that go beyond the professional competence and normal functions of auditors. Many examples can be cited.

In 1955, and for several years following, the audit reports on the Tennessee Valley Authority included statements of opposition to legislation then being proposed which would authorize TVA to sell revenue bonds to finance construction of steam plants and other power facilities. The Comptroller General recommended that "agencies of the Government, other than the Treasury Department, should not be authorized to borrow from the public for purposes of the nature involved in the proposed legislation and that financing of such activities should be by appropriation."[32] Thus the Comptroller General stepped into a policy matter that did not involve probity in the use of funds, or even administrative efficiency, but did involve him in a highly political public-private power controversy. However, he takes the position that any diminution of regular annual congressional control of funds is his business to oppose, regardless of the broader policy objectives involved.

GAO reports have often been highly critical of both policy and ad-

---

[31] Comptroller General, *Annual Report . . . 1962,* pp. 17-26.
[32] Comptroller General, *Annual Report . . . 1956,* p. 145.

ministration of the politically controversial foreign aid programs. Some of its indictments of loose administrative procedures do, indeed, seem well founded. Other reports, however, involve matters of judgment and policy. An audit report of 1959 on the Development Loan Fund, for example, commented adversely on the criteria on which development loans were being made to several countries. Another recent report questioned the procedures by which the Department of Defense and the Joint Chiefs of Staff determined the level of military forces in certain friendly countries that we were aiding. Inasmuch as such decisions involve both military considerations and political maneuvers in the East-West struggle, this hardly seems a sphere for the auditors.

Reports on the Department of Agriculture in recent years provide several examples of GAO's tendency to get into policy matters. In 1959 the Secretary of Agriculture was criticized for setting the export price for cotton at too high a level to bring about a large sale abroad. For foreign policy reasons, the department was refraining from dumping large quantities of cotton on the world market, but the GAO thought such a pricing policy contrary to the intent of Congress. In 1957 the GAO ventured into the perennially controversial topic of the amount of grazing to be permitted on the public lands, and adequacy of the fees charged for such grazing.

In 1962 the Comptroller General told a congressional committee that the GAO had called to the attention of the Secretary of Health, Education, and Welfare the fact that procedures for testing and control of new drug products were different in the biologics program of the National Institutes of Health from those of the drug control programs administered by the Food and Drug Administration.[33] Inasmuch as these programs involve quite different kinds of products, with different technical problems and different historical patterns of government-industry relationships, there is some doubt about the significance of such a discovery by the auditors.

Difficulties arising from the broad scope of the Comptroller General's audit reports are accentuated by the way in which they are handled and used by Congress. There is no single committee of Congress, or in either house, with the sole function of receiving, conducting inquiries, and recommending action on the basis of these reports. The

[33] *Independent Offices Appropriations for 1963,* Hearings Before the House Committee on Appropriations, 87th Cong., 2d sess. (1962), Part 2, pp. 7-8.

Legislative Reorganization Act of 1946 made the Committees on Government Operations of the two houses the principal recipients of these reports, but matters concerning appropriations are reserved to—and jealously guarded by—the two Appropriations Committees; many other committees also request and receive GAO reports from time to time.

Thus there is no single point of responsibility, no systematic and comprehensive review of the GAO's work as a whole. Sometimes the Comptroller General's reports are picked up and provide a basis for important inquiries by the committees. At other times when he reports there seems to be no one listening. Committee chairmen or individual members tend to request or seize on the reports which suit their own purposes—usually those that provide the most anti-executive pay dirt. Thus the tendency of the GAO to stray into policy matters adds fuel to the constitutional conflict between President and Congress or the fratricidal conflict between legislative and executive wings of the majority party.

Parliamentary Control of Expenditure in Great Britain

Before drawing final conclusions about the American system of legislative control of administration through the audit, it will be useful to compare it with the British system, which is fundamentally different.[34] It may be objected that the British system is suited only to a country with a parliamentary form of government, and hence comparisons with similar controls in the United States are of little significance. However, the principles of the British system of audit and legislative control of expenditure have been widely followed, not only by many countries with parliamentary forms of government, but also by a number of American states. These principles are as applicable to one type of constitution as the other.

The British system of legislative control revolves around two key institutions: the Public Accounts Committee of the House of Commons;

[34] For a detailed account of parliamentary control of expenditure in Great Britain, see Basil Chubb, *The Control of Public Expenditure* (1952). See also Joseph P. Harris, "Legislative Control of Expenditure: The Public Accounts Committee of the British House of Commons," *Canadian Public Administration*, September 1959, pp. 113-131.

and an Audit and Exchequer Department, headed by the Comptroller and Auditor General, who reports to the committee.

Created in 1861 on the motion of Gladstone, the Public Accounts Committee was the first, and remains today, the outstanding example of a legislative audit committee. It was established originally to inquire into questions relating to the authority, regularity, and accounting of public expenditure, and to ensure that expenditures and other financial transactions of the executive departments are properly accounted for and in accord with the votes of Parliament. Its functions have since been enlarged to include inquiries into financial and administrative practices and particularly practices or expenditures that appear uneconomical or extravagant. It examines the appropriation and other accounts of the executive departments and agencies, after they have been audited by the Comptroller and Auditor General, and reports its findings and recommendations to the House of Commons. It is thus an indispensable link in the chain of executive and legislative control of expenditure; it provides the sanction for the audits of the Comptroller and Auditor General. The Treasury carries out its recommendations, issuing minutes to the departments instructing them of specific actions to be taken.

The recommendations of the committee are rarely discussed or debated in the House of Commons. Although submitted to the House, they are really directed to the Treasury and the departments, where they receive the most careful attention, and, as a rule, are carried out without question. The committee exercises a subtle but nevertheless effective control over the administrative practices and financial operations of the departments. It provides one of the most notable examples of effective legislative control of administration without encroaching upon the executive function or weakening executive authority. The British financial system is based on the principle that true economy and parliamentary control are best achieved by inquiring into how the departments have used the funds voted to them and by holding the principal department officers strictly accountable for any unauthorized, imprudent, or wasteful expenditure. The Public Accounts Committee has been uniformly praised by select committees of Parliament which have inquired into parliamentary control of finance, and by Prime Ministers, Chancellors of the Exchequer, and other leading members of Parliament, as well as by writers on public finance.

In its early history, the committee devoted its attention primarily to requiring the improvement of the accounting system; it insisted upon accuracy and promptness in submitting the accounts, on strict regularity, and on a classification of accounts that was definite and intelligible. It required the departments to submit explanations of any unusual expenditure, particularly of expenditures which did not correspond to the estimates.[35] After about 1880, however, it broadened the scope of its work and not only considered legal and accounting matters, but inquired into administrative practices which appeared wasteful, extravagant, or unduly expensive. It encouraged the Comptroller and Auditor General to bring to its attention any administrative action which he deemed unsound or uneconomical, and required the permanent heads of the departments, who are designated "Accounting Officers," to explain and defend such actions. The tendency of the Committee to devote its attention primarily to questions of economy and the prudent use of public funds rather than to legality became even more pronounced after World War II. The work of the committee, as the Comptroller and Auditor General stated in 1956, "is largely directed to questions of management, with which economy is intimately connected."[36]

To understand the work of the Public Accounts Committee, it is necessary to review briefly the type of audits conducted by the Comptroller and Auditor General, who heads the Audit and Exchequer Department. He is appointed for an indefinite term and is subject to removal only by the action of the two houses of Parliament. He is always selected from the civil service, usually is a former member of the Treasury staff, and ordinarily has served as the permanent head of a department prior to his appointment. Accordingly, he is well informed on all aspects of administration, but is not an accounting specialist.

The auditing staff of the Audit and Exchequer Department, which consists of about 500 auditors, carries on its work in the several departments and agencies throughout the year, utilizing a test or spot audit to make sure that the departments' internal auditing staffs are doing a competent job. The audit has been described by the Comptroller and Auditor General as including: (1) an "accountancy audit" to es-

---

[35] Chubb, op. cit., p. 45-47.
[36] The late Sir Frank Tribe, in an address at the London School of Economics, Nov. 6, 1956.

tablish that the accounts are a true record of receipts and payments; (2) a "finance audit," which is concerned with the adequacy of the department's internal audit and financial procedures, including contract procedures and store accounts; and (3) an appropriation audit, which is designed (a) to ensure that funds are expended in accordance with the intentions of Parliament when they were voted, (b) to inquire into any variations between estimates and expenditures and the use of transfers, and (c) to ascertain that expenditure conforms to the authority that governs it.[37]

The only sanction which the Comptroller and Auditor General has is to report the results of his audit, with comments, to Parliament. His approval is required for all issues from the Exchequer to the appropriation accounts, but this function, once important, has become largely a formality. Unlike the U. S. Comptroller General, he does not have the power to settle accounts, to disallow expenditures, or to issue opinions or rulings interpreting the meaning and effect of statutes. In his audit reports he certifies as to the accuracy of the accounts, and, in addition, questions any expenditure which he thinks is not authorized, is not in accord with the intentions of Parliament, or does not conform with Treasury or departmental regulations. He also points out any shortcomings in the departments' accounting records and any practices of the departments that his auditors have questioned, giving special attention to such matters as contract procedures, storekeeping, inventories, and controls maintained by the departments. He may report any subjects which he thinks warrant the attention of the Public Accounts Committee, and is expected to bring to its attention practices which appear unduly expensive or wasteful. However, his staff does not conduct efficiency studies or attempt to make general evaluations of the organization and administration of departments, and the Comptroller and Auditor General himself carefully avoids expressing any views on policy.

The Public Accounts Committee, which is now the oldest committee of the House of Commons, consists of fifteen members, divided between the two political parties. By custom the chairman is a member of the opposition party, often a former Financial Secretary of the Treasury, whose experience gives him a thorough knowledge of financial and administrative practice. The committee conducts hearings, usually

[37] *Ibid.*

twice weekly, after the session of Parliament opens and the Comptroller and Auditor General is ready to submit his audit reports on particular departments. The Accounting Officers of each department (ordinarily the permanent secretaries), who appear before it, are required to explain and defend the expenditures or actions that have been questioned by the Comptroller and Auditor General. This places the responsibility for any shortcomings or improper expenditures squarely on the administrative head of the department.

The reports of the committee are written in a dry and factual manner, characteristically restrained and judicial—and understating any criticism of the departments. The committee scrupulously avoids sensational charges and seldom expresses any condemnation of department officials. Ordinarily it calls attention in its report to department practices or procedures that it regards as faulty or unduly expensive and, without prescribing the remedy, calls upon the department and the Treasury to institute inquiries, as well as the needed corrections. The minutes issued by the Treasury directing the departments to carry out the recommendations of the committee are quite specific, however. Although not mandatory, the recommendations are customarily followed by the departments, but the departments may, with Treasury approval, defer action and ask the committee for reconsideration the following year. The committee follows up relentlessly, inquiring of each department how it has carried out the recommendations of the previous year, and the Comptroller and Auditor General reports any failure of departments to follow its recommendations.

The Public Accounts Committee exerts a continuous and highly salutary influence on the day-to-day administration of the departments, whose officials are constantly mindful of the fact that any questionable expenditure or administrative action may have to be defended by the head of the department before the committee. This unquestionably has an important effect in deterring waste, extravagance, and imprudent management. The committee has never made any claims as to the amount of savings which it has accomplished, but over the years it has undoubtedly been instrumental in requiring the departments to exercise economy and prudence in their management.

Parliamentary control of expenditures in Great Britain is thus quite different from the control exercised by Congress. Exercised by a standing committee of the House of Commons with the aid of the legislative auditor, it is primarily concerned with the economical use of public funds rather than technical questions of legality. The Comptroller and Auditor General reports to the Public Accounts Committee only matters of importance that warrant its attention—usually department expenditures or practices which he regards as wasteful or not in accord with accepted financial procedures, though at times he raises questions concerning the authority and legality of expenditures. The British audit system thus promotes economical and prudent management of the departments, while the American system sometimes seems to have the opposite effect because of its preoccupation with questions of legality and the enforcement of the auditing officer's interpretations of the law.

The British system provides a *post*-control over expenditures, while the American system provides a *pre*-control. Since the U. S. Comptroller General may disallow expenditures, prudence requires the executive departments of the United States Government to apply to him for advance rulings if there is any question as to the legality of a proposed expenditure. The British departments are under no similar necessity to secure advance decisions from the Comptroller and Auditor General, who, as a matter of policy, declines to give advance opinions concerning his audits. The latter officer has no authority to prevent expenditures that he regards as unauthorized or improper, a power that his American counterpart regards as absolutely essential to his office. However, it would be a mistake to assume that the British audits have little or no influence on department actions. They are conducted throughout the year on the heels of the actual expenditures, and any questionable expenditure is taken up with the departments without waiting to lay it before the Public Accounts Committee. Ordinarily any type of expenditure which the Comptroller and Auditor General questions is discontinued forthwith, unless the department is able to satisfy him concerning its propriety.

The notable success of the British Public Accounts Committee, with the assistance of the Comptroller and Auditor General, in maintaining effective and salutary control over the expenditures and administration of the government departments may be attributed largely to the following factors: (1) the control is exercised by a single committee of the House of Commons, which speaks with the authority of Parliament itself; (2) the committee devotes its attention primarily to questions of costs and administration rather than to legal technicalities; (3) it refrains from partisan and controversial policy issues; (4) it acts in a judicial manner and avoids sensationalism; (5) it holds the chief administrative officers of the departments to a strict accounting for any unauthorized, imprudent, or unsound activities; and (6) it has the active cooperation of the Treasury, which sees to it that the committee recommendations are carried out. The control exercised by the Public Accounts Committee does not encroach on the executive function; on the contrary, it strengthens and enforces the internal control of each department and the central controls exercised by the Treasury.

Summary: Congress and the Audit

This brief comparison with the British system serves to emphasize how far the American legislative audit deviates from the criteria stated at the beginning of this chapter (pp. 128-129).

The first criterion, independence from the executive and responsibility only to the legislature, is substantially met. Of the Comptroller General's independence of the President and the departments there can be no doubt. And although at times he appears to operate as a law unto himself, his primary audience is Congress, and he is clearly responsible to Congress to the extent that it can or wishes to organize itself to control and supervise him.

The American scheme seriously fails the second criterion, that the audit should be a post-audit. To be sure, there is no longer a pre-audit of the type common in the McCarl era, which required the GAO's approval before each disbursement could be made. Nowadays, the departments can make payments on their own responsibility. However, a transaction does not really become final until the Comptroller General has implicitly approved it in settling accounts; the funds are still subject to recovery from either the recipient or the accountable officer if the Comptroller General disapproves. This power of settlement and disallowance virtually forces the departments to go to the Comptroller General for preliminary discussion and advance approval of any types of expenditure about which there can be any question. In a significant sense, then, the Comptroller General is a party to every transaction of uncertain validity. The system thus dilutes the responsibility of the executive and denies Congress a post-audit report from someone completely detached from the transaction.

The third standard—comprehensiveness, intensity, and promptness —is met in part, but only in part. The Comptroller General has appropriate freedom to make his inquiries as broad and as deep as he deems necessary. If there be any fault, it is in his tendency to extend the scope of the audit to comprehend matters of policy that have little if anything to do with either probity or efficiency in the use of public funds. Promptness of the audits has been greatly improved in the past decade, but many audit reports still deal with matters that the departments claim to have taken care of long ago. Instead of the present pattern of audits and reports at intermittent intervals, it would be preferable to have prompt reports on the state of the accounts of each agency for each fiscal year, such as the GAO submits for government corporations and which is generally the British practice.

Finally, Congress is not adequately organized to receive, consider, and act on the audit reports. The two Committees on Government Operations are the most important in this respect, but the GAO also has close relations with the Appropriations Committees, and from time to time with various subject-matter committees as well. A great deal of work is done for individual members. There is no single point of responsibility in either house for supervising the Comptroller General's work and systematically following up on his reports. The result is that the resources of the GAO are frequently used on investigations for the specialized and highly political purposes of committee chairmen and senior legislators, while the more prosaic but highly important job of reviewing audit reports, holding executive officers accountable, and considering improvements in financial management is neglected. Proposals that the House and the Senate establish special auditing committees or (better yet) a joint committee of the two houses with the sole duty of overseeing the Comptroller General and taking up problems raised in his reports have so far aroused little enthusiasm.

We conclude, then, that the present auditing and accounting system of the federal government violates several generally accepted principles governing such functions. Most serious is the violation of the principle that the post auditor should have no part or voice in the financial transactions which he audits, but his sole functions should be to examine the accounts and financial transactions and report his findings to the legislative body. As a result, executive officers are hampered in their duties by the rulings and regulations of the Comptroller General, which prescribe and limit the activities and methods which they may utilize in carrying out the programs authorized by Congress, and thus their responsibility to their administrative superiors and to Congress is impaired.

The system introduces a high degree of external legal control and red tape in administrative operations, but lessens the responsibility of executive officers for the efficient and economical performance of the functions assigned to them. Emphasis is placed on the meticulous observance of technical legal requirements rather than prudent and frugal use of public funds. In sound auditing systems, accounting and post-auditing functions are clearly separated; the former is the responsibility of executive officers, while the latter is the sole responsibility of the legislative auditor. The basic defect of the legislation establishing the federal auditing system is that the accounting and auditing functions are commingled; as a result executive officers are deprived of authority which they must have if they are to be held responsible for the conduct of the departments, and the legislative body is deprived of true audit reports that it must have to hold executive officers to a strict accounting.

Yet Congress, in whose name the legislative audit is conducted, shows no disposition to make significant changes in the present arrangements. As history shows, Congress has always resisted proposals to modify the functions and powers of the Comptroller General, particularly if they seemed to emanate from the Executive branch. Records of congressional hearings participated in by representatives of the GAO, especially when the Comptroller General himself appears, abound with expressions of mutual appreciation. On Capitol Hill, the Comptroller General is accorded a deference comparable to that given the Director of the FBI.

Why is there so little interest in change? Obviously because the system well serves the interests of Congress as a whole and of individual members *as these interests are presently perceived by most members.* The Constitution, it must be remembered, divides power between Congress and the Executive branch, and predisposes them to conflict. The Comptroller General and his staff are willing and valuable allies in the perennial effort to control, hedge, and harass the Exec-

utive branch—an activity which many members consider their duty under this system. Neither the Constitution nor the party system provides
the sense of mutual dependence and restraint that characterizes relations between the Cabinet and the legislative majority in Great Britain.

Weakness of party leadership in the United States readily trans-
lates itself into weakness of the whole legislature's control over its committees and individual members. The "agent of Congress" becomes in
effect the agent of powerful individual members, or particular parts of
Congress. Committee chairmen and members with influence and seniority deal separately with the GAO, draw on it for reports and services, and by the nature of their interests and responses significantly influence the policy content of the GAO's work. The "market" is not for
dry reports on the state of the accounts, or even for pointers toward
administrative efficiency in the limited sense; rather, it is for reports
that provide raw material for well-publicized investigations or advance
the special policy purposes of individual members. And, by the work-
ings of the seniority system, the members best situated to utilize the
services of the GAO are often least in touch, and least responsive to
the modal policy views of the Congress.

It would be a mistake, however, to assume that a legislative post-
audit system is unsuitable for a government based upon a constitutional system of separation of powers and checks and balances. A considerable number of American state and local governments have
adopted audit systems within recent years which in all essential respects are similar to those used by the British government and by business and industry. In such systems the function of the legislative auditor is confined to conducting a post-audit and reporting his findings to
the legislative body, without the authority to settle accounts, to prescribe the accounting system, to disallow expenditures, or to determine
the legality of expenditures. This movement of state and local governments to adopt a true post-audit system to serve the legislature recog-
nizes that it is unwise to authorize the auditor to dictate administrative
methods and procedures or to pass upon administrative decisions, and
that his true function is to examine the accounts and financial practices
and report his findings to the legislative body.

The present arrangement is useful to key members of Congress,
particularly the chairmen of committees, who often utilize the staff of
the Comptroller General to assist in the conduct of investigations of

the administration of the department, the results of which are often used to attack particular policies and programs of the government. Despite the utility of such investigations in the perennial struggle between Congress and the Executive branch, one may question whether this type of activity is appropriate for a legislative auditor. Congress will be better served if the legislative auditor confines his activities to auditing, and reports to Congress any failure on the part of the departments to account for the funds entrusted to their use, any expenditure or activity not authorized by law, any shortcomings in the accounting system, any financial practices that are not suitable or adequate, and any wasteful or improper uses of public funds. With such reports Congress will be better able to hold executive officers to a strict accounting for their activities and uses of public funds, which is the central purpose of an audit system.

Never before in the history of the country has it been so important for the departments to be administered competently, efficiently, and responsibly; never before have their activities so greatly affected the welfare of the nation and, indeed, of the entire free world. An unsound system hampers efficient administration and fails to serve the real needs of the legislature; a sound audit system is essential. Only when Congress is persuaded that such an audit system will afford it greater, rather than less, real control over the financial management of the executive departments, will it be disposed to revise the present system and make it conform to accepted principles of sound financial practice. A broad inquiry into the present audit system and how it might be revised to better serve the needs of Congress and of the executive departments would be an appropriate first step.

7

Congress and the Civil Service

THE ADMINISTRATION of a modern government depends in large measure on the quality of its public service, the competence, ability, and loyalty of its employees. Without an able, efficient civil service, the policies and programs provided by law will fail to accomplish their purpose. "Improved personnel management," stated the report of the Sixth American Assembly (1954), "is one of the major keys to economy, efficiency, and a higher quality of government service."[1] The President and Congress both have important responsibilities for personnel administration and the public service. The maintenance of high standards, the adoption of needed improvements in policies and administration, and the strengthening of the public service require the joint action of Congress and the departments. Effective teamwork by the two branches of government, mutual respect and trust, and recognition by each of the functions of the other are essential to sound personnel administration. Unfortunately, cooperative relations between Congress and the executive have not always prevailed in this area, and as a result the public service has suffered.[2]

It is the responsibility of Congress, broadly speaking, to determine certain of the most important personnel policies of the government that are not delegated to the President or the Civil Service Commission, and to see that these policies are being faithfully carried out and

[1] The American Assembly, *The Federal Government Service: Its Character, Prestige, and Problems* (October 1954), p. 181.
[2] See Leonard D. White, "Congress and the Civil Service," *Public Personnel Review,* Vol. 5 (April 1944), pp. 65-69.

the public service is being competently managed. However, the President as Chief Executive shares with Congress the responsibility for major personnel policies, and many policy decisions are wisely delegated to the Civil Service Commission. The administration of personnel is the President's responsibility and that of the heads of the departments and agencies, assisted by staff agencies. It is also the President's responsibility to take the initiative in bringing about needed improvements. "The President," according to the American Assembly report, "has the responsibility for leadership of the Federal Government Service in the Executive Branch. . . . This leadership must be acknowledged and supported by the heads and employees of executive departments, by the party leaders, and by the members of the Congress. This leadership must be accepted and exercised by the President, if the business of the National Government is to be efficiently performed."[3]

The Civil Service Committees

The Committee on Post Office and Civil Service of the House of Representatives consists of twenty-five members, and its Senate counterpart of nine (as of 1962). In both houses these committees (referred to hereafter as civil service committees) rank next to the lowest in member preference.[4] Members often serve on them only a term or two, transferring to other committees as soon as they have acquired sufficient seniority to secure preferred assignments. Those who choose to remain rise rapidly to ranking positions. From 1947 through 1960 (80th Congress through the 86th), of the 174 House members appointed to the civil service committee, 81 had not previously served on it. In the Senate, of the 85 members appointed, 40 had not previously served.

When, in successive Congresses, a great many of a committee's members are new, serving a first (and often an only) term, the continuity of the committee's business will obviously be interrupted and diminished, since the novices' knowledge and understanding of the problems dealt with are necessarily limited. The problems of the civil

[3] The American Assembly, *op. cit.*, pp. 181-182.
[4] See George Goodwin, Jr., "The Seniority System in Congress," *American Political Science Review*, Vol. 53 (June 1959), p. 433.

service are important and intricate, yet almost half of the membership of the committees legislating on them in recent years has been inexperienced. Moreover, not all of the senior members who have exercised leadership have displayed an understanding of the needs of the federal service or a desire to bring about its strengthening and improvement, and a few have been among its harshest critics. In the past both committees have included among their members many patronage-minded congressmen who were unsympathetic to the merit system.

It is unfortunate that these committees are assigned jurisdiction over Post Office legislation, which is, in the main, unrelated to personnel administration. (The dual jurisdiction was one result of the Legislative Reorganization Act of 1946.) It is likely that some members have accepted the committee assignments solely because of their interest in postal matters. A large proportion of the membership, especially on the House committee, has always stemmed from rural areas of the South and Midwest, where there are ordinarily few federal employees other than those in the postal service; metropolitan areas, which have the largest concentrations of federal employees, have been but slimly represented. The members who rise to positions of leadership have ordinarily reflected the outlook and attitudes toward the public service that exist in their rural districts. This is no doubt one of the reasons why federal salary scales, especially in the middle and upper brackets, lagged for so long a time behind the salary scales in private industry of the larger urban states.

The low prestige of the civil service committees is due in part to the restricted role which has been undertaken, a role that has placed emphasis upon controlling and policing the civil service instead of seeking to strengthen and improve it. Conceiving their functions narrowly, the members have failed to recognize the important role which the committees might play in building a public service second to none. Yet, at times, under effective leadership, such a role has emerged. Representative Robert Ramspeck of Georgia, chairman of the House committee from 1935 to 1945, achieved national recognition because of his constructive leadership in securing legislation to extend the civil service to practically all positions in the federal government.

A substantial amount of personnel legislation relating to employees of individual departments is enacted without being referred to the civil service committees. Investigations of particular aspects of personnel administration have not uncommonly been conducted by other committees. This unfortunate splintering of responsibility has been due in part to the failure of the civil service committees to report bills granting needed personnel authority to the departments—for example, bills authorizing additional supergrade positions—so that the departments have turned to other committees for special authorizations.

Trends in Personnel Legislation

The United States public service is regulated today by numerous acts of Congress which cover almost every aspect of personnel administration. This is, however, a relatively new development and in distinct contrast to earlier practice. The first civil service legislation in the modern sense was passed in 1871 as a rider to the sundry civil appropriations bill, authorizing the President "to prescribe such rules and regulations for the admission of persons into the civil service of the United States as will best promote the efficiency thereof, and ascertain the fitness of each candidate . . . ; and . . . to employ suitable persons to conduct said inquiries, to prescribe their duties, and to establish regulations for the conduct of persons who may receive appointments in the civil service."[5] The Pendleton Civil Service Act of 1883 similarly delegated authority to the President to administer the law and to issue rules and regulations governing the civil service.[6] "The Pendleton Bill," stated the report of the Senate Committee on Civil Service and Retrenchment, "assumes that the power of appointment to the executive service is vested in the President, and that it is neither legal nor desirable to limit that authority, but simply to provide for its exercise in the manner most beneficial to the public service."[7]

For some fifty years after the passage of the Pendleton Act, Congress enacted only a few statutes dealing with personnel, importantly among them the Lloyd-LaFollette Act of 1912, which granted federal employees the right to organize and to petition Congress, the Retirement Act of 1920, and the Classification Act of 1923. After 1930, however, Congress altered its practice, and the extent to which the civil

[5] 16 Stat. 514.
[6] 22 Stat. 403.
[7] Senate Report 576, 47th Cong., 1st sess. (1882), pp. 5-6.

service is today regulated by statute is indicated by the codification recently prepared (but as of 1963 not yet published) by the Civil Service Commission of more than 1,500 statutes, the majority of them enacted since 1930.

In recent years Congress has enacted from 20 to 25 civil service laws annually, plus many other statutes that carry incidental provisions affecting personnel. In the 85th Congress, 787 civil service bills were introduced, 350 of which related to retirement, the balance to 40 other subjects. The Civil Service Commission received 879 requests from congressional committees for reports on personnel bills and submitted 684 such reports.

It is doubtful that such a mass of legislative detail on all aspects of the civil service is desirable, since many administrative procedures are thus frozen into statute and the President and the departments are deprived of needed discretion and flexibility. It may be noted that in Great Britain the practice is quite different: detailed regulation of the public service is left to the Treasury and to the departments, and statutes have been passed only with respect to retirement. In 1952 the U. S. Civil Service Commission criticized the recent legislative tendency as follows:

> The last few years have seen a growing tendency on the part of Congress to legislate on the details of personnel administration. The Commission believes that by going beyond statements of policy and legislative intent to spell out procedures of carrying them out, Congress often creates a rigidity of operation and administration that interferes with efficient personnel management in the executive branch. Administrative rules and regulations are flexible and easily altered to suit changing conditions. Personnel procedures set by law can be changed only by new legislation after a necessarily lengthy process.[8]

Statutory controls dealing with the civil service have been applied in the following categories: (1) coverage of the civil service and other merit systems and exemptions; (2) organization for personnel administration; (3) classification, pay, and retirement; (4) personnel policies and administration; (5) rights of employees, veterans' preference, employee conduct; (6) miscellaneous restrictions, limitations, and controls, which are often adopted as riders to appropriation acts. Each of

[8] U. S. Civil Service Commission, *69th Annual Report* (1952), p. 20.

these types of legislation is discussed on the following pages. Additional controls over personnel are exercised through investigations, the Senate's confirmation of presidential appointments, and various devices, other than riders, for reducing the size of department staffs. These actions are also discussed briefly below but more fully in other chapters.

Legislation Determining the Coverage of Civil Service[9]

At the outset the Pendleton Act of 1883 applied only to about 10 per cent of the employees in the Executive branch, but the President was authorized to extend the service to other employees by executive order, as he saw fit. Legislation on the coverage of civil service has usually been aimed at exempting certain classes of positions or certain government activities. In creating other merit systems, however, such as those for the Foreign Service, Public Health Service, Tennessee Valley Authority, International Cooperation Administration, Federal Bureau of Investigation, and so on, Congress has determined by law which positions shall be included in each system. The following account deals with the coverage of the civil service as distinct from the other merit systems.

By 1932 approximately 80 per cent of the federal civilian employees in the Executive branch had been placed under the civil service. Starting in that year with the creation of the Reconstruction Finance Corporation, Congress followed the practice for a number of years of exempting positions in new agencies and new activities instituted to cope with problems growing out of the Great Depression. Within four years the number of exempted positions increased from 111,070 to 325,535, while the percentage of total positions within the civil service declined to 60.5. "Never in the history of its civil service legislation," according to Ralph S. Fjelstad, "had Congress made such a sustained and deliberate attempt to undermine the extensions of merit appointments."[10]

---

[9] See Commission on Organization of the Executive Branch of the Government, *Task Force Report on Personnel and Civil Service,* Appendix B, "Highlights in the Growth of the Merit System" (1955), pp. 167-197.

[10] Fjelstad, "Congress and Civil Service Legislation, 1933-1947" (unpublished doctoral dissertation, Northwestern University, 1948), p. 138.

The exemption of personnel in these new activities was defended on the grounds that the programs were temporary and staffs could be recruited more quickly outside of civil service. At this time the examining procedures of the service were cumbersome and slow, so that it was probably true that the Commission was not equipped to undertake the large volume of employment required by the new activities of the government. Without doubt, however, Congress was also reacting to the tremendous pressures being put on it for appointment openings, both because of the enormous unemployment produced by the depression and because the time had been long since Democrats had last been favored for offices. Moreover, civil service was not then held in high esteem by most members of Congress. It should nevertheless be noted that, although many appointments to exempted positions were used as patronage, many others were made on the basis of merit. The Tennessee Valley Authority Act (1933), for instance, required the TVA Board to establish a merit system of its own, and prohibited patronage appointments. The personnel of the Social Security Board, created to administer a permanent program, was placed under the civil service, except for experts and attorneys, who were not covered until a few years later.

During the first term of the Franklin D. Roosevelt administration, even while legislation was seeming to undermine the principle of merit appointments, there was a resurgence of public demand for civil service reform. In 1935 the Commission of Inquiry on Public Service Personnel, a distinguished private body, published its report, *Better Government Personnel*, urging the adoption of the career system in the public service at all levels and the extension of the federal civil service to exempted positions. The National Civil Service Reform League, the League of Women Voters, and other organizations joined in the movement for the strengthening of the civil service. Both the Democrats and the Republicans promised extension of the civil service in their platforms of 1936, and Republican candidate Landon made this an issue in his presidential campaign. In 1937 the President's Committee on Administrative Management urged the extension of the merit system "upward, outward, and downward" to include all positions in the government except a very few of the higher posts that are principally policy determining.[11] The time had come for Congress to con-

[11] *Report, with Special Studies*, p. 4.

sider legislation to reverse the trend which had obtained during the five years preceding.

In 1938, Congress passed the Ramspeck-O'Mahoney Act (52 Stat. 1076), which ostensibly placed postmasters of the first three classes under the civil service—but in fact made no real change in the previous practice of political appointments. Members of Congress of the party in office continued to select the temporary appointees when vacancies occurred in their districts and these political appointees almost invariably received regular appointments after the examinations were conducted. In other districts the selection was made by the local party organization. The act did make two desirable changes: appointments were for indefinite terms instead of four years, and postmasters were prohibited from engaging in partisan activities. Concurrently with signing the act, President Roosevelt issued an executive order extending the civil service to practically all positions not exempted by statute, and on the same day issued another order making the most thorough revision of the civil service rules since 1903 (Executive Orders 7916 and 7915).[12]

The President by this action went as far as he could in extending the merit system; the next step was up to Congress. Chairman Ramspeck of the House civil service committee had for a number of years been urging legislation to extend the system; in 1937 his committee had conducted hearings on such an extension. In 1940, Congress passed the Ramspeck Act (54 Stat. 1211), authorizing the President to cover under the civil service nearly 200,000 positions previously exempted by law. The act also authorized the extension of position classification under the Classification Act of 1923 to the field service and provided for the revision of the efficiency rating system. President Roosevelt at once began issuing a series of executive orders that eventually placed almost all of the previously exempted positions under the civil service. By early 1943 approximately 95 per cent of the nearly 2 million federal employees were working under some version of the merit system.[13]

Several bills which would have seriously curtailed the scope of the civil service were before Congress in the following years, among them the defense bill reported in 1940 by the House Military Affairs Committee which provided that civilian appointments could be made with-

[12] See Paul P. Van Riper, *History of the United States Civil Service* (1958), p. 338.
[13] See *ibid.*, p. 344.

out regard to the civil service laws. Through the effective intervention of Civil Service Commissioner Arthur S. Flemming and the willingness of the Commission to adapt its rules and procedures to meet the greatly increased personnel requirements of the government during the emergency, this threat was headed off.

Legislation on
Organization for Personnel Administration

Whether the Civil Service Commission should be responsible to the President or be independent of his direction has recently become an issue in federal personnel administration. A related issue is whether a commission or a single administrator should be used. During the debate preceding passage of the Pendleton Act in 1883 statements were repeatedly made that the act would not curtail the appointing power of the President and that under the Constitution the central personnel agency must be responsible to the President. The act placed the Commission directly under the President and provided that its members should be appointed by him and serve at his pleasure. Moreover, they were directed to "aid the President as he may request in preparing suitable rules for carrying this act into effect." The power to issue rules and regulations governing the civil service was granted, not to the Commission, but to the President.

For fifty years after the passage of the Pendleton Act the Commission was regarded as a presidential agency. In recent years its functions have been greatly increased by numerous acts of Congress, as well as by executive orders, and its contacts with congressional committees have multiplied. The Commission today occupies a somewhat ambivalent position: although it continues to regard itself as the agency of the President, responsible to him for its policies and administration, it is under considerable pressure from congressional committees to take an independent position and to resist presidential direction and control.

As a bipartisan body of three members, the Commission was never able to function completely as a staff agency of the President in developing improved personnel policies and practices throughout the government. With this difficulty in mind, the President's Committee on Administrative Management recommended in 1937 that the three members be replaced by a single administrator and that a nonsalaried, advisory board be created to act as the "watchdog of the merit system," inquiring into personnel policies and administration and making recommendations for their improvement to the President and to Congress.[14] This plan failed to secure the approval of Congress, and in the Reorganization Act of 1939, which granted the President power to reorganize executive departments, the Civil Service Commission was among the agencies specifically exempted from the power.[15]

In consequence President Roosevelt created the position of Special Assistant on Personnel Administration in his Executive Office, and over the years many of the recommendations which the Committee on Administrative Management had made for the improvement of personnel administration were adopted. Largely as a result of the dynamic and untiring efforts of Commissioner Arthur Flemming, during World War II the Commission greatly expanded its activities to meet the enlarged personnel needs of the government. Since then its functions and prestige have continued to increase, its relations with both Congress and the President have become closer, and, especially in recent years, it has exercised greater leadership in bringing about improvements in personnel administration.

Several important changes in its organization took place in the postwar period. In 1949, on the recommendation of the first Hoover Commission, the president of the Civil Service Commission was designated chairman and given the responsibility for its administration, assisted by an executive director. In 1953, President Eisenhower took the further step, also recommended by the Hoover Commission, of appointing the chairman to serve also as personnel adviser to the President. The effect was to bring the work of the CSC into close relationship with the President and his Executive Office, but the plan attracted criticism, and the Task Force on Personnel and Civil Service of the second Hoover Commission recommended its abandonment. When Chairman Philip Young, who had served in this dual capacity, resigned from the Commission in 1957, President Eisenhower reverted to the former arrangement of appointing someone other than the CSC chairman to the office of Special Assistant to the President for Personnel Administration in the Executive Office.

[14] *Report, with Special Studies,* pp. 9-11.
[15] 53 Stat. 561.

The role of the Civil Service Commission and its relations to the President, to the executive departments and agencies, and to the civil service committees of Congress were the subject of a report issued by the House civil service committee in 1956.[16] Rejecting the view that the Commission was a staff agency of the President, the report emphasized that it was "the executive agency established by law to administer civil service laws, rules, and regulations," adding that "Congress expects to hold it entirely accountable." The Commission was warned against presidential control of its activities, and instructed to "insist upon and practice complete independence of action and freedom of influence or domination by any other [executive] agency." This independence, however, was not advocated in respect to the civil service committees of Congress; on the contrary, the Commission was urged to bring plans, programs, and proposed regulations for consultation and advice before putting them into effect, and the report indicated that the House committee, at least, expected to exercise close legislative oversight.

Not content merely to exhort, the committee proposed several steps to give the Commission greater independence. One of the steps would provide six-year, overlapping terms for the Commissioners, previously serving at the pleasure of the President; another would transfer the authority to approve super-grade positions from the chairman to the Commission itself, acting by majority vote. These provisions were subsequently added as a rider to the Executive Pay Bill of 1956, which was passed near the end of the session; the President signed them into law rather than defeat the pay bill he had urged upon Congress. Nevertheless (as noted in Chapter 2), the Commission itself still tends to operate as a staff agency of the President.

The Senate civil service committee tends to take the position that personnel administration is the responsibility of the President and the department heads rather than of the Commission. In 1958, Senator Joseph S. Clark of Pennsylvania, a member of the committee, introduced a bill (S.3888) to create an office of personnel management, in the Executive Office of the President; it would be headed by a director and would take over most of the functions of the Commission. The Commission would be retained as an independent agency to protect

---

[16] *The Civil Service Commission*, House Report No. 1844, 84th Cong., 2d sess. (March 1956).

employee rights by hearing appeals, and to administer the Hatch Act and investigate the administration of personnel, reporting findings and recommendations to the President and Congress. The bill partially embodied the recommendations of a survey conducted for the Senate civil service committee by a special staff headed by James R. Watson, executive director of the National Civil Service League,[17] and was based on the following principles: (1) that personnel administration is an executive function for which the President is given responsibility by the Constitution; (2) that the President should have a staff agency, comparable to the Bureau of the Budget and headed by a single director, to assist him in developing and maintaining high standards of personnel administration throughout the government; and (3) that wider authority and responsibility for personnel administration could be delegated to the departments.[18]

Hearings were conducted on the bill in 1958 and 1959. Those who testified in favor of it maintained that personnel administration is an essential part of management, and that a single director of personnel administration under the President would enable him to bring about needed improvements. The opposing witnesses expressed the view that an independent commission is needed to safeguard the merit system against patronage pressures. Spokesmen for employee unions were afraid that the plan would lessen the rights of employees, while veterans' organizations were fearful that veterans' preference would be impaired. The administration endorsed the objective of the bill, but otherwise took no stand.[19]

The Clark bill was reported in June 1960, but was not called up for action in the Senate.[20] Three members of the Senate committee submitted a minority report in which they agreed that personnel administration is the responsibility of the President, but contended that

[17] *Administration of the Civil Service System,* Report to the Senate Committee on Post Office and Civil Service, 85th Cong., 1st sess. (1957). Recommendations similar to those of the report had been made in 1937 by the President's Committee on Administrative Management.

[18] See *To Provide an Effective System of Personnel Administration,* Report of the Special Subcommittee on S.3888, Senate Committee on Post Office and Civil Service, 85th Cong., 2d sess. (October 1958).

[19] *Hearings Before a Subcommittee of the Senate Committee on Post Office and Civil Service on S.3888,* 85th Cong., 2d sess. (June 1958); and on S.1638, 86th Cong., 1st sess. (May and June 1959).

[20] Senate Report 1545, 86th Cong., 2d sess. (1960).

needed improvements could be accomplished by strengthening the Civil Service Commission.

Legislation Relating to
Pay, Classification, and Retirement

One of the earliest recorded examples of pay legislation was an act of the Continental Congress in 1775 providing for the payment of $176.26 to a Mr. Alexander "for riding express divers times." If Mr. Alexander were a federal employee today he would not have to secure a special act of Congress to be paid, but the amount which he would receive would be subject to highly detailed statutory provisions, and would depend upon which of the numerous federal pay systems applied to him. An interdepartmental committee reported in 1957 that the government had 77 different pay plans for civilian employees—16 statutory and 61 local wage board plans under various statutes. Civilian employees covered by the major statutory plans included the 950,000 being paid in accordance with the Classification Act, the 440,000 under the key job description system of the Postal Field Service, and the 116,000 others under a number of systems used variously by such agencies as the AEC, TVA, Foreign Service, and VA Medical. Some 770,000 employees were paid under the wage board plans at rates fixed by local boards in conformity with prevailing locality rates.[21]

The use of numerous pay plans with different rates has resulted in variations of pay for the same type of work, piecemeal revisions, and failure to maintain rates that are competitive with outside employment. The first Hoover Commission criticized this multiple system as "inequitable and complex," "a system for compensating employees which varies not only from agency to agency but also within individual agencies." It declared that "a comprehensive pay administration policy for the entire executive branch is long overdue," and pointed out that the government was losing many of its best personnel to private enterprise because of the low salary ceilings. The Commission recommended that Congress: (1) enact a comprehensive pay administration policy for the

[21] Interdepartmental Committee on Civilian Compensation, *Report on Civilian Compensation in the Executive Branch of the Federal Government* (November 1957), pp. 4-5.

entire executive branch, (2) raise the salary ceilings, and (3) delegate the fixing of individual pay scales, including salary adjustments from time to time, to the Civil Service Commission, subject to the approval of the President.[22]

These recommendations met with little favor in Congress. Unwilling to give up the detailed control made possible by fixing individual salary rates under the several pay plans by statute, Congress was not prepared to adopt a comprehensive, government-wide, salary policy and simplified pay administration. It raised salary rates, created three new top grades (which unfortunately came to be called super-grades), and extended the Classification Act of 1923 to the field, but this was as far as it was willing to go in revising the civilian pay system.

The salary adjustments made in 1949 proved to be only a stopgap solution, and further revisions soon became necessary. In the following decade numerous salary surveys and studies were conducted, reflecting the growing criticism of the pay rates and administration and the increasing difficulties of the government in recruiting and retaining competent personnel.

Federal salaries of white-collar workers, especially those in the higher grades, failed to keep pace with salaries in private employment, while federal wages paid to blue-collar workers, which are set by local wage boards, advanced with the wage rates in private industry. In many instances supervisors were being paid at a lower rate than workers whom they supervised; in making salary adjustments, the rates of increase Congress has granted to employees in the lower grades, who are numerous and represented by strong employee organizations, have often been higher than those for the upper grades.[23] As a result, the salary spread from the lowest to the highest grades had gradually declined and the scales were no longer suited to federal personnel requirements. From 1942 to 1958 the entrance rates of the first five grades

[22] Commission on Organization of the Executive Branch of the Government, *Personnel Management* (1949), pp. 4, 22-27; *Task Force Report on Federal Personnel* (1949), pp. 45-58.

[23] In the debate on the postal pay bill in 1958 one senator pointed out the tendency to raise the pay of clerks and carriers but not of supervisors: "The thing that impressed me most was the failure, time and time again, of the Senate committee to provide for supervisors. . . . It was . . . because the carriers and the clerks had very able and effective representation and they had much greater numbers." See *Congressional Record*, Vol. 104, Pt. 3, 85th Cong., 2d sess. (Feb. 28, 1958), p. 3135.

more than doubled, while those of the top three normal grades increased by only about one third.

To correct these defects, the Interdepartmental Committee on Civilian Compensation recommended that "a modern, coordinated, total pay program" be established in place of the current statutory pay systems, and that the President should have "full responsibility for pay determination and administration for employees below the level of assistant secretary, subject to reasonable congressional control."[24] In 1958, President Eisenhower urged Congress to establish a joint legislative-executive commission to study broadly the problem of civilian compensation in all three branches of the government, stating:

> During recent years it has become more and more difficult for the Federal Government to recruit and retain competent employees because its salary scales have not remained competitive with those of non-Federal employment. The recent debates in the Congress on the postal and classified pay bills have emphasized the problems inherent in a system which depends exclusively on the legislative process for the periodic adjustment of salary schedules. . . .
> The fact of the matter is, the Federal Government has no comprehensive, uniform pay policy. . . . The rigidity in the pay of top Government officials has had the effect of depressing the salaries of career employees in the upper grades and has resulted in a gradual but progressive distortion of what were orginally sound salary structures. . . . The piecemeal approach to this problem has put an excessive demand on the time of the Congress and has subjected it to a variety of pressures.[25]

The President's recommendation received little support in Congress, and was not acted upon.

On February 20, 1962, President Kennedy sent a special message to Congress proposing a new pay plan under which federal employees would receive comparable salaries to those paid in industry for the same level of duties and responsibilities. To implement this policy, he proposed substantial increases of the salaries of employees in the highest grades, raising the maximum rate from $18,500 to $28,000 within three years. Smaller increases were proposed for the lower grades, which, in the main, were already comparable to those in industry. The

[24] *Report on Civilian Compensation* . . . (1957), pp. 21, 31.
[25] *Congressional Record,* Vol. 104, Pt. 11, 85th Cong., 2d sess. (July 15, 1958), p. 13837.

plan called for other reforms, including the equalization of wage rates for the same level of duties throughout the federal service, greater increases within grade to encourage employee initiative and high levels of performance, and greater differentials between grades. To maintain federal salary rates that are comparable to those in industry, the plan called for an annual salary adjustment based upon an annual report to the Congress by the President on prevailing industry rates.

In 1962 Congress enacted pay legislation adopting, with modifications, the major features of the President's recommendations. It raised salaries in the top levels, but not as much as the President had recommended, and raised those in the lower levels more than he had recommended. The legislation directs the President to report annually to Congress his recommendations for salary revisions to maintain federal pay scales comparable to those paid in private industry. Congress also authorized additional positions in the three highest grades, but retained its control over the number of positions in these grades, although certain professional positions were exempted from this numerical limitation. Congress thus retained its control over federal pay scales. Only time will tell whether it will adjust them periodically to make them comparable with salaries paid in private industry.[26]

Since 1949 Congress has placed statutory limits on the number of positions assigned to the three top grades. It raised the top salary levels in 1949 on the recommendation of the first Hoover Commission, but limited the number of positions that could be assigned to the three new "super-grades" to 400. Only 25 were permitted to be assigned to the highest grade. Prior to 1949, Congress had fixed the qualification standards and salary rates of each grade by statute, but had not placed arbitrary statutory limits on the number of positions that could be assigned to each grade.

This arbitrary limitation on the number of upper-grade positions has proved to be unwise. The number of "super-grades" initially allowed was seriously inadequate to meet the requirements of the vast federal service, and many positions which met the standards could not be allocated to these grades because of the limits. Each year has seen the number increased, in most cases by legislation or appropriation riders applicable to individual departments. Favored agencies, such

[26] See John W. Macy, Jr., "Personnel Developments on the U.S. Federal Level," *Public Personnel Review*, Vol. 24 (January 1963), p. 12.

as the FBI, the Federal Aviation Agency, and the National Aeronautics and Space Agency, as well as the Defense Department, have been well provided for, while others have not fared so well. In addition, certain positions have been placed in super-grade categories by statute. These special statutory authorizations of higher grade positions to individual departments made it impossible to maintain uniform standards and effective controls throughout the service. Certain departments have been authorized also to appoint specified numbers of engineers and scientists at salaries above those fixed in the Classification Act.

The President and the Civil Service Commission have repeatedly urged Congress to repeal these statutory limitations on the number of top-grade positions and to permit their classification according to their duties and responsibilities. Congress, however, has been unwilling to give up this form of control, though it has increased the number of positions authorized in these grades from year to year.

Legislation Relating to Personnel Policies

Almost every aspect of personnel administration is today covered by statutes, including such subjects as eligibility, examinations and appointments, apportionment, hours of work, holidays, leaves of absence, training, employee ratings, employee relations, medical and other services, awards, promotions, layoff and separation, and retirement. No attempt is made here to summarize this voluminous body of laws. Instead, there follow case studies of recent action by Congress on two important personnel programs: (1) the Training Act of 1958 and (2) the Career Executive Program, which was instituted by Executive Order of the President in 1958 and subsequently blocked by Congress. These two cases illustrate the difference in points of view of the legislative and executive branches and raise some of the problems involved in detailed statutory regulation of personnel administration.

The Training Act of 1958

The Government Employees Training Act of 1958 (P. L. 85-107) is one of the most important recent statutes dealing with personnel administration. Prior to its passage most departments had been handicapped because clear-cut authority to carry on training programs was lacking. Training authority had been granted piecemeal to a few departments and agencies, but there was no government-wide authorization or policy. The Comptroller General had ruled that the departments could not assign employees to take training in universities or other institutions without specific statutory authorization, and his rulings also cast doubt on whether the departments could spend funds for certain other training activities. The purpose of the 1958 legislation was to grant training authority to all departments, including training off the job, and to establish government-wide policies.

The earliest ruling concerning the use of federal funds for training appears to have been a decision of the Comptroller of the Treasury in January 1910 which held that the salaries and travel expenses of forest rangers assigned to attend short courses in forestry at universities could not be paid. The Comptroller stated that there was "nothing . . . in the law . . . which, in my judgment, lodges with you the power to send these rangers to college at the Government expense. . . . Unless there is something in the law to the contrary, it is presumed that officers and employees of the Government when appointed and employed have the necessary education to perform the duties for which they were appointed or employed."[27]

The doctrine of the auditors that government employees are fully qualified when they are appointed and hence may not be given further training at government expense, especially training off the job, continued in effect for nearly fifty years. A decision by the Comptroller General in 1939, for instance, held that "government officers or employees may not, in the absence of specific statutory authority, be furnished educational courses or other training at Government expense, as all expenses of qualifying for a Government position are considered personal."[28] Such decisions hampered the development of training programs, and this was especially serious during World War II and in the period after the war when government activities were undergoing rapid expansion and change.

As noted above, however, Congress from time to time passed piecemeal legislation granting training authority of various kinds to certain

[27] *Hearings Before the House Committee on Post Office and Civil Service on H.R.6001,* etc., 85th Cong., 1st sess. (May and June 1958), pp. 105-106.
[28] *Decisions of the Comptroller General,* Vol. 18 (May 11, 1939), p. 843.

departments. Furthermore, the Comptroller General at times modified earlier rulings to permit a limited amount of training off the job without specific statutory authority, provided it could be shown to his satisfaction that the training was essential to the work of the agency. But he ruled that employees could not be assigned to take work in public administration at a university, attend conferences on management at public expense, or accept fellowships from private foundations to take outside training, and he advised the departments to seek general legislation authorizing expenditures for these purposes.[29]

The first Hoover Commission reported in 1949 that many agencies were "reticent to conduct in-service training officially" because of the uncertainty of their legal authority to make expenditures for this purpose, and that the negative attitude which prevailed concerning training and employee development impaired the development of the career service. It recommended that legislation be passed clearly setting forth the policy of the government on the conduct of training programs and authorizing all agencies to carry on in-service training and to use their appropriations for this purpose, and that the Civil Service Commission should assist the agencies in developing training.[30]

In 1953 the Senate civil service committee issued a report on training, recommending comprehensive legislation to authorize all departments to conduct training off the job as well as in-service training on the job, and in 1954 the House committee issued a special report making similar recommendations, but no legislation was passed.[31] In 1955 the second Hoover Commission and its Task Force on Personnel and Civil Service recommended legislation to authorize training throughout the government, both on the job and off the job at universities or other nongovernmental facilities. Without waiting for the passage of legislation, President Eisenhower issued a directive (January 11, 1955), to the departments instructing them to institute training and employee development programs. The Civil Service Commission, having is-

[29] For a review of the leading decisions of the Comptroller General on Training, see *Hearings Before the Committee on Post Office and Civil Service on H.R.6001,* etc., 85th Cong., 1st sess. (1958), pp. 105-109.

[30] Commission on the Organization of the Executive Branch of the Government, *Personnel Management* (1949), p. 23; *Task Force Report on Federal Personnel,* pp. 35-36, 42.

[31] *Training and Education in the Federal Government,* Senate Document No. 31, 83d Cong., 1st sess. (March 1953); *Training of Federal Employees* (House Civil Service Committee), 83d Cong., 2d sess. (December 1954).

sued several studies on training and executive development, in its 1955 *Report* urged the enactment of legislation authorizing training in nongovernmental facilities.[32]

In 1956 the administration renewed its effort to secure training legislation. An administration bill (S.3287) was introduced by Senator Olin D. Johnston, chairman of the Senate civil service committee; reintroduced as S.385 in the spring of 1957, it passed without opposition. It granted broad authority to all departments to carry on training within the departments and through interdepartmental programs, thus removing the question concerning the legality of in-service training, and also of training off the job in nongovernmental facilities, subject to regulations of the President.

The House civil service committee did not take up the Senate bill until the next year, when a subcommittee conducted hearings on it in conjunction with two House training bills (H.R.6001, H.R.1989). The subcommittee actually gave scant attention to the Senate bill and concentrated almost wholly on the Rees bill (H.R.6001), which was highly detailed and placed numerous restrictions and limitations on training in nongovernmental facilities. It specified, for instance, that no employee could be given off-the-job training unless he had served at least a year within the agency concerned, and any employee assigned to take such training was required to sign an agreement to reimburse the government if he did not stay with the agency for three years after the training period. Not more than 1 per cent of total employee time per agency could be given to training, and an individual employee could not be given more than one year of training in ten years of service.

The Rees bill also authorized the Civil Service Commission to issue any other regulations and restrictions which it deemed appropriate. Departments and agencies were required to submit highly detailed reports on any employee assigned to take outside training, and to defend the training by showing its relation to the duties of the employee, estimated economies that would be achieved, and other details. It was evident that the House committee, in favoring the Rees bill, was more intent upon safeguarding against possible abuses than upon promoting training programs. However, in recognition of the possibility that some

---

[32] U. S. Civil Service Commission, *72d Annual Report* (1955), pp. 33-38.

of the restrictions would work hardships and thus defeat the purpose
of the legislation, the bill did give the CSC authority to waive them
in individual cases if in the public interest.

Administration spokesmen objected strongly to the Rees bill's statutory restrictions and limitations on training. The CSC chairman stated
that they "would inevitably complicate operations and make administration of training more cumbersome than it need be."[33] Similarly, the
Director of the Bureau of the Budget testified that he did not consider
the danger of wrongdoing by the departments sufficient to warrant
writing into the statute "inflexible criteria" which might hinder the development of training.[34] The members of the subcommittee, however,
took the position that the bill should include all possible restrictions
and limitations, especially on training in nongovernmental facilities, in
order to prevent abuse of the authority by the departments.

THE HISTORY OF the Training Act of 1958 affords signficant insights
into the problems and difficulties attending detailed statutory control
of personnel administration. President Truman's recommendations for
training legislation were made in 1947; thus, eleven years had elapsed
before Congress took action on them. During these eleven years the
government service was alternately increased and decreased, being adjusted from a temporary wartime basis to a permanent status and back
again; techniques and methods of work were undergoing rapid change
owing to changed programs and increasing use of automatic and electronic equipment. Yet the departments and agencies were hampered
in developing training programs because of the uncertainty of their
authority.

In 1957 and 1958, when Congress finally got around to considering
general training legislation, the two civil service committees differed
widely from each other in their attitudes toward such training—and
hence on the form the legislation should take. The Senate committee
regarded training as an essential part of administration and favored
legislation that would facilitate training throughout the government;
its bill accordingly granted broad training authority to the President
and the departments with very few restrictions, leaving detailed regu-

[33] House Committee on Post Office and Civil Service, House Report No. 1951,
to accompany S.385, 85th Cong., 2d sess. (June 1958), p. 11.
[34] Hearings . . . on H.R.6001, etc. (1958), p. 74.

lation to the President. The House committee, fearful that the departments would abuse the authority to conduct training off the job, wrote numerous restrictions and limitations into its bill; this was the bill that Congress passed, despite administration protests.

The act's restrictions and limitations appear bound to hamper rather than facilitate training programs. Obviously some government-wide regulation of off-the-job training is required, but it makes a great difference whether it is written into statute or provided by administration rulings which may be revised from time to time on the basis of experience. Statutory restrictions and limitations are difficult to revise, and are strictly interpreted and enforced by the Comptroller General, even when their effect is to impede good administration.

The Career Executive Development Program

A major recommendation of the second Hoover Commission in 1955 for the improvement of personnel administration in the government was the establishment of a "Senior Civil Service" of highly qualified administrators.[35] The purpose of the plan was to strengthen top management in the government by providing that a carefully selected, experienced, and proved group of nonpolitical executives would be available to administer the departments and agencies under the direction of the political executives appointed by the President. Members of the proposed Senior Civil Service would be available for appointments to the top career positions requiring administrative or managerial abilities, including administrative assistant secretaries, bureau chiefs and assistant chiefs, some division chiefs, the heads of such staff offices as budget and personnel; members would also be available to serve as professional assistants to political executives. The number of such positions in the government services was estimated at more than 3,000 as of 1955. It was believed that the creation of a Senior Civil Service would make the federal service more attractive to persons of promise and ability, and would aid in the early identification and development of persons in junior and middle grades who possessed executive abilities.

The Hoover Commission Task Force pointed out in its report that

[35] Commission on Organization of the Executive Branch of the Government, *Personnel and Civil Service* (1955), Chap. 3; *Task Force Report on Personnel and Civil Service* (1955), Chap. 3.

although the government is the "largest employer with the greatest continuing need for managerial competence, it has no system by which it identifies men and women of great capacity within the Government," and no means of officially recognizing competence or of providing adequate incentives to encourage persons with outstanding talents to make the government service a career. "There is no positive governmentwide program to supply management talent at any level, and especially the highest level."[36]

While the objectives of the plan proposed by the Hoover Commission were universally lauded, the details were the subject of much discussion and differences of opinion in academic and civil service circles following the issuance of the report early in 1955.[37] Two members of the House who served on the Hoover Commission, Clarence J. Brown and Chet Holifield, dissented from the recommendation for a Senior Civil Service. Representative Brown opposed creating a "civilian 'elite corps,'" fearing that the addition of "lifetime security and tenure" would "strengthen and further entrench the bureaucracy," and tend "to destroy government by representation." Representative Holifield, "although sympathetic to the objective of strengthening top career management," thought the details of the plan somewhat impractical and doubted that it would be attractive to eligible civil servants.[38]

The proposal for a Senior Civil Service received strong support from President Eisenhower and his staff aides. In August 1957 the President created a Career Executive Committee by executive order and instructed it to prepare a definite plan for a career executive program. The objectives of the program were stated as follows: (1) to improve the civil service system in the selection, compensation, and effective use of top career civil servants; (2) to make the civil service more at-

[36] *Ibid., Task Force Report on Personnel and Civil Service*, p. 49.

[37] See Paul T. David and Ross Pollock, *Executives for Government* (1958), Chap. 4; Leonard D. White, "The Case for the Senior Civil Service," pp. 4-9, *Personnel Administration*, Vol. 19 (January-February 1956); Herman M. Somers, 'Some Reservations about the Senior Civil Service," pp. 10-18, *ibid.*, and "The Editor's Say: Executive Development Conference Debates the Senior Civil Service," pp. 2-3, *ibid.*; Paul P. Van Riper, "The Senior Civil Service and the Career System," *Public Administration Review*, Vol. 18 (Summer 1958), pp. 189-200; William Pincus, "The Opposition to the Senior Civil Service," *ibid.* (Autumn 1958), pp. 324-331; George A. Graham, *America's Capacity to Govern* (1960), Chap. 4; Herman Finer, *The Presidency: Crisis and Regeneration* (1960), p. 251 ff.

[38] Commission on Organization of the Executive Branch of the Government, *Task Force Report on Personnel and Civil Service* (1955), pp. 90, 93-95.

tractive as a career to able men and women; and (3) to provide for the planned development of employees at all levels and to increase the number of individuals who would qualify under the career executive program.

The committee's report, made in December 1957, followed closely the 1955 recommendations of the Hoover Commission. It proposed the creation of a "Career Executive Service," which in some respects was comparable to the "Senior Civil Service" proposed by the Hoover Commission. At the outset, appointments to the service were to be limited to executives in Grades GS-16 and higher. The committee recommended that the President establish the service by executive order and create a part-time, bipartisan Career Executive Board, whose members would be individuals "of high reputation from within and outside the Federal service," to administer it in cooperation with the Civil Service Commission. The board would assist the departments and the Civil Service Commission in executive development plans and programs, select persons to be appointed to the Career Executive Service, and develop records and procedures for placement and transfer of members of this service to meet pressing management needs of the government.

On March 4, 1958, President Eisenhower issued an executive order (No. 10758) to put these recommendations into effect, except those which required legislation. The President's action came under attack almost immediately by the House civil service committee, whose Subcommittee on Manpower Utilization started hearings on the program on April 30, 1958. In opening the hearings, Chairman James C. Davis stated that the subcommittee proposed to examine the need for "this so-called elite corps of career executives," which might usher in an era of personal patronage.[39] Members of the subcommittee saw little or no merit in or need for the program, and took administration witnesses to task for its establishment by executive order instead of by legislation. Strong exception was taken to the idea of an "elitist corps" that could be moved from one department to another, and throughout the hearings various members expressed their fear that the Career Executive Board and its director might become dictators of the civil service and overshadow the Civil Service Commission. It was also suggested

[39] *Manpower Utilization in the Federal Government (Career Executive Program)*, Hearings Before the Subcommittee on Manpower Utilization of the House Committee on Post Office and Civil Service, 85th Cong., 2d sess. (April and May 1958), pp. 7-8.

frankly that a President who wanted to play politics by using the board to control the higher federal positions could do so very easily.[40]

At the end of the hearings the subcommittee passed a resolution requesting the President to suspend the program until it had been authorized by legislation. When the President failed to comply, other steps were taken to block the program. In the spring of 1959, at the request of members of the House civil service committee, the House Committee on Appropriations struck the modest budget request of $52,500 for the Career Executive Board and its staff for fiscal 1960, and attached a rider to the appropriation for the Civil Service Commission prohibiting the use of funds for this purpose.

IT IS UNFORTUNATE that the career executive program, which was the result of four years of study and planning, was thus nipped in the bud by the House civil service committee. The most important function of the Career Executive Board would have been to advise and make recommendations on the legislation, policies, and procedures that were needed to improve and strengthen executive development programs. If the board had been able to secure the support of Congress, as well as that of the administration and the departments, it would doubtless have made in time a substantial contribution to strengthening the civil service.[41]

Veteran Preference Legislation

Another important area of civil service legislation relates to the rights of employees and is concerned with such matters as political activities, union membership, representation in labor-management relations, hearings and appeals in disciplinary or other personnel actions, job retention and reinstatement, and veteran preference. As a case study in this area, we will review veteran preference legislation.[42] The

[40] *Ibid.*, p. 79.

[41] In 1961 the Civil Service Commission established a Career Executive Roster which was intended to accomplish the same purposes as the defunct Career Executive Board.

[42] See U. S. Civil Service Commission, *History of Veteran Preference in Federal Employment, 1865-1955* (1955), upon which the author has drawn heavily in preparing the following account.

first law giving federal employment preference to veterans was passed on March 3, 1865, and provided:

> That persons honorably discharged from the military or naval service by reason of disability resulting from wounds or sickness incurred in the line of duty, should be preferred for appointments to civil offices, provided they shall be found to possess the business capacity necessary for the proper discharge of the duties of such offices.[43]

No mention was made of veteran preference in the 1871 rider which authorized the President to institute civil service examinations, but the Pendleton Act of 1883 adopted the provisions of the 1865 act by reference. The administration of these and later provisions was governed by civil service rules issued by the President instead of by law; Congress confined its action to the determination of policy.

From 1883 to 1919 the few changes that were made in the preference rulings resulted from executive orders. Though the Grand Army of the Republic for a number of years urged legislation that would accord preference to all northern Civil War veterans, Congress did nothing to change the original restrictions of the 1865 act. Whether preference should be accorded Confederate veterans was a controversial issue never resolved, and veterans of the Spanish-American War—which GAR members regarded as a mere skirmish—were not granted the special privileges. Therefore, since those who could qualify for preference were thus narrowed down to include only Civil War veterans of the northern armies who had been discharged for disabilities in the line of duty, the number who applied for and were appointed to federal positions was relatively small.

At the end of World War I the recently formed veterans' organizations pressed for legislation that would grant preference to all veterans. Congress responded by repealing the 1865 statute in a rider to the Census Act of March 3, 1919, which granted preference to all honorably discharged soldiers, sailors, and marines and to their widows if they were qualified to hold the positions; in July the act was amended by a rider to the Deficiency Act of 1919 extending the preference to the wives of injured veterans, "who themselves are not qualified, but whose wives are qualified to such positions."[44] Again the determi-

---

[43] 13 Stat. 571.
[44] 40 Stat. 1293 (March); 41 Stat. 37 (July).

nation of the manner in which preference should be accorded and the administration of the law were left to civil service rules issued by the President.

The Veterans' Preference Act of 1944

The civil service rules issued by the President between 1919 and the beginning of World War II had gone considerably farther in extending preference to veterans than legislation required, and there was no reason to assume that the veterans of World War II would have cause for complaint. Nevertheless, the veterans' organizations pressed for additional legislation which would strengthen preference and write the rules into law. Attempts in the late 1930's to secure passage of such legislation had been blocked by the inability of the three major organizations to reach consensus on a bill they would support, but in 1943, in consultation with the Civil Service Commission, they agreed upon a bill which all three were willing to back before Congress.

In 1944, Representative Joe Starnes introduced the bill (H.R.4115), testifying that its purpose was to "give legislative sanction to existing veterans' preference to the rules and regulations in the executive branch of the Government, and to broaden and strengthen those preferences."[45] President Roosevelt endorsed the bill, stating that its passage was necessary to assure "those who are in the armed forces that when they return special consideration will be given them in their efforts to obtain employment."[46] The bill passed the House on April 17 with only one dissenting vote and was approved by the Senate unanimously. The President signed it into law on June 27, 1944.

In addition to writing into statute the existing civil service rules relating to preference, thereby removing the authority of the President to revise them, the 1944 Veterans' Preference Act (58 Stat. 387) extended the preference benefits in several important respects and made other significant changes in civil service rules not directly related to preference. One aspect of the act which was to have serious effects on personnel administration was its statutory provision of the "rule of three" in certifying eligible candidates to appointing officers. The rule of three—which had often been criticized by leading personnel au-

[45] U. S. Civil Service Commission, *History of Veteran Preference* . . . , p. 16.
[46] *Ibid.*, p. 15.

thorities and administrators—had been in use under civil service rulings since 1885, but it would always be waived if appointing officers presented evidence that the three top-ranked candidates, from among whom the choice was supposed to be made, did not have the necessary qualifications for particular jobs. With the rule written into law (58 Stat. 389, sec. 8), the Civil Service Commission was prevented from waiving it when necessary for good administration. What was even worse, the law prevented the flexible examining and rating procedures that were needed in the postwar years, and required the use of ranked, closed registers, and percentage scoring of candidates.

The act also required an appointing officer who passed over a veteran to submit a statement of reasons to the CSC for its review, and to furnish the veteran with a copy at his request. In 1953 the law was amended to make the findings of the Civil Service Commission mandatory on the appointing officer (67 Stat. 581). This provision broke sharply with previous practice, for until this time the departments had had the final determination in making appointments.

The existing civil service rules which granted a 10-point preference in competitive examinations to disabled veterans, as well as to wives, widows, or mothers of disabled veterans who were themselves unable to qualify, were written into the 1944 act. Those who passed the examinations (with the added 10 points) were placed at the top of the registers, except for scientific and professional positions with a basic salary of $3,000 or more. The 10-point absolute preference led shortly to serious difficulties. Many registers became clogged at the top with disabled veterans whom appointing officers were reluctant to choose because they regarded them as unqualified, while other candidates with higher scores, including many nondisabled veterans, could not be reached and were thus prevented from receiving appointments. Among those who benefited by the 10-point preference were many whose disabilities were only slight and often not service connected. In some cases departments declined to make any appointments at all rather than employ persons whom they regarded as unqualified. Several attempts were made by the Truman administration to secure a modification of the rule, but to no avail. Having been written into the statute, it could not be revised by executive order.

In 1953, however, an amendment to the 1944 act was finally approved that remedied the situation to some extent. It required all veterans to pass examinations with an earned score of 70 points before re-

ceiving additional preference points, and it limited the 10-point absolute preference to veterans who had service-connected disabilities of
at least 10 per cent. Despite these changes, the absolute preference
rule remains one of the serious weaknesses of the federal personnel
system.

A new absolute preference granted all veterans by the 1944 act
applied to examinations for the positions of guard, elevator operator,
messenger, and custodian, and the President was authorized to add
other positions to the list for a limited period. The earlier rules requiring the reopening of examinations for 10-point veterans were written
into law and somewhat enlarged. Among other new provisions was the
exemption of veterans from age and physical requirements, unless the
requirements were essential to the performance of the duties of the
position. Of even greater importance, the act prohibited the CSC from
setting any educational requirements for examinations, except in the
case of scientific, technical, and professional positions—and even for
these, educational requirements could be established only if the CSC
found that the duties involved could not be performed by a person
without such education. Furthermore, the CSC was required to place
in its public records a statement justifying its decision. This limitation
on the discretion of the Commission reflected an outmoded point of
view and a lack of understanding of the very basis of a career system.

Especially significant changes were made in the civil service laws
by the provision of the act that granted to veterans who were dismissed
for cause the right of appeal on substance to the CSC, which was authorized to report its findings to the agency, but not to order reinstatement. In 1947 an amendment (61 Stat. 723) made the CSC decision
binding on the agency. Nonveterans could appeal only on procedural
matters; in essence, then, the 1944 act created two distinct classes of
employees with different rights, leading to a dual personnel system inconsistent with democratic principles. However, in 1962 the inequity
was remedied by Executive Order No. 10988, sec. 14, which gave
all employees covered by civil service the right of appeal on substance.

THE MISCHIEVOUS EFFECTS that are often the consequence of enacting detailed rules and regulations into law are well demonstrated by
the Veterans' Preference Act of 1944. Prior to its passage Congress had
usually confined its legislation on veteran preference to general policies.
The civil service rulings issued by the President faithfully carried out

the legislative policy but could be revised when necessary for good administration. Thus preference was accorded to veterans in a manner that in general protected the integrity of the public service. All of this was changed by the 1944 Act. As we have noted, a number of its detailed provisions proved to be seriously harmful to the federal service in ways not anticipated, but, having been written into statute, they could be revised only with great difficulty and over the opposition of veterans' organizations. Many of the shortcomings of federal civil service administration in the postwar years can be laid at the door of the act. Moreover, it was a turning point in legislation on the civil service, being followed by other statutes prescribing personnel procedures in considerable detail.

Personnel Restriction by Rider

Congress has also exercised control over civil service procedures by forcing reduction of staff through statutory limitations and restrictions on personnel, usually attached as riders to appropriation acts. The leading recent examples of such personnel limitations through riders include the following: (1) personnel staffing ratios, which restrict the number of personnel workers; (2) the Jensen riders of 1950-1953, which limited the number of vacancies that could be filled; and (3) the complex Whitten Amendment, first adopted in 1950 and still partially in effect.[47]

Personnel Office Staffing Ratios

For a number of years after 1950, riders applicable to individual departments and agencies were used by certain appropriations subcommittees to set maximum ratios of personnel workers to total employees, varying from 1 to 105 to 1 to 125. The effect was often to force drastic reductions of personnel staffs, leading to the assignment of personnel work to operating officials without special training. In some agencies important personnel programs had to be curtailed or discon-

[47] See Paul Stephen Greenlaw, "Legislative Riders and Federal Personnel Administration: A Case Study of the Jensen, Thomas, and Whitten Amendments" (unpublished doctoral dissertation, Syracuse University, 1955). Extensive use has been made of this study in the following account.

tinued entirely. At the very time these forced reductions were being made, other legislative riders greatly increased the work of personnel offices. The Senate civil service committee, which investigated the effects of the personnel ratios in 1952, reported:

> Our findings to date reveal that the major effect the ratios have had on agency programs is the forced curtailment, and in many cases the complete abandonment, of those vital functions of personnel management which are designed to increase the efficiency and quality of the organization and work force. Savings in salaries of personnel employees resulting from the ratios are more than offset in lowered morale, high turnover, reduced productivity, and ineffective utilization of manpower. Moreover, there is an alarming tendency to transfer personnel functions to operating officials. This lessens their time for program activities and results in staff increases under various disguises to carry the burden of unfamiliar personnel functions.[48]

The committee concluded that personnel office staffing ratios were arbitrary, disregarded the different personnel tasks of agencies, and were unworkable and incompatible with the management improvement goals of both the Executive branch and Congress. It accordingly recommended that their use be discontinued. Personnel staffing ratios have since been largely abandoned, but still apply to a few agencies.

The Jensen Riders

The Jensen riders, which were attached to nine major appropriation acts from 1950 to 1953, were designed to force the departments to reduce their personnel in a manner which was believed to be relatively painless—by not filling vacancies. No employee would lose his job because of the rider, and, on the assumption that executive departments were invariably overstaffed, it was believed that reductions could be accomplished without impairing essential activities. Although varying from each other in some details and exemptions, each of the riders provided that not more than one vacancy in four could be filled by a new appointment, or by transfer from another department, until an arbitrary 10 per cent reduction of budgeted personnel had been achieved. Thereafter the rider became inoperative and all vacancies could be filled. (The first rider passed by the House required a 20 per

[48] *Effect of Personnel Office Staffing Ratios on Manpower Utilization,* Senate Document No. 28, 83d Cong., 1st sess. (March 1953), p .1.

cent reduction before vacancies could be filled, but this was reduced in conference to 10 per cent, the figure used in subsequent riders.)

The riders originated as amendments offered on the floor by Representative Ben F. Jensen of Iowa. The administration strongly opposed them on the ground that they would cripple the work of certain units which had a high rate of employee turnover. Although the House Appropriations Committee also objected to them, and various other members attacked them as arbitrary, "meat-ax" reductions of personnel, they were pushed through to passage by an economy-minded House. The Senate rejected all but one of the riders, but each one was restored in conference because the House conferees refused to yield.

The objection that the Jensen riders would seriously disrupt the work of certain departments or units was met by exempting specific agencies or types of position. Eventually more than half of the federal service was exempted—including the armed services, which employ more than half the total number of civilian employees in the government, the Veterans Administration, the FBI, General Accounting Office, presidential appointees who were confirmed by the Senate, legislative and judicial employees, personnel engaged in scientific and technical work, hospital employees, and the two lowest grades (principally messengers, elevator operators, and custodial employees).

The riders had numerous undesirable effects that were not foreseen when they were passed. Although adopted as economy measures, they resulted in added administrative costs because of the additional records, controls, and personnel adjustments that were required. They also led the departments to resort to various undesirable personnel practices; for instance, on the theory that a poor employee is better than none at all, incompetent employees who might otherwise have been dismissed were retained. Since vacancies could not be filled, a strong effort was made to retain employees by giving salary raises and upgrading positions, in some instances without justification. Whenever possible, vacancies were filled from within the agency, a procedure that in some cases resulted in the assignment of employees to jobs for which they were not adequately qualified. The inability to replace employees engaged in essential operations disrupted the work of some divisions and proved to be highly expensive to the government. Worst of all, the agencies penalized most severely by the riders were those that had already reduced their staffs rather than those that were overstaffed. Therefore, as long as the riders remained in effect there was little incentive for departments and agencies to trim their personnel estimates; in fact, it was soon recognized that the inclusion of a personnel cushion in the budget was the best way to resist forced reductions. Fortunately, the Jensen riders were dropped in 1953.

The Whitten Amendment

Of the various appropriation riders placing restrictions and limitations on personnel administration, the original Whitten Amendment, adopted in 1950 after the outbreak of hostilities in Korea, has attracted most attention. No other rider illustrates so well the difficulties and unfortunate effects that flow from detailed legislative limitations and restrictions on personnel, however laudable their objectives. Intended to accomplish several different purposes during the emergency, the amendment included various detailed restrictions, some of which were still in effect as of 1961—still hampering personnel administration, although the departments have found ways of operating under the restrictions.

Many members of Congress feared in 1950 that the Korean war would result in permanent increases in personnel, indiscriminate upgrading of positions, and unduly rapid promotion of employees. As a safeguard against these assumed dangers and to encourage the transfer of federal employees from nondefense to defense agencies, the Whitten Amendment was adopted as a rider to the Supplemental Appropriation Act for 1951 (64 Stat. 1066). It provided that the number of permanent employees of covered departments and agencies could not exceed the number on September 1, 1950, banned permanent transfers, promotions, and reinstatements during the emergency period, and directed the departments, as far as possible, to make only temporary new appointments.

To clarify the appointment situation, it was necessary for the President to issue an Executive Order (No. 10180) in November 1950, directing that all appointments thereafter, with certain exceptions, should be temporary. The effect of the ban on permanent appointments, according to a 1953 report of the Senate civil service committee, was to handicap the government in recruiting personnel in certain professional categories, including scientists and engineers, in competition with private industry. The report also pointed out that the government would be faced at the end of the emergency with the necessity of going through another expensive reconversion program.[49]

The amendment had also been intended to facilitate the war effort by encouraging transfers from nondefense to defense agencies, but the ban on permanent transfers had the opposite effect. (This ban was later rescinded.) The provision that gave transferred employees the right to return to their former jobs and forbade the departments to fill these positions except with temporary appointees gave rise to serious administrative difficulties.

In 1951 the act was amended to require a minimum period of service of one year in grade before an employee was eligible to be promoted to the next higher grade. Although this rule appeared simple and easily enforcible, and obviously was enacted to curb reported administrative abuses, in practice it proved to be difficult to administer, as is often the case with such legislation. In some cases two-step promotions are the standard practice, there being no classifications at the intermediate grades. In many other situations the inflexible rule greatly hampered good administration by preventing departments from promoting the best-qualified persons to vacant positions. After these and similar problems were pointed out, a long and complex section was added to the rule authorizing the Civil Service Commission to make exceptions under certain conditions. The loophole thus provided made the difference between tolerable and intolerable legislation.

The Whitten Amendment required all departments and agencies annually (1) to review all positions which had been created or placed at a higher grade during the preceding year, (2) to abolish positions found to be unnecessary, (3) to readjust those retained, and (4) to report the results of the survey to the House and Senate civil service and appropriations committees. Although the required annual classification survey might appear to be reasonable and salutary, in actual operation it proved to be expensive and of little value. Some agencies and departments, having insufficient staff to conduct the survey without neglecting more urgent work, made only perfunctory studies. According to the Senate civil service committee's 1953 analysis, the requirement had created "unnecessary cost, red tape, and administra-

[49] *Analysis of the Whitten Amendment*, Senate Document No. 35, 83d Cong., 1st sess. (March 1953), pp. 2-3.

tive inconvenience. It has put into law what is properly an administrative problem."[50]

EXPERIENCE INDICATES THAT the imposition of arbitrary restrictions and limitations on personnel administration is undesirable and has harmful effects on departmental administration. The expected economies are seldom produced; on the contrary, such legislation has often made government operations more expensive. As we have seen in the above discussion, the restrictions and limitations of the Jensen and Whitten riders created serious administrative difficulties, necessitated extra records and controls, increased red tape, and resulted in excessive centralization. As Arthur S. Flemming testified before the Senate Civil Service Committee in 1951, "the end result of such riders can be nothing more or less than to tie personnel administration up in a knot."[51]

Other Controls of Personnel

Loyalty Programs

Although the loyalty-security program for civilian employees which began in the late 1940's was established by executive order rather than legislation, Congress played a vital part in its development, not only authorizing but also virtually forcing executive action. The Truman "Loyalty Order" of March 21, 1947 (Executive Order 9835), which for the first time required an investigation of the loyalty of all civilian employees, was undoubtedly issued to forestall objectionably drastic legislation. Similarly, Executive Order 10450 issued by President Eisenhower on April 27, 1953, which initiated a reorganization of the program, was doubtless in response to pressures from members of Congress.

Beginning in 1939 with the Hatch Act (section 9A), numerous statutes had been passed barring the employment by the government

[50] *Ibid.*, p. 14.
[51] *Bills to Implement Recommendations of the Commission on Organization of the Executive Branch of the Government,* Hearings Before Subcommittees of the Senate . . . Civil Service Committee on S.1135, S.1148, and S.1160, 82d Cong., 1st sess. (August and September 1951), p. 15.

of persons "who have membership in any political party or organization which advocates the overthrow of our constitutional form of government in the United States." (The phrase, or some variation of it, was primarily aimed at proscribing the employment of Communists or members of Communist-front organizations, although during the war years it applied also to Nazi or fascist organizations.) The Congress indicated its support of loyalty-security programs by voting appropriations to carry them on, but its major activity in this area has been an almost continuous series of inquiries into the alleged employment of Communists by the government. The earliest investigations were conducted by the House Un-American Activities Committee, but other committees, especially the Senate Internal Security Subcommittee and the Senate Permanent Investigating Subcommittee, were soon in action. At the height of the loyalty ferment, almost any hearing on proposed legislation or department budgets might be turned into an inquiry about the employment of alleged Communists or Communist sympathizers.

It is probable that Congress has given more of its attention since 1939 to the issue of loyalty and security in the federal service than to any other aspect of personnel administration. The issue quickly degenerated into a political controversy, in which sweeping charges were made that the federal service was infiltrated by Communists. The charges were eventually shown to be gross exaggerations, but not before serious injury had been inflicted on the service. No attempt will be made here, however, to discuss the operation of the several federal loyalty-security programs carried on during and since World War II and their impact on the federal service. This aspect of the subject, about which much has been written, is beyond the scope of this study.[52]

It is, however, significant to the study to point out that the British civil service has not been subjected to sweeping charges of disloyalty and subversion, and that the government has confined its loyalty investigations to persons in sensitive positions. In Great Britain and in Canada, Communists are not barred from employment in nonsensi-

[52] The literature on loyalty-security is extensive. Leading studies include the following: Eleanor Bontecue, *The Federal Loyalty-Security Program* (1953); Special Committee of the New York City Bar Association, *The Federal Loyalty-Security Program* (1956); *Report of the Commission on Government Security* (1957); Ralph S. Brown, *Loyalty and Security* (1958).

tive positions. Yet the threat of communism in Great Britain is surely as great as it is in the United States, and there is no evidence to indicate that its public service is freer than ours of potentially disloyal persons. A major reason for the British policy is that the public service is held in high esteem and has traditionally been free from scurrilous attacks. Politicians in Parliament attack one another but not the civil service—unless they are willing to incur the disapproval of their colleagues and condemnation by the press and public. In the United States, the public service has had difficulty in acquiring prestige and has always been considered fair game for political attack. There can be little doubt that a majority of the charges that disloyalty was rife among federal employees were made largely for political purposes, and were continued as long as they could be used to political advantage.

The recent struggle over the loyalty issue has been a part of the perennial contest between the legislature and the Executive branch under our constitutional system. Congressional investigations and charges of Communist infiltration of the public service have been episodes in this struggle. Their effect was often to weaken the President and the executive departments concerned, and, at least temporarily, to stengthen the power of the members of Congress who directed the attacks.

Confirmation of Presidential Appointments

The Senate exercises a special control over personnel through its power of confirmation of appointments made by the President. Although intended by the framers of the Constitution to apply only to the major policy offices in the Executive branch—the heads of departments and agencies and their immediate assistants, now numbering about 1,000—the requirement of confirmation by the Senate has been extended to well over 100,000 positions, including officers of all ranks of the armed services, foreign service officers and similar positions in other career systems, postmasters of the first three classes, and many minor administrative posts. Requiring senatorial confirmation for these thousands of civilian positions prevents their being placed under the civil service and restricts the promotional opportunities of career employees. This is especially true of the postal service, where the 15,000 postmasterships of the first three classes are reserved for political appointment, despite the pseudo-merit system which was put into effect by the Ramspeck-O'Mahoney Act of 1938 (52 Stat. 1076).

The use of Senate approval of appointments, including promotions, with regard to the officer grades of the armed services, the Foreign Service, the Public Health Service, and other career services, has become largely an empty formality. With respect to federal field officers, however, such as postmasters, marshals, and collectors of customs, the requirement has perpetuated patronage appointments; the harm done to the public service is obvious. Every major survey of the administration of the government during the last fifty years has recommended that such field officers be placed under the civil service.

Through the unwritten rule of senatorial courtesy, the nominating power with respect to these field positions, as well as to the position of federal judge and district attorney, has been transferred from the President to the senators of his party for appointments in their own states. Further, by long established custom, members of the House of Representatives of the President's party are permitted to name the postmasters in their districts. This practice was not altered by the Ramspeck Act of 1938, under which postmasters thus selected must pass a civil service examination before receiving a regular appointment.

Although senatorial confirmation of top-level political executives deprives the President of a free hand in the selection of his chief assistants, exposes him at times to secret influences in making the appointments, and reduces the responsibility that can be fastened on him for his choices, it does have the merit of giving the appointees a special status and of providing the Senate with an assurance that these officers are agreeable to a majority of its members—at least when appointed. Less defense can be made for the requirement of Senate approval of assistant secretaries, under secretaries, and other political executives, for it often deprives a department head of the choice of his own chief assistants, and requires him to accept political appointees not of his own choosing, whose loyalty may be divided. The requirement of Senate confirmation of the appointments of thousands of subordinate executive employees should be abandoned and these positions placed under the civil service or other merit systems.[53]

[53] The history and operation of senatorial confirmation of appointments are reviewed in my study, *The Advice and Consent of the Senate* (1953).

Staff Reductions

A major concern of Congress with respect to personnel administration is to establish controls that will prevent overstaffing by the departments and agencies. Charges of inflated staffs and ineffective personnel controls are perennially heard, especially during periods of expansion of government activities. Congress has attempted to cope with this problem in many ways, but the present size and complexity of the federal government make the maintenance of workable personnel controls difficult at best. As we have seen, arbitrary personnel restrictions and staffing ratios are not the solution. The most effective congressional control of staffing has undoubtedly been that exercised by the appropriation subcommittees in their reviews of the department budgets. A better legislative control probably cannot be found.

The Joint Committee on Reduction of Nonessential Federal Expenditures, with Senator Harry F. Byrd as chairman, has long conducted a campaign for the reduction of the number of federal employees, utilizing for this purpose periodic reports on the number of employees in each department and agency, with especial attention to whether the trend of federal employment is up or down. Using this information, Senator Byrd has frequently issued press releases urging reductions, but it is doubtful that the committee has had any noticeable effect on the size of department staffs. Statistics on the number of employees in the numerous departments and agencies give little or no indication of whether there is, in fact, overstaffing. Any control to be effective must be based upon much more detailed information and assessment of the work loads and the personnel practices of individual agencies.

The Subcommittee on Manpower Utilization of the House civil service committee has within recent years conducted investigations and hearings on manpower utilization and personnel controls of the departments in an effort to require them to exercise tighter controls. The departments are required to submit periodical reports on their personnel practices to the subcommittee, which serve as the bases of subsequent hearings at which department officers testify. In addition, the subcommittee's staff has conducted a number of special studies in an attempt to establish personnel norms, as, for example, in financial administration. Although the department witnesses testify that they have installed tight personnel controls and have adopted management improvements which reduce personnel requirements, it is doubtful that the efforts of the subcommittee have had much effect. Department officers generally regard the required reports as burdensome and of little value. A weakness of the procedure is that the subcommittee attempts to inquire into staffing practices throughout the government, and hence is not able to make intensive investigations of individual departments, which would reveal specific instances of overstaffing and lack of effective personnel controls. The task undertaken is probably too vast and complex to be performed effectively by any congressional committee, and can possibly be carried on effectively only within the Executive branch. However, it must be said that the personnel ceilings established by the Bureau of the Budget under authority of law during World War II were not, on the whole, very successful.[54]

Conclusions

One of the greatest needs of the federal civil service is the establishment of closer and more cooperative relations between the civil service committees of Congress and the executive officers in charge of personnel administration. Too often in the past the relationship has been marked by suspicion, distrust, and misunderstanding. Mutual respect and understanding that will contribute to more effective teamwork are essential if needed improvements are to be made in the service and if it is to be maintained at a high level of competency and efficiency. Congress is unable to pass wise personnel legislation and authorize needed programs and improvements without the advice and counsel of the executive officers, who in turn are unable to perform their tasks effectively without the confidence and cooperation of the civil service committees of Congress.

The first step toward achieving better relations and greater cooperation is the recognition and acceptance by each branch of its proper role in personnel administration. It is the function of Congress to determine the broad personnel policies of the government, to delegate the necessary authority to executive officers, to lay down guide lines

[54] See Edgar B. Young, "The Control of Government Employment," in *Civil Service in Wartime*, Leonard D. White, ed. (1945), Chap. 8.

and standards, and to check on the administration of executive departments to ensure that these policies and standards are being effectively carried out. It is the function of the President and the departments to administer the public service under the policies and authority granted by law, to take the leadership in effecting needed improvements and in recommending new policies and programs that require legislation. This division of responsibilities between the legislative and executive branches was the basis of the Pendleton Act of 1883, in which Congress provided by law for the general policies to govern the civil service and left the detailed rules and administration to the President. For more than fifty years Congress generally followed this practice, but recently it has enacted many administrative details into law. In the words of the Sixth American Assembly: "Congressional intervention in the details of personnel management deprives the President and the heads of departments and agencies of needed discretion in the use of a vital tool of management. Such intervention impedes administrative effectiveness and efficiency by freezing procedure in a rigid pattern."[55]

Congress should return to its former practice of confining legislation, as a rule, to general policies, leaving the issuance of detailed rules and regulations to the President and the Civil Service Commission. This is essential if personnel administration is to be conducted efficiently, if executive officers are to be held responsible for their performance, and if Congress is to get on with its important work of considering new personnel programs and policies and needed improvements in the civil service. In recent years Congress has enacted much significant new legislation on such subjects as training, retirement, group health insurance, and vacation rights and fringe benefits; in addition, it has conducted important inquiries into executive development programs, the Hatch Act, employee relations, manpower utilization, and the organization and administration of the civil service. It is in this area of important legislative policy that Congress will make its greatest contribution to the strengthening of the federal civil service.

[55] The American Assembly (1954), *op. cit.* (see footnote 1, above), p. 182.

8

The Legislative Veto

IN 1932, CONGRESS FIRST experimented with a form of control over administration that had been unknown during the preceding years of the Republic. The distinguishing characteristics of this device, now termed the "legislative veto" and increasingly used in recent years, are as follows: (1) certain specified executive decisions are required to be submitted to Congress or to its committees for a waiting period—usually sixty days—before going into effect; (2) Congress reserves the authority during the waiting period to disapprove the proposed action by a concurrent resolution, by a simple resolution of either house, or, since the mid-1940's, by the action of standing committees; (3) Congress limits its action, or the action of its committees, to the approval or disapproval of the executive proposal without amendment. If Congress fails to act during the waiting period, the proposed executive action becomes effective, though in a few instances affirmative action by Congress or its committees is required. The most significant feature of the whole process is that the action of Congress or its committees is taken in a form that does not require the signature of the President, and hence is not subject to his veto.

The legislative veto was initially and somewhat tentatively applied when Congress was forced by the growing complexity of the government in the 1930's to delegate reorganization authority to the President —an action it had never been willing to take except in wartime. The new device was insurance to Congress that its always jealously guarded control over the structure of the executive organization would still reside where Congress believed it belonged—in its own hands. The device emerged from its experimental stage when President Franklin D. Roosevelt signed the Reorganization Act of 1939 without questioning the constitutionality of its provision (Section 5) that, prior to the end of a sixty-day waiting period, Congress could disapprove of the President's proposed reorganization plans by concurrent resolution. By this procedure Congress had made sure that it could set aside the plans by a majority vote of both houses. A precedent having thus been established, the legislative veto was soon being applied to executive actions other than reorganization, and a few years later Congress provided that either house could exercise the veto by simple resolution. The next step was to delegate the disapproval power to individual standing committees without requiring either house to pass a resolution of disapproval; since the end of World War II the legislative veto has usually taken this form.

In a message of March 1961, President John F. Kennedy proposed to Congress a new use of the legislative veto in an area that is clearly legislative in character. He recommended that the Soil Conservation and Domestic Allotment Act be amended to delegate authority to the Secretary of Agriculture, in consultation with advisory committees, to prepare agricultural commodity programs which, after being approved by a two thirds vote of the farmers affected, would be laid before Congress. Within sixty days either house of Congress could set aside such a commodity program proposal; otherwise it would go into effect as though enacted by law. The procedure, had it been adopted, would have strengthened the position of the President and the Secretary of Agriculture. The Executive branch would have had the initiative and the task of formulating the specific programs; Congress would have retained the power of disapproval by either house, but would give up its power to amend the executive proposal. The form of the legislative veto was the same as that used by Congress earlier, but in this instance it was proposed specifically as a substitute for legislation. In the subsequent Agricultural Act of 1961 Congress did authorize the use of advisory committees (75 Stat. 295) but refused to consider the legislative veto aspect of the proposal.

The legislative veto, in providing a new and highly significant form of control of the Executive branch by Congress and its committees, may revise the historic concept of the functions of these two branches of government. From the beginning of the Republic until the new control was devised, although the two branches had often overlapped and each had sometimes appeared to usurp certain of the other's prerogatives, it was generally accepted that Congress and its committees could not participate in the execution of the laws, which the Constitution assigns to the Executive branch. The legislative veto has therefore been widely criticized as contrary to the constitutional principle of separation of powers. Further, it is subject to serious criticism on practical grounds (to be discussed later in this chapter), although it does meet an important need by facilitating broad delegations of authority to executive officers to cope with problems that have become increasingly difficult to solve by legislation.

Numerous bills which include legislative veto provisions are introduced annually, and, since 1941, more than forty such bills have been enacted into law. Presidents Truman and Eisenhower strongly opposed this tendency, and in some cases sent vigorous veto messages to Congress protesting the encroachment on the executive function, but both signed certain bills, even though they carried the provision, when the legislation was urgently needed.[1]

The Legislative Veto by Resolution

Executive Reorganization

Throughout the history of the Republic it has been the practice of Congress to create and alter executive departments and agencies by statute. The principal exceptions to this rule have occurred in wartime,

---

[1] The leading publications on the legislative veto include the following: Robert W. Ginnane, "The Control of Federal Administration by Congressional Resolutions and Committees," *Harvard Law Review*, Vol. 66 (February 1953), pp. 569-611; William E. Rhode, *Congressional Review of Administrative Decision-Making by Committee Clearance and Resolutions* (doctoral dissertation, Michigan State University, 1958); Peter Page Schauffler, *A Study of the Legislative Veto* (doctoral dissertation, Harvard University, 1956); John D. Millett and Lindsay Rogers, "The Legislative Veto and the Reorganization Act of 1939," *Public Administration Review*, Vol. 1 (Winter 1941), pp. 176-189; Cornelius P. Cotter and J. Malcolm Smith, "Administrative Accountability to Congress: The Concurrent Resolution," *Western Political Quarterly*, Vol. 9 (December 1956), pp. 955-966; Howard White, "The Concurrent Resolution in Congress," *American Political Science Review*, Vol 35 (October 1941), pp. 886-889; Joseph Cooper, "The Legislative Veto: Its Promise and Its Perils," *Public Policy; A Yearbook of the Graduate School of Public Administration, Harvard University*, Vol. 7 (1956), pp. 128-174; Peter Schauffler, "The Legislative Veto Revisited," *ibid.*, Vol. 8 (1958), pp. 296-327; Joseph and Ann Cooper, "The Legislative Veto and the Constitution," *George Washington Law Review*, Vol. 30 (March 1962), pp. 467-516.

when the President has been granted authority to establish temporary agencies for the conduct of war activities, but it may be noted that the Department of Health, Education, and Welfare was created in 1953 by a presidential reorganization plan. With respect to bureaus and other subordinate units within the departments and agencies there is no uniform rule; in some cases they have been created and their functions and chief officers have been prescribed by statute, while in other cases establishment has been by executive action.[2] The major determination of executive organization, however, particularly the establishment of departments and independent agencies and the determination of their functions, has always been regarded by Congress as a legislative function which should not be delegated to the President.

In the early 1930's, Congress was nevertheless obliged to recognize that the task of reorganizing the departments and agencies and of reassigning functions and activities when necessary to secure more effective coordination and more efficient operation had become too complex to be accomplished through ordinary legislation. Therefore, President Hoover was authorized in the Legislative Appropriation Act of 1932 (Title IV) to reorganize departments and agencies, but the authority was made subject to the provision (Section 407) that the executive orders must be submitted to Congress sixty days before going into effect and could be set aside by a resolution of either house.[3] When the President submitted his proposals to Congress during the ensuing lame duck session, they were all disapproved by the House of Representatives.[4] Section 407 was later questioned on constitutional grounds by Attorney General William G. Mitchell.[5]

In the Economy Act of 1933 (Title IV), Congress granted President Roosevelt the authority to reorganize the executive departments and agencies by executive order. Proposals for a legislative veto were offered in both Senate and House, but the final bill reflected congressional acceptance of Attorney General Mitchell's opinion: it did not provide that the executive orders could be set aside by Congress, but did require them to be reported sixty days in advance of becoming effective. President Roosevelt made extensive use of the authority, and in one instance withdrew a reorganization order because of congres-

[2] See Chapter 2.
[3] 47 Stat. 413, 414.
[4] House Resolution 334, 72d Cong., 2d sess.
[5] *Opinions of the Attorneys General,* Vol. 37, pp. 63-64.

sional opposition, though no vote was taken. The authority was not renewed when it expired in 1935. In 1937, Roosevelt sent to Congress with his approval the report of his Committee on Administrative Management, which recommended that the President be granted a permanent authority to reorganize the executive departments and agencies. The committee did not propose a legislative veto of the President's reorganization orders, assuming that it would be unconstitutional.

After a bitter legislative struggle that extended over two years, Congress granted the President a limited authority in 1939 to reorganize executive agencies, but exempted numerous agencies and provided for the legislative veto in a new form. In order to get around the constitutional objections, the 1939 Reorganization Act provided that the President should submit executive reorganization *plans* instead of executive orders to Congress, and that these plans could be set aside within sixty days by a concurrent resolution.[6] Thus the objections of Attorney General Mitchell to the 1932 act were partially met, but the constitutionality of a legislative veto by concurrent resolution was still subject to serious question. Nevertheless, President Roosevelt signed the act and proceeded to make use of the reorganization authority granted to him. As noted earlier this statute became the precedent for subsequent legislation.

The reorganization authority of the President was not renewed when it expired two years later, but eleven days after Pearl Harbor, Congress granted the President sweeping authority to reorganize the executive agencies during the war, without any provision for the legislative veto. Roosevelt made repeated use of the authority to reorganize the war agencies, and early in the war ordered a sweeping reorganization of the War Department.

In 1945, when the war was drawing to an end, President Truman sought and secured legislation renewing the peacetime authority of the President to reorganize the executive departments. Congress, however, was unwilling to make a permanent grant of the authority, as recommended by Truman; following the precedent of the 1939 act, it exempted a number of agencies and provided that the reorganization plans might be disapproved by a concurrent resolution during the sixty-day waiting period.[7] When the authority expired in 1948, Congress re-

[6] 53 Stat. 562, Sec. 5.
[7] 59 Stat. 615, 616. See Joseph P. Harris, "Wartime Currents and Peacetime

fused to renew it, but in 1949 passed a similar act which authorized either house by a majority vote of all members to set aside the President's reorganization plans.

During his second term President Truman submitted forty-one reorganization plans, many of which were designed to carry out the recommendations of the first Hoover Commission; twelve were rejected by the action of one house. A proposal to create a Department of Health, Education, and Welfare was twice rejected by Congress. (A similar plan submitted by President Eisenhower shortly after he took office was permitted to go into effect.) Truman's plan to create a unified Department of Defense was rejected, but Congress passed an act intended to accomplish the same purpose. In 1952, the President attempted to make an unusual use of the reorganization authority by submitting plans to bring collectors of internal revenue, collectors of customs, marshals, and postmasters of the first three classes under the civil service. All were strongly opposed in the Senate and only the plan to abolish the office of collectors of internal revenue and reorganize the service was approved.[8]

President Eisenhower secured a renewal of the reorganization authority in 1953, and again in 1955, 1957, and 1959. In 1957, Congress amended the previous statute to permit either house by simple resolution, passed by a majority of those voting, to set aside a reorganization plan, thus returning to the form of the legislative veto which Attorney General Mitchell had held to be unconstitutional. President Eisenhower submitted twelve reorganization plans in his first two years in office, most of which were noncontroversial, and all were sustained. Thereafter he made little use of the power, but several of the few plans he did submit during this period were set aside by one house. It is significant that his 1958 proposal to reorganize the Defense Department was submitted in the form of proposed legislation and not as a reorganization plan.

The subsequent Defense Reorganization Act of 1958 authorized the Secretary of Defense to transfer, reassign, consolidate or abolish functions within the department (but not to create new units to re-

Trends" (Part II of "Federal Executive Reorganization Re-examined"), *American Political Science Review*, Vol. 40 (December 1946), pp. 1146-1149; John D. Millett, *Government and Public Administration* (1959), p. 130.

[8] See Joseph P. Harris, *The Advice and Consent of the Senate* (1953), pp. 332-355.

ceive merged functions), and required such action to be reported to the Armed Services Committees while Congress is in session, and be subject to disallowance by a resolution of either house.[9] This appears to be the only instance of the delegation of authority to a department head to reorganize and shift functions within the department, notwithstanding statutory assignment of functions, subject to legislative veto. In signing the act, President Eisenhower objected to the procedure, which bypassed his office, and stated that he was instructing the Secretary of Defense that any proposed reassignment of functions should be transmitted to the President.

Veto of Other Executive Actions

The precedent created by the 1939 Reorganization Act had been quickly extended to other legislation. The Alien Registration Act of 1940 authorized the Attorney General to suspend the deportation of aliens of good moral character if deportation would result in hardship to dependents who were legal residents. Suspensions for more than six months were required to be reported to Congress at the beginning of the next session; if not set aside by concurrent resolution during the session, they would become permanent.[10] From 1940 to June 30, 1947, the Attorney General reported 20,444 suspensions, none of which were set aside by Congress.[11]

In 1948 the act was amended to require affirmative action by concurrent resolution of Congress to suspend deportation. According to the Senate Judiciary Committee, the change was made because, under the previous procedure, deportation cases were "almost automatically shelved in favor of other matters in which affirmative action is required. The committee cannot bring itself to the view that Congress should relinquish its prerogative to pass upon these referral cases."[12] After the change in the law, Congress rejected a few suspensions in individual cases, but at the end of each session a large number of cases would be pending. These delays led Congress to amend the law in 1952, and again in 1956, to return to the former procedure, except when the alien

[9] 72 Stat. 514, Sec 3. Also see Chapter 2.
[10] 54 Stat. 672. And see Harvey C. Mansfield, "The Legislative Veto and the Deportation of Aliens," *Public Administration Review*, Vol. 1 (Spring 1941), pp. 281-286.
[11] See Ginnane, *op. cit.*, p. 583.
[12] Senate Report No. 1204, 80th Cong., 2d sess. (1948), p. 4.

was deportable for criminal acts or association with a subversive organization, in which case the affirmative approval of Congress was required. An act of 1957 authorizing the Attorney General to change the status of up to fifty persons from temporary to permanent residents required that each case be reported to Congress, and could be set aside by a resolution of either house.[13]

An act of 1946 authorizing the Secretary of the Navy to transfer title of obsolete vessels and other articles of war to states and other designated bodies required all such transfers to be reported in advance to Congress, subject to its disapproval.[14] Similarly the Rubber Plants Disposal Act of 1953 required all contracts for the disposal or sale of these plants to be reported to Congress, and authorized either house to set aside all or a part of any proposed contract.[15]

A legislative veto by concurrent resolution was provided by an act passed in 1958 that amended the Atomic Energy Act of 1954. The act was especially significant because it illustrated the problem that Congress increasingly faces: under the necessities of a rapidly changing world it must delegate extraordinary powers to executive agencies, despite its legitimate desire to retain an effective voice so that legislative power will not be weakened. The President was authorized to enter into agreements with other nations for the exchange of military information and atomic energy materials, provided that such agreements were laid before Congress sixty days before going into effect, and were not set aside by concurrent resolution.[16] The Joint Committee on Atomic Energy stated in its report on the bill that, after considering various alternatives to provide "close congressional review over the extraordinary and sensitive powers authorized to be carried out by executive agencies," it had come to the conclusion that this procedure should be followed when the exchange of military information and materials was proposed, but not in other cooperative agreements. It rejected a proposal which would have given either house the power to disapprove such agreements by a simple resolution, stating that after due consideration it had "concluded that proposed international agreements for cooperation should not be disapproved by the Congress un-

[13] 71 Stat. 643. The act was intended to apply to high-ranking diplomats and United Nations officials.
[14] 48 Stat. 564.
[15] 67 Stat. 408.
[16] 72 Stat. 276.

less both Houses should join in the concurrent resolution."[17] In May 1959, President Eisenhower submitted to Congress agreements under the act with Great Britain and France, which became effective after the required waiting period.

The Trade Agreements Extension Act of 1958 included a novel legislative veto provision whereby Congress could, by concurrent resolution, override a decision of the President *not* to act. The act provided that if the President rejected the recommendations of the Tariff Commission to raise import duties to protect domestic producers against serious injury, Congress could within ninety days overrule the President and put the recommendations of the Tariff Commission into effect by adopting a concurrent resolution by a two thirds majority.[18] This appears to be the only instance of the legislative veto which requires a two thirds majority vote of Congress. The President accepted the provision as a corollary of the power of Congress to override the President's veto of legislation by a two thirds majority.[19]

Other Uses of Concurrent Resolutions

Numerous wartime statutes granting unusual authority to the President, starting with the Lend-Lease Act of 1941, contained provisions for termination by concurrent resolution. Several of the foreign aid acts passed since the end of World War II have contained similar provisions, some providing that Congress may by concurrent resolution discontinue aid to any country. The use of concurrent resolutions to repeal or to modify previous acts of Congress is subject to serious constitutional objections, but has not been tested in the courts. Congress has also provided in a number of acts that certain statutory provisions will become effective upon the passage of concurrent resolutions.[20]

[17] House Report No. 1849 on H.R. 12716, 85th Cong., 2d sess. (1958).
[18] 72 Stat. 676.
[19] The Senate rejected an amendment offered by Senator Robert S. Kerr, and recommended by the Senate Finance Committee, that would have deprived the President of the power to override the recommendations of the Tariff Commission, unless Congress passed a concurrent resolution within 90 days sustaining his decision. The amendment was criticized by the *Washington Post and Times Herald* (July 11, 1958) as "thoroughly unacceptable," "cumbersome," and a provision that would "transfer to the legislative branch a foreign policy function which can be effectively administered only in the executive branch."
[20] For reviews of this type of legislation, see Ginnane, *op. cit.*, and Howard White, "Executive Responsibility to Congress via Concurrent Resolution," *American Political Science Review*, Vol. 36 (October 1942), pp. 895-900. President Franklin D. Roosevelt in a confidential memorandum to his then Attorney General, Robert

An amendment to the Universal Military Training and Service Act adopted in 1951 (65 Stat. 75, 80) provided that Congress thereafter could by concurrent resolution reduce the terms of service or eliminate the requirement of compulsory service for any age group. Similarly, the Federal Highway Act of 1956 (70 Stat. 379, sec. 108), which contained a new formula for allocating federal highway aid to the states after 1960, required that the allocations to the several states be reported to Congress and be approved by concurrent resolution before going into effect.

In 1958 Congress passed a bill authorizing the armed services to settle certain types of claims for damages, acting under regulations to be issued by the Secretaries of the three departments. The bill required that the regulations be submitted to Congress sixty days before taking effect, during which period they might be amended or disapproved by concurrent resolution. President Eisenhower vetoed the bill on September 6, 1958, stating that this provision unconstitutionally deprived the President of his review.

Before the legislative veto was established as a precedent, Congress had tried at least twice to provide for the removal of a public official by resolution. The budget and accounting bill of 1920 provided that the Comptroller General, regarded as an agent of Congress, could be removed by concurrent resolution; President Wilson vetoed the bill because he considered this provision unconstitutional. In 1933 the tactic was used again, when the Tennessee Valley Authority Act provided that members of the TVA Board of Directors could be removed by concurrent resolution. Subsequently the provision was held not to interfere with the President's power of removal.[21]

Veto by Committee

Unofficial Committee Control of Administration

Long before the committee veto of recent years was developed, congressional committees had exercised unofficial and informal controls over the departments and agencies which come before them to secure legislation or appropriations. Since these controls were exercised by the

H. Jackson, went on record that the concurrent resolution provision in the Lend-Lease Act of 1941 was unconstitutional; see Robert H. Jackson, "A Presidential Legal Opinion," *Harvard Law Review*, Vol. 66 (June 1953), pp. 1353-1361.

[21] *Morgan v.TVA*, 115 Fed. (2d), p. 990 (6th Cir. 1940).

committees in connection with their assigned legislative functions, behind the informality there was always the sanction of official control through statutes, appropriations, and investigations. The committee veto, which has developed since 1944, plays a relatively small part in committee supervision of administration; its significance lies not in its extent but rather in its portent.

Unofficial committee controls over the executive—in contrast to official controls, which are written into statutes and appropriation acts—are conveyed to department officers through oral directions and instructions during hearings and at other times. They are not subject to review and consideration by the houses of Congress, as are the official controls that are written into statute, and are often exercised by key members of the committees, especially the chairman, rather than the committee as a whole. They are obviously more readily subject to abuse than official controls, and there is no doubt that they have frequently been used to further personal or provincial ends. The directions given to department officers may not reflect the judgment of Congress or of either the House or Senate—or even of the membership of the committee concerned. Thus this type of committee control is bound to weaken executive responsibility, and in a very real sense also weakens rather than strengthens congressional control over administration.

The unofficial controls are usually more important and pervasive than the official controls. Departments are placed under obligation to consult with the committees or their chairmen when making important decisions, and especially when changes become necessary in plans that have been presented to the committees. These advance consultations enable a committee to enter objections to or require modification of contemplated decisions; they also protect department officers against future criticisms. Most committees insist upon consultations about important decisions, though there is a wide variation in practice depending upon the relationships between the committee and the department, the nature of the activity, and other factors.

A department customarily consults with its appropriations subcommittee before making an expenditure that does not conform to the detailed budget estimates submitted earlier. On important variations the chairman of a committee or subcommittee is usually consulted, but minor matters are taken up with the committee staffs. Committee hearings are occasionally held on the more important decisions, but more often the chairman acts for the committee.

Department or agency officers are not bound to accept the directions of committees, unless they are written into law, but it is highly unusual for a department to proceed with an action that has been objected to by a committee which passes on its legislation or appropriations. In rare instances an agency may insist that the committee directions be written into legislation, thus appealing to Congress as a whole, but the more common appeal is to the corresponding committee of the other house. It is not uncommon for the committee of the second house to countermand the instructions of the first, or to issue conflicting instructions, which relieves the department of the necessity of following either, but may make it impossible for it to act at all. In the majority of cases departments do carry out the wishes of the committees, or work out a mutually acceptable compromise solution.

The control which standing committees are thus able to exert over the departments has often been criticized, although few detailed studies have been made of the impact of standing committees on department administration. The major criticism is that the committees are able to dictate department decisions for which they are not accountable, and are thus in the position of exercising power without responsibility. Another criticism is that members of the committees, not being in daily touch with the operations of the departments, are not sufficiently informed about them to make day-to-day decisions, and that the decisions required of the departments by the committees are apt to be dictated by personal, local, and political considerations. Since the executive departments and agencies are under necessity of getting along with the committees that pass upon their legislation and appropriations, they are normally obliged to defer to committee wishes, even those that they consider unwise and possibly contrary to the public interest.[22]

[22] For an illustration of committee control of administration, see Ralph K. Huitt, "The Congressional Committee: A Case Study," *American Political Science Review,* Vol. 48 (June 1954), pp. 340-365. Concerning the control exercised by the Senate Committee on Banking and Currency over the OPA in 1946, Huitt wrote (p. 349): "The Committee thus constituted itself a kind of super-administrative agency, intervening capriciously and depending upon business to initiate the process. Capehart got assurance that a price increase would be granted the cheese industry, and Taft a promise of immediate action on evaporated milk. In some cases the outcome was

A leading critic of committee intervention in administration was Woodrow Wilson, who wrote in 1885: "I know not how better to describe our form of government in a single phrase than by calling it a government by the chairmen of the Standing Committees of Congress." Congress, he declared, "has entered more and more into the details of administration, until it has virtually taken into its own hands all the substantial powers of government. . . . There is no distincter tendency in congressional history than the tendency to subject even the details of administration to the constant supervision, and all policy to the watchful intervention, of the Standing Committees."[23]

Wilson attributed the growth of congressional control of administration to the development of the committee system. The next sixty years, however, witnessed a swing in the pendulum from congressional to executive control of administration. The powers of the President were greatly strengthened, while congressional committees with inadequate staffs found themselves handicapped in attempting to exercise detailed controls over the executive departments, which were constantly increasing in size, functions, and complexity. At the end of World War II a counter movement set in, and with the passage of the Legislative Reorganization Act of 1946, which authorized enlarged committee staffs, the committees were enabled to cope more effectively with the operations of the departments. The trend in recent years has been in the direction of greater rather than less committee control over administration, due in large part to the greatly increased committee staffs.

It is not easy to draw the line between legitimate, useful, and mutually helpful consultations and relations the standing committees of Congress may have with the executive departments, and committee encroachment on executive functions. It is highly desirable for committee members to become informed about the operations of departments which come before them for legislation or appropriations, but committee dictation of executive decisions is undesirable for it destroys the accountability of executive officers and injects political influence in

---

ambiguous, as with Capehart's efforts in regard to the price of butter and oil, and Millikan's attempt to 'get an airtight promise out of OPA to decontrol poultry.' " See also Morgan Thomas, *Atomic Energy and Congress* (1956), and Holbert N. Carroll, *The House of Representatives and Foreign Affairs* (1958).

[23] Wilson, *Congressional Government* (1913 ed.), pp. 102, 45, 47.

operating decisions. Legislative oversight of the departments is best exercised through committee inquiries into department policies and administration in order to hold the executive officers accountable. Informal committee controls of administration are in some respects more objectionable than the formal committee veto of executive decisions, for the informal controls are exercised usually by a few members without any effective review.

The Committee Veto

After the precedent of the legislative veto by simple or concurrent resolution had been established in 1939 and extended in the early 1940's, the next step was to delegate the same authority to individual committees without requiring a resolution to be passed by either house. The committee veto was first established as a working precedent by a statute passed in 1944 which required the Secretary of the Navy to "come into agreement" with the Naval Affairs Committee of each house before entering into real estate transactions acquiring, disposing, or leasing land or facilities for naval installations.[24] At intervals before this, however, various statutes had authorized committees to exercise certain controls over executive action.

One of the first of these was a statute of 1919 which empowered the Joint Committee on Printing "to adopt and employ such measures as, in its discretion, may be deemed necessary to remedy any neglect, duplication, or waste in the public printing and binding and the distribution of Government publications."[25] The following year an appropriation rider provided that thereafter no journal, periodical, or similar government publication should be issued or discontinued without the approval of the Joint Committee on Printing, and authorized it to prescribe regulations governing such publications.[26] The bill was vetoed by President Wilson. He stated:

> The Congress has the right to confer on its committees full authority for purposes of investigation and the accumulation of information for its guidance, but I do not concede the right, and certainly not the wisdom, of the Congress of endowing a committee of either house or a joint committee of both Houses with the power to prescribe "regulations" under which the executive departments

[24] 58 Stat. 190.
[25] 40 Stat. 1270.
[26] H.R. 12610, 66th Cong., 2d sess. (1920).

may operate. . . . I regard the provision in question as an invasion of the province of the Executive and calculated to result in unwarranted interference in the processes of good government, producing confusion, irritation, and distrust.[27]

The rider did not become law, but the joint committee has continued to exercise control over executive department printing, and its powers have been enlarged by statutes from time to time. Its control had originated in an act of 1895 which required the executive departments to use the recently expanded facilities of the Government Printing Office for all printing.[28] Because the joint committee had supervised the GPO (created in 1860 to do printing for Congress), the 1895 act brought department printing also under its supervision. It was not long, however, before this control over executive printing was nullified by the development of other reproduction processes, such as duplicating, which did not come under the committee's jurisdiction. In 1949, the loophole was closed by a statute that extended the control,[29] and since that date the committee has issued regulations governing all departmental printing and duplicating. Its regulations cover, for example, the processing and distribution of all government documents, and its approval is required for the establishment of printing plants, purchase and disposal of printing equipment, the letting of contracts to private printers, and the use of photographs or color printing in excess of $500.

In 1949, President Truman criticized control by a congressional committee over the departments' printing and duplicating and urged the enactment of legislation by which Congress would determine the major policies concerning printing, but leave the administration to the departments. Objecting to the mixing of legislative and executive responsibilities and the "invasion of the rights of the Executive branch by a legislative committee," the President also pointed out that most of the printing laws were obsolete, having been passed long before the introduction of modern duplicating processes. In 1950 he submitted legislation to carry out his recommendations, but Congress took no action.[30]

[27] *Congressional Record,* Vol. 59, Pt. 7 (May 13, 1920), pp. 7026-7027.
[28] 28 Stat. 622.
[29] 63 Stat. 405.
[30] The above account is based on Richard T. Greer, "Control of Administration by Congressional Committees" (master's thesis, Georgetown University, July 1958), pp. 43-46.

The control exercised by the Joint Committee over executive printing operations is typical of requirements that developed as incidental to the controls Congress exercises over its own housekeeping and administrative services and which therefore set no precedents. The official committee veto of proposed executive decisions was and is a much more intentional control.

Legislation providing for the committee veto has taken several forms, but in all cases the departments have been required to submit advance reports on their proposed actions. The precedent-setting statute of 1944 required the Navy Department to "come into agreement" with the congressional committees—in other words, committee approval was necessary before the department could carry out its proposed action—and for a time subsequent legislation providing for committee approval or disapproval was of similar effect.

"Come Into Agreement" Legislation. Prior to World War II it was the practice of Congress to authorize individually each Navy installation or public works project, but during the war the volume of construction became so great and the time element so urgent that handling projects in this manner was no longer feasible. In 1942, on the understanding that all proposals for acquisitions of land and leases would be submitted informally in advance to the Naval Affairs Committee of each house for its approval, the two committees recommended and Congress voted a general authorization in lump sum without specifying the individual projects. The Navy Construction Authorization Act of 1944, accordingly, wrote into law the practice of advance submission which had previously been followed by informal understanding.[31]

This arrangement was agreed to by the Secretary of the Navy and was not objected to by President Roosevelt when he signed the bill into law. Roosevelt did object to another bill of 1944 which authorized the Secretary of the Navy to enter into contracts for the production of oil from naval reserves, but required prior consultation with the Naval Affairs Committees, and presumably their approval of such contracts.[32] Although the President signed the bill, he issued a statement to the

[31] Statement of Representative Vinson, *Congressional Record,* Vol. 97, Pt. 4, 82d Cong., 1st sess. (May 17, 1951), p. 5435.
[32] 58 Stat. 282.

press expressing his disagreement with this feature. This delegation to the two committees of Congress, he declared, disregarded "principles basic to our form of government. Efficient and economical administration can be achieved only by vesting authority to carry out the laws in an independent executive, and not in legislative committees. This act, in my opinion, impinges deeply upon this fundamental principle of good government embodied in the Constitution."[33]

In 1949 an act authorizing the armed services to acquire land for use as a proving ground for guided missiles or other weapons required them to come into agreement with the Armed Services Committees.[34] In 1951, during the Korean War, a construction authorization bill applying to all three services provided that all acquisitions of real property, all leases having an annual rental of more than $10,000, all transfers of government-owned real property, or reports of excess government-owned real property for disposition could be made only after the agency had "come into agreement" with the committees. Because of objections of the Corps of Engineers, river improvements and harbor and flood control projects were specifically exempted, as were grazing permits on military lands. In proposing such a bill in 1949, Representative Carl Vinson, chairman of the House Armed Services Committee, stated:

> Well, I think it is a fine control. I want this committee to have something to do with running the departments instead of the departments just telling the committee what they are going to do . . . when we are guiding the destinies of the Navy we feel that the committee should have a hand in a great many things.[35]

During the debate on the 1951 bill he declared that it would save "millions and millions of dollars" and enable the committee "to keep close tabs on what goes on in the departments."[36]

President Truman vetoed the bill, saying that the "legal requirement for the submission of countless real estate transactions to the scrutiny of congressional committees . . . would result in the imposition

---

[33] *New York Times*, June 18, 1944, p. 30.
[34] 63 Stat. 66.
[35] *Organization of the Armed Services Committee*, Hearing No. 1, House Committee on Armed Services, 81st Cong., 1st sess. (Jan. 25, 1949), p. 10.
[36] *Congressional Record*, Vol. 97, Pt. 3, 82d Cong., 1st sess. (April 23, 1951), p. 4189.

of a severe and unnecessary administrative burden on the Department of Defense," and lead to serious delays that would be a serious impediment in defense procurement. He also pointed out that the bill would "force a substantial degree of centralization in Washington of real estate transactions that could otherwise be more efficiently handled in the field," but he offered to supply the committees with full information on any real estate transactions in which they were interested. In conclusion, the President stated:

> Finally, I am concerned by what appears to me to be a gradual trend on the part of the legislative branch to participate to an ever greater extent in the actual execution and administration of the laws. Under our system of government it is contemplated that the Congress will enact the laws and will leave their administration and execution to the executive branch.[37]

A notable debate took place in the House before it voted 312 to 68 to override the veto. In defense of the bill Representative Vinson stated that its objective was to keep control in Congress over the land acquisitions and disposals of the Defense Department. Asked whether the bill would result in a trespass on executive functions, he replied in the negative, saying ". . . instead of delegating to a bureau [you] delegate it to yourselves, delegate it to a committee here in Congress. . . . It is Government property and Congress should have some control over Government property."[38]

Declaring that the bill would authorize the Armed Services Committees to administer the law, Representative Abraham J. Multer of New York inquired, "When has the Constitution been changed so as to give this Congress the right to administer the laws that it enacts?" The same point was made by Representative Boyd Tackett of Arkansas, who said that the legislation would permit the committees of Congress "to administer the very laws this Congress adopts . . . to supervise the purchasing and selling of property by the defense agencies." Representative Wright Patman of Texas maintained that the handling of real estate transactions was an executive function which Congress should not undertake, saying: "I do not believe we should get into the execu-

[37] Ibid. (May 15, 1951), pp. 5374-5375. The Washington Post stated in an editorial commenting on the vetoed bill: "The real question is whether Congress is overstepping its proper function of supervising administrative action. We think it is."
[38] Ibid. (May 17, 1951), p. 5437.

tive branch of government any more than the executive branch should get into the legislative branch. . . . We have plenty to do in the legislative branch. We should do our own job better before attempting to run the executive branch."[39]

The Senate did not attempt to pass the bill over the President's veto, but four months later, as the session neared its end, the House Armed Services Committee attached the same requirement of committee approval to another military construction authorization bill. The bill was passed, and because of the urgent need for the legislation, President Truman signed it. The act provided that the Defense Department "shall come into agreement" with the Armed Services Committees on all real estate transactions involving in excess of $25,000, or an annual rental of $25,000. No time limit was provided for committee approval.[40] The next year an act was passed requiring committee approval of the cost of construction of military works, "including those real estate actions pertaining thereto."[41]

The review of the proposed real estate transactions specified in the various statutes is conducted by subcommittees of the Senate and House Armed Services Committees. Proposals are examined initially by a member of the subcommittee staff, and then referred to the member of the House from the district concerned and to the senators of the state to ascertain if there is any objection. If no objection is received, they are routinely approved. Hearings are conducted by the subcommittees when a sufficient number of projects have been submitted to warrant it—usually 15 to 20. For each project, the Defense Department submits a written summary, and officials are present at the hearings to answer questions and supply additional information. Between 150 and 200 projects are passed upon annually, probably averaging in total value, including improvements, about $500 million. From 1951 through 1959, the House Real Estate and Construction Subcommittee passed upon a total of 1,510 real estate projects, divided about equally among the three armed services. Only a very few were rejected, although some were held up for further information.

The management of the real estate holdings and properties of the armed services, with an estimated value in 1955 of over $28 billion,

[39] *Ibid.*, pp. 5437-5441.
[40] 65 Stat. 765.
[41] 66 Stat. 606, 626.

is a proper concern of Congress, but efficient management is not notably encouraged by the present procedure. The subcommittees are not able to conduct any real examination of these transactions which involve properties all over the country and abroad, and necessarily rely on information supplied by the Defense Department and on advice of the local congressmen. A post-audit or examination of real estate transactions, conducted with the aid of a field investigation by the subcommittee staff or the General Accounting Office, would be a more effective procedure to determine whether the armed services are competently and efficiently managing their real property. This would enable the subcommittees to hold the services to a proper accounting for their management, and to inquire, for example, whether installations that are no longer needed are being closed.

When the "come into agreement" requirements were established during a period of rapid expansion of the armed services they probably served a useful purpose, despite the delays occasioned, but they can hardly be justified in normal times. In recent years the transactions have been, for the most part, disposals of installations and land no longer needed. The requirement of advance approval by congressional subcommittees enables members of Congress to resist the closing of military installations in their districts, and it cannot be doubted that the effect is to force the retention of installations that in the interest of economy should be closed.

The procedure was strongly criticized by the second Hoover Commission and its Task Force on Real Property Management as "cumbersome," "a deterrent to orderly and efficient real property management," because of the delays—frequently of a year or more—in securing the approval of the two committees. The commission also condemned "congressional participation in the executive function of operation as an invasion of the executive by the legislative branch," and recommended repeal of the requirements.[42]

President Eisenhower repeatedly opposed "come into agreement" provisions as unconstitutional. Finally, in 1960, he stated in his budget message that if the provision was not repealed he would direct the Secretary of Defense to disregard it, thus forcing a test of its constitution-

[42] Executive Commission on Organization of the Executive Branch of the Government, *Real Property Management* (1955), p. 35-36; Task Force Report, *Real Property Management* (1955), p. 94.

ality. Subsequently, the House Armed Services Committee reported an amendment that repealed the objectionable provision, and substituted in its place the requirement that all real estate transactions of more than $50,000 be reported in advance to Congress, and be subject to disapproval by a simple resolution of either house within the following thirty days. If Congress adjourned before the expiration of the thirty days without acting on the proposed transactions, the Secretary of Defense was authorized to enter into transactions so reported, provided he certified that the national defense would be imperiled by further delay.[43] The change in the act was one of form rather than substance. It is safe to predict that it will not affect the practical operation of the law.

In 1954 and 1956 President Eisenhower vetoed bills with "come into agreement" provisions on constitutional grounds. The 1954 bill authorized the Secretary of the Army to transfer federally owned lands within Camp Blanding Military Reservation to the State of Florida after "coming into agreement" with the Armed Services Committees. The veto message stated:

> The practical effect would be to place the power to make such agreement jointly in the Secretary of the Army and the members of the Committees on Armed Services. In so doing the bill would violate the fundamental principle of the separation of powers prescribed in Articles I and II of the Constitution, which place the legislative power in the Congress and the executive power in the executive branch. The making of such a contract . . . is a purely executive or administrative function. . . . Congress may not delegate to its members of committees the power to make such contracts either directly or by giving them power to approve or disapprove a contract which an executive officer proposes to make. Moreover, such a procedure destroys the clear lines of responsibility which the Constitution provides.[44]

Congress then passed a new bill which omitted the provision, and this was signed by the President.

Despite the 1954 veto of the Camp Blanding bill, Congress passed a bill in 1956 with similar provisions. Two sections of it—one authorizing the construction of family unit dwellings for the use of military or civilian personnel, and another authorizing funds for the construction

[43] House Report No. 1307, 86th Cong., 2d sess. (March 2, 1960), pp. 43-45.
[44] House Document No. 430, 83d Cong., 2d sess. (May 26, 1954).

of Talos missile facilities—required the Defense Department to "come into agreement" with the Armed Services Committees. Chairman Vinson defended the requirement with respect to housing on the ground that it would enable the committee to "re-enter" this important military field, and said that the committee would fail "to perform its function if it does not, from time to time, give the departments guidance in certain areas of activity."[45] In vetoing the bill President Eisenhower stated:

> The provision would also compel the Secretary of Defense, an executive official, to share with two committees of the Congress the responsibility for carrying out the Talos missile authorization. This procedure would destroy the clear lines of authority which the Constitution provides.[46]

Congress repassed the bill, omitting the provisions, but accomplished the same result by requiring plans to be submitted to Congress six months in advance, unless earlier approved.[47] The following year this requirement was dropped and specific authorization of such housing was required by act of Congress.

An extraordinary form of the legislative veto was used in a provision of the Supplemental Appropriation Act for fiscal 1953, passed in 1952, which has since been repealed. The act gave the regulations of the Bureau of the Budget relating to housing allowances (Circular A-45) the effect of law, but provided that any amendment or revision of the regulations should be approved by the chairman of the House Appropriations Committee. Thus the veto was to be exercised, not by a committee of Congress, but by one member of a committee. The provision placed the Bureau of the Budget in a quandary, since it wished neither to acquiesce in the propriety or the constitutionality of the requirement, nor to defy the powerful chairman of the House Appropriations Committee. As a result, the regulations were not revised for several years. In 1959, President Eisenhower recommended in his budget message that the section be dropped, and this was done in the appropriation act of that year.

[45] *Congressional Record*, Vol. 102, Pt. 5, 84th Cong., 2d sess. (April 10, 1956), p. 5595. The *Washington Post and Times Herald* (July 18, 1956) called the bill an "indefensible encroachment" on the President's authority.
[46] *Congressional Record*, Vol. 102, Pt. 9, 84th Cong., 2d sess. (July 16, 1956), p. 12958.
[47] 70 Stat. 1018.

The Termination of Business Enterprises. In 1955, Congress attached a rider to the Defense Appropriation Act (69 Stat. 321, Sec. 638) giving the two appropriations committees the power to pass upon proposed terminations of commercial type activities in the armed services and transfer of the work to private auspices.[48] Under the act the Defense Department was required to submit to the two committees all decisions to shut down business activities that had been in operation three years or more. Either committee, within the ensuing ninety days, could disapprove such termination. The provision was dropped in 1956 in the expectation that the veto power would be transferred to the Armed Services Committees, and a bill to that effect did pass the House but died in the Senate.

During the year the provision was in effect, the Defense Department reported plans to discontinue operation of 112 business enterprises, including the famous ropewalk at Boston, which had manufactured rope and cable for the Navy since its establishment by act of Congress in 1834, a chain forge factory, coffee roasting plants, several cement mixing plants, two paint manufacturing plants (for a special type of paint used on the bottoms of ships), and various other activities, some large and many very small. The House Appropriations Committee disapproved nine plans, and the Senate committee disapproved one. The other plans, generally relating to small operations, became effective.

For many years the armed services have operated a variety of manufacturing or other plants, including shipyards, arsenals, powder and ammunition plants (which date from the Revolution), and repair facilities, as well as establishments providing services for troops, including cleaning plants, cobbler shops, and others. In 1954 the Defense Department engaged in forty-seven categories of business activity, including manufacture of clothing, paint, ice cream, chain, and chlorine; operation of sawmills, bakeries, furniture repair shops, auto repair shops, tree nurseries, air and sea transportation fleets, and so on.

The degree to which the government was engaging in business or industrial activity began to be seriously questioned after the close of World War II. This concern gave rise to a so-called "decompetition

---

[48] This section of the chapter has drawn heavily on the case study by Edith Carper for the Inter-University Case Program, *The Defense Appropriation Rider* (1960).

program" in the Department of Defense—that is, a program of closing down certain of the military's business operations which produced goods or services that could be purchased from private business. In carrying out the program, the department acted under administration policies which had originated in at least three quarters: (1) campaign promises made by the Republicans in 1952 to "get the government out of business"; (2) representations from national trade and business associations; and (3) the widely publicized reports of the first and second Hoover Commissions' recommendations that the government's business-type operations be curtailed.

Three congressional committees joined the effort to speed decompetition. The House Government Operations Committee, after lengthy hearings in 1953, concluded that the extent of the government's commercial activities constituted "a step toward socialization" and recommended that with few exceptions these activities be turned over to private enterprise. The Senate Small Business Committee and the Senate Appropriations Committee also urged government departments to curtail activities in competition with private firms. Nevertheless, Congress was later to assert controls slowing down the process.

The Department of Defense had actually initiated the decompetition program by a 1952 directive, under which in early 1953 it ordered the armed services to survey commercial and industrial-type activities and to discontinue those in competition with private enterprise. One of the first operations singled out for shutdown was the venerable Boston ropewalk. Local groups immediately protested, and the Boston Chamber of Commerce took a firm stand against the shutdown. The aid of Representatives Thomas P. O'Neill, whose district encompassed the ropewalk, and John W. McCormack, whose district adjoined it, was sought. The combination of local and congressional pressure resulted in the closure plan being shelved.

In 1954 the plan was revived, although the Navy—the "proprietor" of the ropewalk—had been taking strong exception to the Defense Department's recommendation and proposed that, at the very least, operation at the ropewalk should continue on a reduced basis for research and development purposes. In early 1955, however, the Navy gave in, announcing that the operation would be "phased out completely within six months." Again there was protest in Boston, and Representative McCormack, now again House majority leader, took up the cudgels for the ropewalk. But on February 28 he told the House that his campaign was unsuccessful, and cited the message he had sent earlier to his Massachusetts constituents: "If they had left it at the legislative level, I know I could block it. I blocked it in the last Congress, which was Republican controlled, and I know I could block it in this Congress, which is Democratic controlled, but it is going to be action by the Executive branch."

The decompetition program moved into high gear by May 1955, at which time the Defense Department was able to announce that 171 commercial activities in various regions had been discontinued. However, local opposition, especially from members of government unions facing loss of their jobs, had been mounting. Constituents lodged protests at an increasing rate with their congressmen, and the congressmen in turn sought to block each projected shutdown.

Robert Sikes of Florida, a member of the House Appropriations Committee and the Defense Appropriations Subcommittee, who represented the district encompassing Pensacola Air Force Base, endeavored to reverse the decision of the Navy to transfer the telephone exchange and other base activities to commercial operation. Failing in his attempt, in March 1955 he had introduced legislation (H.R.5115) to give Congress a veto over such decisions, but the House Armed Services Committee, to which the bill was referred, shelved it after receiving an unfavorable report on it from the Defense Department. Sikes then took his bill to the Defense Appropriations Subcommittee, and with the support of other members with similar problems in their own districts, was able to persuade the subcommittee to attach the gist of it as a rider (Section 638) to the annual defense appropriations bill.

Debate on the bill began in the House on May 11, 1955. Sikes' provision was strongly opposed by Chairman Carl Vinson of the Armed Services Committee. Vinson characterized it as an "unconstitutional invasion of an executive function." This was, indeed, an extraordinary argument coming from a leading advocate of the legislative veto. The rider was, however, vigorously defended by members who feared that the termination of business activities in their own districts would lead to unemployment, and on May 12 the Vinson amendment to delete Section 638 was rejected on a roll call vote of 184 to 202.

The Senate Appropriations Committee reported out a revised version of Section 638 that gave the Defense Department more discretion than did the House draft. Under it, only those installations in existence twenty-five years or longer needed to be cleared with the appropriations committees. In conference, however, the Senate committee representatives gave in and agreed to the House provision.

Because of the urgent need of the armed services for funds (the act appropriated over $31 billion), President Eisenhower signed the bill, but protested Section 638. In a message to Congress on July 13 he said that the Attorney General had advised him that the provision was unconstitutional and that "the Congress has no right to confer upon its committees the power to veto Executive action or to prevent Executive action from becoming effective." Stating that he regarded this encroachment on executive authority as a "dangerous precedent," he served notice that the Executive branch would regard the section as invalid unless otherwise determined by a court of competent jurisdiction.

The President's message was angrily protested by members of Congress. Representative Sikes declared that the President was seeking to place himself above the law, and Majority Leader McCormack called it nullification. Representative Porter Hardy of Virginia obtained assurances that the Comptroller General would enforce the law by disallowing expenditures made in contravention of Section 638. The St. Louis Globe Democrat, however, termed the section a "shotgun rider," a "political shenanigan" designed to prevent the removal of "shipyards, arsenals, even . . . paint plants from the bailiwicks of influential congressmen."

Despite the President's instructions to the contrary, the Defense Department concluded that it had no alternative but to observe the provisions of the rider. The Boston ropewalk was included in the first list the department sent up to Congress under Section 638. (Operations had continued at the ropewalk pending the outcome of the congressional debate). At hearings conducted by the House Appropriations Subcommittee, five Massachusetts congressmen—two Democrats and three Republicans—testified in opposition to the plan to close the ropewalk and a chain forge factory in Boston, and representatives from other states accompanied by union representatives of the employees affected appeared in opposition to plans to close activities in their respective districts. The House Appropriations Committee forbade closing the Boston ropewalk and chain forge, paint plants in California and Virginia, and several other minor activities—nine altogether —but permitted the other plans to go into effect. The committee's report complained that the Department had overcomplied with the act by reporting plans to terminate picayune activities, several of which involved less than one full-time employee.

The following year the rider was dropped from the defense appropriation bill in the expectation that the authority would be continued in another bill awarding the veto to the two Armed Services Committees. When the latter bill failed to pass the Senate, the committee veto came to an end.

Veto Via Authorization of Appropriations. Since the "come into agreement" provision had increasingly resulted in presidential vetoes, on constitutional or other grounds, Congress found a new committee veto formula. This device required committee approval of proposed actions before funds could be appropriated for them. It was first used in the Public Buildings Contract Purchase Act of 1954.[49] An earlier bill passed in 1952, which authorized the Postmaster General to enter into lease-purchase contracts for the construction of post office buildings, required him to "come into agreement" with the Public Works Committee and the Post Office and Civil Service Committee of each house. This bill (H.R.6839) was pocket-vetoed by President Truman with the statement that it would infringe on the Executive branch: "I do not dispute the right of Congress and its committees to take an interest in real-estate transactions made by the executive branch of the Government, but I do question the propriety and wisdom of giving committees the veto power over executive functions."[50]

The 1954 bill authorized the Administrator of General Services and the Postmaster General to enter into lease-purchase contracts for the construction of public buildings. As passed by the House, it required that reports of such contracts be submitted to the Public Works Committees thirty days in advance, but the Senate Public Works Committee brought in an amendment to require the executive officers to "come into agreement" with the committees before a contract could be ex-

[49] 68 Stat. 518.
[50] *Congressional Record*, Vol. 98, Pt. 7, 82d Cong., 2d sess. (July 19, 1952), p. 9756.

ecuted. Senator Everett Dirksen of Illinois strongly opposed this provision:

> ... this measure, in its present form, would ... vest in two committees of the Congress a function which the Constitution does not sanction. It gives two committees a veto over actions of the executive branch which have been authorized by congressional enactment. Nowhere in the Constitution is mention made of committees of the Congress. ... The only authorized congressional action is action by both Houses of Congress and not by committees.[51]

An amendment offered by Senator Dirksen to strike the "come into agreement" provision and to substitute merely the requirement of advance reports on proposed lease-purchase contracts was defeated. In conference, however, the section was dropped because of constitutional objections and in its place provision was made that no funds could be appropriated for annual payments in excess of $20,000 on any lease-purchase contract unless the contract had been approved by the Public Works Committee of each house. The conference committee assured the two houses that this language retained "the same degree of legislative responsibility as the Senate amendment." The President signed the bill on the advice of the Attorney General that the new provision was within the power of Congress, and this act became the accepted pattern thereafter for the committee veto.

The results achieved under the lease-purchase act during the three years it was in effect were meager. Although 146 proposed projects, involving an estimated cost in excess of $700 million, were approved by the committees, the General Services Administration actually placed only one contract and the Post Office Department only three. All proposed projects, with a single exception (which was deferred), received committee approval. The committees followed the practice of referring proposed projects to the congressman from the district and to the senators from the state, who invariably recommended approval. Because of these meager results the act was permitted to expire in 1957.

The Watershed Protection and Flood Prevention Act of 1954 was another statute requiring committee approval before funds could be appropriated. It authorized the Secretary of Agriculture to make grants to cooperating state and local authorities for this purpose, but with the

---

[51] *Congressional Record,* Vol. 100, Pt. 4, 83d Cong., 2d sess. (April 14, 1954), p. 5095.

requirement that plans be approved by the agriculture committees of the House and Senate before an appropriation may be made.[52] In practice, lump-sum appropriations are made for this program, but the Secretary of Agriculture secures the approval of the committee of each house before entering into a contract.

The program proved to be popular and in recent years has involved annual expenditures of about $60 million. Payments are made to land owners who follow the prescribed soil conservation practices in watershed areas. By 1959 approximately a hundred projects had been approved, and none rejected. The reason given for requiring committee approval was to assure that a fair distribution was made among the several regions of the country. The requirement has resulted in increased congressional pressures on the department to approve projects within the district of the member concerned, but otherwise has had little visible effect.

The Small Projects Reclamation Act of 1956 provided that grants to local authorities be reported sixty days in advance to the Senate and House Interior Committees, and authorized either committee within this time to disapprove such grants.[53] President Eisenhower signed the bill, but entered a protest against this provision, stating that the program would not be carried out until the law had been amended to omit this objectionable feature. "Although the Congress may prescribe the standards and conditions under which executive officials may enter into contracts," he said, "it may not lodge in its committees or members the power to make such contracts, either directly or by giving them the power to approve or disapprove a contract which an executive officer proposes to make."[54]

The act was amended at the next session of Congress by striking the provision objected to by the President and by adding another having exactly the same effect. The amendment provides that no funds shall be appropriated for any project which either committee has disapproved.[55] Although on constitutional grounds this procedure is less objectionable than the earlier provision, it is administratively more objectionable, for it imposes excessive delays. The House Appropriations Committee has persistently declined to vote funds for a project until it has been laid before the committees for the specified time, imposing

[52] 68 Stat. 667.
[53] 70 Stat. 1045.
[54] *Public Papers of the President: Dwight D. Eisenhower, 1956*, p. 650.
[55] 71 Stat. 49.

a delay of a year or more before funds can be secured. By the summer of 1958 only one project had been authorized and funds voted under this procedure.

The Requirement of Advance Reports. Another legislative device which enables committees to review proposed executive actions is the requirement of advance reports, without mention of a veto power. Such reports are customarily required from thirty to ninety days before the action may be taken, but under some acts the committees may reduce the waiting period by earlier approval of the proposed action. The effect of the requirement is the same as though a formal veto power were granted, since the advance report puts a committee on notice and enables it to inquire into proposed actions or plans. If the action is questioned by a member of the committee or its staff, or by other members of Congress, the department will usually be asked to supply additional information, and the committee may conduct hearings. If the committee objects to the proposed action, the departments invariably suspend action or modify the plans to meet the wishes of the committee.

The first such statutory requirement of advance reports of executive decisions appears to have been an appropriations rider of 1927, which provided that tax refunds in excess of $75,000 must be reported to the Joint Committee on Internal Revenue Taxation sixty days before being paid. This rider was passed as a result of criticisms and charges of irregularities in connection with the large refunds which were paid in the years following World War I when Andrew Mellon was Secretary of the Treasury. As of 1961, the provision was still in effect, although the act has been revised to reduce the waiting period to thirty days, and to increase the minimum refund required to be reported to $100,000.

In an average year there are approximately 250 tax refunds of more than $100,000, each of which under law must be reported to the Joint Committee on Internal Revenue Taxation thirty days before they are paid. The total averages about $250 million annually, or slightly less than 10 per cent of all tax refunds.[56] In practice, the Internal Revenue Service does not pay these refunds until they have been cleared by the committee staff, and the thirty-day waiting period is extended when necessary to permit the staff to complete its examination. Although the committee and its staff are not authorized to disallow payments, In-

---

[56] Information supplied to the author by the Internal Revenue Service.

ternal Revenue accepts their ruling as binding upon it, and will not pay—except on a court order—when there has been objection.

To pre-audit the refunds the committee utilizes a staff consisting of four attorneys, whose offices are located in the Internal Revenue building. Their examination is concerned primarily with the accuracy of Internal Revenue's tax determination, whether the evidence submitted in support of a claim is sufficient and in correct form, and whether correct interpretations have been made of the tax laws. Although comparatively few disallowances result from the examination, the staff often raises questions or takes exceptions that lead to revision of the determinations. If agreement is not reached between the committee staff and Internal Revenue, the case is referred to the chief counsel of the Joint Committee, who reviews the case and may hold a hearing to permit Internal Revenue to present oral argument. His decision may be appealed to the Joint Committee, though this is rarely done.

The requirement of advance reporting of large tax refunds to the committee was established following serious charges of irregularities in the years before the Internal Revenue Service had established the thorough internal checks and reviews that are used today. It is questionable whether the external pre-audit of large tax refunds by the committee's staff is still needed. It may also be questioned whether this form of examination, limited to large refund cases—which make up only a miniscule fraction of the millions of all types of tax cases each year, which involve some hundreds of millions of dollars—adequately meets the needs of Congress for a check on the administration of the tax laws.

Although it is understandable why this particular type of tax case was originally subjected to congressional scrutiny, the reasons are not applicable today. An independent check of the administration and interpretation of the tax laws is undoubtedly a proper function of a legislative body. However, the examination conducted by the legislative staff should not be limited to large refund cases, which are in no respect a good sample of the tax determinations made by the Internal Revenue Service, but should include a sample of the various types of tax cases, and the examination should be conducted as a post-audit rather than as a pre-audit. The Comptroller General, it should be noted, is not authorized to examine the determination of tax cases or to interpret tax laws, but does audit Internal Revenue accounts.

In defense of the present procedure, it may be said that the pre-audit of all large tax refund cases prior to payment provides an added precaution against errors and incorrect interpretations of the law, thus avoiding excess payments. On the other hand, because of the external pre-audit, the Internal Revenue Service has instituted more elaborate checks and reviews of such cases than would otherwise be used, and a voluminous record and report is prepared for each case. These additional checks and reviews involve added administrative expense and delays. Payment on the tax refunds which come under the scrutiny of the Joint Committee staff are delayed, on the average, a year and a half, involving an annual interest charge of over $40 million. In a recent year the interest charges on tax refunds audited by the Joint Committee staff averaged 9 per cent, while the interest charges on other refunds averaged only 0.6 per cent.[57] Thus, the savings that may be attributed to the refund audit by the committee staff and to the additional checks made by Internal Revenue in handling these cases would appear to be more than offset by the added interest charges and administrative expense. (It may be noted, however, that not all of the increased time in handling large tax refunds is the result of the committee staff's pre-audit, for in any event more elaborate checks and reviews would be used for large tax refunds than for small ones, most of which are paid out prior to the audit.)

A review of the experience during some thirty-five years of advance reports to Congress of large tax refunds is significant to this study because it shows that advance reporting has substantially the same effect as a committee's formal veto of executive decisions. The Internal Revenue Service accepts the determinations of the Joint Committee staff, though not legally bound to do so, and will not pay refunds to which exception has been taken. It is also significant that the Joint Committee has delegated the examination and determinations almost wholly to its staff. In a recent three-year period only one case was referred back to the Joint Committee.[58] Congressional committee oversight has in this case become largely staff oversight. And the staff's present examination, in being concerned only with the accuracy with which large tax refunds are determined, bypasses the more important

[57] Information supplied by the Internal Revenue Service.
[58] Interview with Russell C. Harrington, Commissioner of Internal Revenue, August 1958.

and proper legislative function of checking the administration of the tax laws to ascertain whether they are being correctly interpreted, the taxes properly assessed and collected, and adequate internal checks utilized—the kind of check that would enable the Joint Committee to hold the executive officers accountable.

The Atomic Energy Commission is the leading example of an executive agency whose operations are closely supervised by a congressional committee through the requirement of advance reports on many of its activities and plans, and, in fact, on all aspects of its operations. By means of the reports the Joint Committee on Atomic Energy is advised about the work of the commission and is able to participate in important decisions. The original Atomic Energy Act of 1946 provided that the commission must "keep the Joint Committee fully and currently informed with respect to the Commission's activities." This requirement was strengthened in the 1954 Act and extended to the Defense Department.[59] The committee's report on the 1954 bill stated that it is the "intent of Congress that the Joint Committee shall be informed while matters are pending, rather than after action has been taken."[60]

Subsequent acts have further required advance reports of many of the most important actions of the AEC, including the sharing of secret information with other countries, plans for cooperative arrangements with other countries, the construction of demonstration reactors and other projects not previously approved by the Joint Committee, the classification of "source materials" and "special materials," regulations governing the disposal and price of nuclear materials for nongovernmental use, and long-term utility contracts for electric service. In most cases a waiting period of forty-five days while Congress is in session is required before such decisions may take effect, but in a 1958 amendment to the Atomic Energy Act of 1954 cooperative arrangements with other countries were required to be laid before the committee for sixty days, and in this case disapproval by concurrent resolution is authorized.[61] These requirements of advance reports were enacted despite objections from the AEC, which pointed out that it was already

[59] 68 Stat. 919.
[60] Quoted in Morgan Thomas, *Atomic Energy and Congress* (1955), p. 153. The following account draws heavily on this book.
[61] 72 Stat. 277.

required by the Atomic Energy Act of 1946 to keep the committee currently informed.

In view of the nature of the atomic energy program and its importance to the nation, and especially because of the uncertainties about future development in the early years of the program, it was to be expected that Congress would exercise close supervision over the policies and administration of the AEC. The Joint Committee was set up precisely for this purpose. It was impossible in the early years to foresee and to authorize by law the various activities which would be carried on by the AEC. Without the close oversight exercised by the Joint Committee, Congress would not have been willing to delegate to the AEC the authority and flexibility necessary to the development of the program. The major task of the Joint Committee has been to act as the arm of Congress in formulating and proposing legislation authorizing new programs and establishing policies, which has required it to keep in touch with the work and plans of the AEC.

The experience since 1946, however, does not indicate that this form of close oversight of administration should be extended to other fields. The Joint Committee has made its greatest contribution in the development of policies and programs rather than in its supervision of administration—and its relationship with the AEC on administrative matters has often produced friction and frustration on both sides. The AEC has often been placed in the unhappy situation of being subject to conflicting directions from the President and his Executive Office, on one hand, and the Joint Committee on the other. The controls exercised by the Joint Committee—for example, in its preoccupation with security measures—have often been negative and hampering rather than helpful and constructive. If the AEC is to be held truly responsible for its administration of the program in the future, it needs to be released from some of the detailed controls that have been exercised in the past.

A number of statutes which require frequent and detailed reporting of specified administrative actions have about the same effects as those requiring advance reports. An act of 1953, for example, which authorized the transfer of certain naval vessels to Italy, France, and other friendly nations, charged the Secretary of Defense to "keep the respective Committee on Armed Services of the Senate and the House

of Representatives currently advised of all transfers and other disposi-
tions" under the act.[62]

In one case, which involved reports on the disposal of surplus property without competitive bidding, the statutory requirement of reports
was held by the committee to mean reports *in advance.* Moreover, an
agreement was secured from the Administrator of General Services
that he would not carry out any disposals in this manner that were objected to by the committee. In describing this procedure, the Senate
Government Operations Committee stated that its practice was to refer such disposals to the senators from the state where the property was
located "for their consideration and recommendation."[63] This case is a
good illustration of the common practice which turns the committee
veto into a device whereby individual senators and representatives
pass upon government activities within their states or districts.

The requirement of detailed and frequent reports of certain activities or decisions, which are referred to the appropriate committees,
provides an additional means whereby these committees may supervise
the work of the departments. The details required indicate the activities over which the committees wish to exercise surveillance. The device is not very effective, for the committees seldom have the time or
staff to examine the reports carefully, and often make little use of them.
At times detailed reporting requirements are made at the behest of opponents of a program in order to secure information which may later
be used to attack. The administrative costs of preparing such reports
are often disproportionate to the use that is made of them.

The Constitutional Issue

The legislative veto by Congress of executive actions by concurrent resolutions or by a resolution of one house has been challenged by
a number of writers, first, as an unconstitutional infringement of the
President's veto power; second, as contrary to the specific provisions

[62] 67 Stat. 363. For examples of numerous other acts of this kind, see J. Malcolm
Smith and Cornelius P. Cotter, "Administrative Accountability: Reporting to Congress," *Western Political Quarterly,* Vol. 10 (June 1957), pp. 405-415.
[63] Senate Report No. 1284, 85th Cong., 2d sess. (1958), p. 3. See also Rhode,
*Congressional Review of Administrative Decision-Making by Committee Clearance
and Resolutions* (see footnote 1 above), p. 41.

in the Constitution concerning the manner in which Congress shall exercise its legislative powers; and, third, as contrary to the constitutional division of powers among the three branches of the government. The recent innovation of using concurrent resolutions to terminate or to bring into effect statutory grants of authority and to modify statutes is even more questionable on constitutional grounds, while the use of simple resolutions by a single house for these purposes is objectionable on additional grounds.

The President's veto power is stated in the Constitution in the most explicit terms. Article I, Section 7, paragraph 2 provides that "every bill which shall have passed the House of the Representatives and the Senate shall, before it becomes a law, be presented to the President of the United States" for his approval or disapproval, and if disapproved, shall not become law unless repassed by a two thirds vote of each house. During the debate in the Constitutional Convention on this clause, James Madison pointed out that "if the negative of the President was confined to *bills*, it would be evaded by acts under the form and name of resolutions, votes, etc." The following day the Convention added the third paragraph of Section 7:[64]

> Every order, resolution, or vote to which the concurrence of the Senate and House of Representatives may be necessary (except on a question of adjournment) shall be presented to the President of the United States; and before the same shall take effect shall be approved by him, or being disapproved by him, shall be repassed by two thirds of the Senate and the House of Representatives, according to the rules and limitations prescribed in the case of a bill.

The debates in the Constitutional Convention and the contemporary discussion of the veto power indicate that the power was granted to the President primarily to enable him to defend himself against legislative encroachments, and only secondarily as a safeguard against bad laws. Alexander Hamilton wrote in *The Federalist* (No. 73) that without the veto power the President would be

> . . . absolutely unable to defend himself against the depredations of the latter [the legislative branches]. He might gradually be stripped of his authorities by successive resolutions, or annihilated by a single vote. . . . The primary inducement to conferring the power in ques-

---

[64] Jonathan Elliot, ed., *Debates on the Adoption of the Federal Constitution*, Vol. 5 (1861), p. 431.

tion upon the Executive is to enable him to defend himself; the secondary one is to increase the chances in favor of the community against the passing of bad laws, through haste, inadvertence, or design.

The veto was regarded as one of the most important powers granted to the President. The language of the Constitution indicates beyond doubt that the power was intended to apply to all actions of Congress which have the effect of law. "It would be difficult to conceive of language and history which would more clearly require that all concurrent action of the two Houses be subject to the President's approval or veto."[65] The only exception, which was specifically mentioned in the Constitution, was a vote on adjournment. It was the early practice of Congress to use concurrent resolutions, which are not submitted to the President for his signature, only for the internal management of Congress itself, such as printing; for creating joint committees; for the expression of opinions which have no legal effect; and for submitting constitutional amendments to the states, a power granted to Congress alone. The rules of both houses limited the use of concurrent resolutions to these purposes. A report of the Senate Judiciary Committee in 1897 on the use of joint and concurrent resolutions concluded:

. . . "whether concurrent resolutions are required to be submitted to the President of the United States" must depend, not upon their mere form, but upon the fact whether they contain matter which is properly to be regarded as legislative in its character and effect. If they do, they must be presented for his approval; otherwise, they need not be.[66]

In defense of the constitutionality of the legislative veto, it has been contended that, since Congress is free to grant or withhold authority of executive officers, it may attach such conditions and requirements as it sees fit, including the requirement that it must be consulted in advance before the authority may be used, and may reserve the right to reject proposed executive actions. Congress has often enacted legislation contingent upon future events, upon the findings of specified facts by executive officers, or in the case of certain agricultural programs, upon the favorable vote of the farmers affected. Why then, it is

[65] Ginnane, "The Control of Federal Administration by Congressional Resolutions and Committees," *Harvard Law Review,* Vol. 66 (February 1953), p. 573.
[66] Quoted in *ibid.,* p. 574.

asked, may not Congress similarly specify, as a condition to the exercise of authority, that proposed actions be laid before it, subject to its disapproval within a specified time?

The analogy is easily seen to be defective. It is one thing for Congress to enact legislation which is contingent upon the occurrence of certain events, or upon the determination of certain facts by executive officers, or even the vote of certain groups of the population; it is quite another thing for Congress to reserve to itself the right to determine in the future whether an executive decision made in pursuance of law shall be carried out. In one case the condition is external to Congress and its action is complete when the legislation is enacted; in the other case the condition involves the future decision by Congress itself, and in a manner not sanctioned by the Constitution. Congress has the power to set aside or to reverse executive decisions, provided it acts in accordance with the Constitution, but it cannot subvert the Constitution through the guise of attaching conditions to laws which it enacts.

The legislative veto of executive decisions which have been made under statutory authority—for example, the decision concerning the deportation of aliens, or the contracts for the disposal of rubber plants —appears clearly invalid. The Constitution does not sanction legislative participation in executive actions, nor does it authorize Congress to take actions having legal effect in this manner. To terminate statutes, discontinue foreign aid to particular countries, and revise regulations concerning military service—all by concurrent resolution—is likewise contrary to explicit provisions of the Constitution.

The constitutionality of the legislative veto as applied to executive reorganization plans stands on quite different grounds than other uses of the device. There can be no question of the authority of the President to submit recommendations or plans to Congress, which is granted to him in the Constitution. Similarly, Congress undoubtedly has the authority to delegate authority to the President to reorganize the executive departments. The legislative veto in this instance is a novel combination of these two constitutional procedures. In permitting an executive reorganization plan to become effective—a plan which sets aside previous acts of Congress—Congress is using the procedure as a substitute for legislation that would otherwise be required. Other uses of the legislative veto by congressional resolution or by committee action, however, enable Congress or its committees to pass upon individual executive acts in a manner not authorized by the Constitution. Furthermore, the veto of executive reorganization plans by a single house is subject to serious constitutional as well as practical objections. Recent experience indicates that under this procedure the authority granted to the President is too limited to enable him to effect needed reorganizations.

There are also serious constitutional objections to the delegation of authority to congressional committees to exercise a veto over specific executive decisions which have been made under authority of law. The committee veto is patently contrary to the principle of separation of powers. Throughout the history of the country it has been generally accepted that the function of passing the laws belongs to the legislative branch, while the function of executing the laws belongs to executive officers. By the Constitution, the President is granted certain legislative powers, especially the veto power, which was intended to protect him against legislative encroachment, and Congress is delegated certain executive functions, notably the confirmation of appointments, to restrain the Executive. But apart from such exceptions, specifically authorized by the Constitution, the principle of separation of powers prohibits either branch from undertaking the functions of the other.

In an early case Chief Justice John Marshall described the division of functions between the three major branches of government in the following words: "The difference between the departments undoubtedly is, that the legislative makes, the executive executes, and the judiciary construes the laws."[67] In the leading case on the separation of powers, *Springer* v. *Philippine Islands,* the Supreme Court held invalid an act of the Philippine legislature vesting the power to vote stock owned by the government in a commission consisting of the Governor General and the presiding officers of the two houses of the legislature. Said the court:

> Legislative power, as distinguished from executive power, is the authority to make the laws, but not to enforce them or to appoint agents charged with the duty of such enforcement. The latter are executive functions.[68]

The reasons for the separation of functions of the legislative and ex-

[67] *Wayman* v. *Southard,* 23 Wheat. 1, 44 (1825).
[68] 277 U. S. 189, 202 (1928).

ecutive branches were cogently stated by President Woodrow Wilson in a veto message in 1920:

> The Congress and the executive should function within their respective spheres. Otherwise efficient and responsible management will be impossible and progress will be impeded by wasteful forces of disorganization and obstruction. The Congress has the right and power to grant or deny an appropriation, or to enact or refuse to enact a law; but once an appropriation is made or a law is passed, the appropriation should be administered or the law executed by the executive branch of the Government. In no other way can the Government be efficiently managed and responsibility definitely fixed.[69]

Although the line between legislative and executive functions not only cannot be sharply drawn but also changes over a period of time, a basic distinction persists. The distinguishing characteristic of the executive function is the application of laws to individual cases. Such matters as the letting of contracts, the acquisition or sale of real estate, the granting of permits and concessions in the national parks, the fixing of prices of fissionable materials are undoubtedly executive functions under the Constitution. It would hardly be contended that such activities may be assigned to congressional committees.

The action of a congressional committee in approving or disapproving a proposed executive action before it is put into effect, is in principle indistinguishable from the assignment of the function directly to the committee. If a committee participates in the decisions and makes the final determinations, the role which it plays is essentially the same as that of an executive officer who passes upon the recommendation of subordinates. It has been pointed out repeatedly in presidential veto messages that the committee veto requires executive officers to share their responsibility for executive decisions with congressional committees. Concerning the committee veto of terminations of commercial-type activities in the armed services, Attorney General Herbert Brownell, Jr., stated:

> The practical effect of these provisions is to vest the power to administer the particular program jointly in the Secretary of Defense and the members of the Appropriations Committees, with the overriding right to forbid action reserved to the two Committees. This,

[69] *Congressional Record*, Vol. 59, Pt. 7, 66th Cong., 2d sess. (May 13, 1920), pp. 7026-7027.

I believe, engrafts executive functions upon legislative members and thus overreaches the permitted sweep of legislative authority.[70]

Another objection to the committee veto is that it delegates authority to individual committees of Congress, which are not mentioned in the Constitution, to make final determinations on behalf of Congress, and thus deprives the President of his veto power. On one occasion Representative Vinson of Georgia, chairman of the House Armed Services Committee, admitted that "the weakness of our position is that it is not Congress, but it is the committee" that passes on real estate transactions.[71] The constitutional objections to the committee veto were summarized by Attorney General William P. Rogers in 1957 as follows:

> Legislative proposals and enactments in recent years have reflected a growing trend whereby authority is sought to be vested in congressional committees to approve or disapprove actions of the executive branch. Of the several legislative devices employed, that which subjects executive department action to the prior approval or disapproval of congressional committees may well be the most inimical to responsible government. It not only permits organs of the legislative branch to take binding actions having the effect of law without opportunity for the President to participate in the legislative process, but it also permits mere handfuls of members to speak for a Congress which is given no opportunity to participate as a whole. An arrangement of this kind tends to undermine the President's position as the responsible Chief Executive.[72]

The constitutionality of the more recent formula—the requirement of committee approval before funds may be voted for projects—has been defended on the ground that the requirement merely revises the rules by which Congress authorizes appropriations, and hence does not encroach on executive functions. The fallacy of this contention is apparent. Congress authorizes appropriations by legislation, which must be passed by both houses and submitted to the President for his signature. It cannot delegate this function to one house alone or to committees. Congress must exercise its powers in the manner prescribed by the Constitution, and it cannot legitimatize committee encroachment on executive functions by changing its rules.

[70] *Opinions of the Attorneys General,* Vol. 41, No. 32 (July 13, 1955).
[71] See footnote 35 above.
[72] *Opinions of the Attorneys General,* Vol. 41, No. 47 (Aug. 8, 1957).

Conclusions

Although its constitutionality may be questioned, the legislative veto by concurrent resolution of the President's executive reorganization plans has provided a suitable device to permit the President and the Congress to cooperate in effecting needed executive reorganizations. The procedure gives the President the initiative in formulating such plans, which his position as Chief Executive warrants. Congress is required to act upon his plans within sixty days, and to accept or reject them without amendment. Although much can be said for an outright grant of executive reorganization authority to the President without any legislative strings other than advance reporting, the provision of the legislative veto by concurrent resolution leaves the President with adequate authority to effect needed executive reorganizations.

Under the 1949 Executive Reorganization Act, however, and subsequent statutes which permitted either house acting alone to set aside the President's reorganization plans, the authority of the President was greatly weakened. Of the forty-one plans submitted by President Truman during his second term of office, mostly to carry out recommendations of the first Hoover Commission, twelve were set aside. President Eisenhower had little difficulty in securing congressional assent to his reorganization plans, which were largely noncontroversial, during his first two years in office when the Republicans were in the majority in both houses of Congress, but thereafter he made little use of the authority and a number of his plans were set aside.

Any executive reorganization plan of the President is likely to face opposition, especially by the agencies affected, by their clienteles who fear that a change of organization may affect agency policies, and by members of Congress who are advocates of the agencies' programs. In addition, political adversaries of the President in his own as well as the opposition party are apt to join in the contention to embarrass the President and reduce his power. Aware of the possibility of rejection by one house, which would weaken his prestige and leadership, the President is reluctant to submit reorganization plans that are likely to be opposed by any influential group. If the concurrence of both houses is required to set aside his plans, the President is in a much stronger position, for he can marshal his strength and defend his plans in the second house, since it often happens that the reasons of one house for opposing a given plan are not shared by the other house.

The extension of the legislative veto to other executive decisions, particularly to specific executive acts such as the suspension of deportations of aliens, the disposal of surplus property, or cooperative arrangements in atomic energy with other countries, is much less defensible. The requirement of advance reports, coupled with all the other controls which Congress is able to exercise over the executive departments, would appear to be adequate to enable Congress and its committees to exercise effective legislative oversight.

The committee veto of executive decisions, which has arisen since the end of World War II, is subject to serious practical as well as constitutional objections. It cannot be doubted that if this form of legislative control comes to be widely used it will result in a fundamental change in our form of government. Initially used as a substitute for legislative authorization of naval installations and public works, it has developed into a means whereby committees are authorized to pass upon specific executive decisions. The committee veto takes various forms, but all have the same result—namely, to enable the committees to share with executive officers the authority to make executive decisions. The requirement of advance reports without any provision for a formal veto by congressional committees has about the same effect as the formal veto, though it is less objectionable on constitutional grounds.

In defense of the committee veto it may be pointed out that Congress has been faced with the necessity of making increasingly broad delegations of authority to the executive departments because of the size and complexity of their operations in recent years. To compensate for these broad delegations of authority, Congress has sought means whereby it may retain a voice in the use of the authority and exercise more effective controls over the executive. The committee veto provides such a device. In addition, it streamlines the legislative process by permitting committees to act on behalf of Congress without the necessity of enacting legislation. Public works projects may be authorized in broad legislation, subject to the approval of individual projects by the legislative committees. The committee veto has been used largely, but not exclusively, with regard to public works authorizations, over which Congress has always jealously guarded its control.

In addition to the constitutional objections reviewed in the last section above, there are at least five major grounds for criticism of the committee veto. *First,* since its effect is to bypass the President and his office and substitute the supervision of congressional committees over departments and bureaus, it weakens the authority of the President—a serious matter in today's world when strong executive leadership is sorely needed. *Second,* it divides responsibility for executive decisions between department heads and congressional committees, thereby defeating the accountability of executive officers. As Representative Chet Holifield of California stated in the debate on a committee veto provision in 1951:

> The surest way to destroy responsibility and accountability in the administration is to make a committee of the Congress a party of each and every administrative act of importance, such as this bill does. . . . The Congress and any appropriate committee of the Congress is entitled to criticize any or all of these transactions. It is entitled to get full information; but it is not entitled in my humble judgment to sit as a party in the making of the transaction. This is a basic violation of those tenets of government to which we have tried to adhere through the years.[73]

Third, the committee veto has harmful effects on administration. In 1951, President Truman objected to the committee veto of real estate transactions of the armed services, because it would lead to excessive centralization of operations that should be delegated to field officers, and would increase red tape and delay. In 1955 the second Hoover Commission reported that the requirement had these foreseen effects and recommended its repeal. The requirement of committee approval of executive decisions may occasionally safeguard against ill-considered or hasty action, but in the long run this advantage will be far outweighed by the harm done to administration by the imposition of extra checks and delays that not only discourage executive officers from accepting responsibility but also make them unduly cautious in seeking improved methods and introducing needed innovations.

Fourth, the committee veto increases the political pressures by members of Congress on the departments with respect to the location of public works, the discontinuance of military installations, and other decisions affecting the members' own districts or states. In many instances,

[73] *Congressional Record,* Vol. 97, Pt. 4, 82d Cong., 1st sess. (May 17, 1951), p. 5441.

a committee will refer proposed actions to the representative or senator locally concerned for his consideration and recommendation, thereby, in effect, virtually transferring the veto power to individual members of Congress.

Fifth, it may be pointed out that congressional committees are seldom equipped to conduct the kind of inquiry necessary to ascertain whether proposed executive decisions should be approved, and are often forced to act without adequate information. Furthermore, a committee's attempt to pass judgment upon day-to-day executive decisions may be futile, for such decisions at this stage often can be judged only by executive officers who are in daily touch with operations.

The President should strongly resist attempts by Congress to encroach on the executive functions by extending the legislative or committee veto to executive actions other than reorganization plans. This he may do by the use of his veto power, for which purpose it was designed, and also by forcing a decision on the constitutionality of the committee veto before that device becomes any more firmly established.

It is unfortunate that a test case on this matter has not (as of 1963) been taken to the courts, a move which only the President can instigate. Congress should exercise its great powers in the manner sanctioned by the Constitution. It has adequate means whereby it can exercise all needful and desirable legislative oversight of the activities of the executive departments. There are doubtless subjects on which advance reports to Congress of major executive decisions are justified, but this requirement should be used sparingly so as not to weaken the administrative arm and impair executive accountability.

9

Control by Investigation

THROUGHOUT ITS HISTORY, Congress has relied on investigation of administration as one of its tools for exercising control over the executive departments. Since the end of World War II, however, this particular tool has increased greatly in importance as a technique of legislative oversight, partly because of the impetus given to committee in vestigations by several provisions of the Legislative Reorganization Act of 1946, which were based on major recommendations in the 1946 report of the La Follette-Monroney Joint Committee on the Organization of Congress.

To equip Congress with better facilities for "surveillance" of the execution of the laws, the report proposed (Part I, Recommendation 4) "that the standing committees of both houses be directed and empowered to carry on continuing review and oversight of legislation and agencies within their jurisdiction; that the subpoena be given them; and that the practice of creating special investigating committees be abandoned"; further (Recommendation 9) "that each reorganized legislative committee be authorized to employ four staff experts in each particular province . . . qualifying under prescribed standards." In support of its recommendations the Joint Committee stated:

> While the Constitution directed the separation of powers between the executive and legislative branches, it did not intend them to go separate ways and in opposite directions. Each year the gulf between Capitol Hill and the departments widens. And without effective legislative oversight of the activities of the vast executive branch,

249

the line of democracy wears thin. Only one man out of 3,000,000 Federal employees is elected by and is directly responsible to the people.[1]

The Legislative Reorganization Act as signed into law by President Truman on August 2, 1946, embodies most of the substance of these proposals and others pertaining to them (to be discussed later in this chapter), except for the abandonment of special investigating committees. In the form passed by the Senate, the act prohibited special committees, but the House struck the provision out; nevertheless, the spirit of the act gave firm statutory approval to investigations by standing committees, and in successive years after 1946 the use of special committees noticeably diminished, especially in the Senate.

Thus strengthened in staff and authority, the standing committees of both houses were equipped to participate in the great expansion of congressional investigation that has marked the period since 1946. In this chapter, after reviewing the history of the investigatory function, we will be concerned especially with these recent trends and with a question that takes its reference from both past and recent experience: are committee investigations the most efficient means of inquiring into administrative problems?

The importance and utility of congressional investigations of administration as a safeguard against executive maladministration, incompetence, and abuse of authority cannot be gainsaid, just as it cannot be denied that maintaining such a safeguard is a duty charged to Congress by the Constitution. But it can be—and has repeatedly been—questioned whether a form of investigation that runs the risk of being unduly influenced by partisan considerations is an effective or even a permissible way to discharge a constitutional obligation. Committee investigations always run this risk, despite the fact, as our review will show, that some of them have been of great benefit to administration. Over the years, a number of critics have advanced various proposals for wider delegation of the investigative function and for other reforms. These will be discussed at the end of the chapter.

[1] *Report of the Joint Committee on the Organization of Congress*, Senate Report No. 1011, 79th Cong., 2d sess. (March 1946), pp. 5, 9, and 6.

Early History of Investigations:
1792-1861

The first congressional investigation of administration was conducted in the spring of 1792, when the House of Representatives decided to look into the disastrous defeat of General St. Clair's expedition against certain Indian tribes in the Northwest Territory. On March 27, an initial resolution requesting President Washington to institute the inquiry was voted down as a violation of the separation of powers. The House then adopted a resolution to establish a select committee to make an investigation, a move that was defended by James Madison on the ground that Congress had the right to conduct investigations respecting the expenditure of public money.

The select committee's first action was to call upon Secretary of War Henry Knox for all original letters, orders, and other papers relating to the expedition. Knox laid the request before President Washington, who called a meeting of the Cabinet to consider the matter. On April 2 the Cabinet decided unanimously that it was within the province of the House to conduct such inquiries and to call for papers, and that the President ought to submit "such papers as the public good would permit" and ought to refuse those the disclosure of "which would injure the public,"[2] a rule which succeeding Presidents have followed. It was agreed that all of the papers relating to the St. Clair expedition should be produced, and Washington instructed the Secretary of War accordingly.

The report of the investigation, which was submitted by the select committee to the House on May 8, 1792, absolved General St. Clair and placed the blame on the War Department—especially the quartermaster and contractors—for gross mismanagement, neglect, and delays in supplying the necessary equipment, clothing, and munitions. The report was never acted upon by Congress, and the Federalists in the house prevented its publication, because they thought it reflected on Secretaries Knox and Hamilton. For twenty years St. Clair pled in

[2] *Papers of Thomas Jefferson,* Vol. 1 (1950 ed.), pp. 189-190.

vain for its publication as his exoneration. For twenty years also, Congress rejected his claim for reimbursement of a considerable amount of personal funds which he had advanced out of his own pocket during the campaign. Finally a pension of $60 per month was voted him—not long before his death. Many years later Congress voted a substantial sum to his heirs.[3]

This first congressional inquiry into an action of the Executive branch is of significance because it set precedents for subsequent investigations. It established the right of Congress to investigate administration and to send for papers, and the right of the President to withhold papers which he regarded as not in the public interest to supply. Partisan considerations probably led to the creation of the investigating committee, and most certainly prevented the publication of the report. Here too a pattern for the work of subsequent investigations was being set.

Until 1861, however, relatively little use was made of investigations. During the first twenty-five years of the new government, for example, only thirty investigations were conducted, all but three by the House.[4] Most of these were concerned with the traditional privileges of a legislature, such as charges against members, but a few related to conduct of the departments. In 1800, Oliver Wolcott, Secretary of the Treasury, demonstrated that the Executive branch acknowledged the right of Congress to inquire into the expenditures of public moneys when he requested and secured an investigation by the House of his administration because of the criticisms that had been made of it. A select committee absolved him of all charges of misconduct.[5]

Andrew Jackson, like several later Presidents, vigorously resisted some of the investigations of his administration. In January 1837 a House committee's request for information of various kinds, including lists of all officers or agents or deputies appointed without "authority of law," and of all "innovations" made without legal authority, evoked a blistering letter from the President in which he stated that the committee was assuming that he and the heads of departments were guilty of the "charges alleged" and was calling upon them to furnish the evidence to convict themselves. Likening the inquiry to a Spanish inquisi-

[3] The above account is based largely on Telford Taylor, *Grand Inquest* (1955), Chap. 2.
[4] Marshall Edward Dimock, *Congressional Investigating Committee* (1929), p. 58.
[5] Ernest J. Eberling, *Congressional Investigations* (1928), p. 53.

tion, he made it clear that he esteemed it his "sacred duty" to resist "all such attempts as an invasion of the principles of justice, as well as of the Constitution." Six of the nine members of the committee agreed with him and voted to drop the inquiry, reporting that, so far as the investigation had revealed, the departments had been conducted with ability and integrity.[6]

The Joint Committee on the Conduct of the Civil War

Military operations have always been a favorite field for investigations by Congress; only the Spanish-American War of 1898 escaped, owing to the timely establishment of an inquiry by President McKinley before Congress was able to act. One of the most famous of such inquiries was carried on by the Joint Committee on the Conduct of the Civil War. Authorized in December 1861 by a concurrent resolution giving it sweeping powers, the committee ranged far and wide, investigating "past, present, and future—defeats, the orders of executive departments, the actions of generals in the field, and the questions of war policies."[7]

During the summer and autumn of 1861 the radical Republicans in Congress had become sorely dissatisfied with President Lincoln's conduct of the war and with his refusal to utilize his war powers to abolish slavery. Apparently obsessed with the fear that a cabal of Democratic and conservative Republican generals would establish a military dictatorship, they demanded that generals be placed in charge who shared their radical views, and chafed at any delay.

When Congress met in December, motions were immediately introduced in both houses to establish a select committee to investigate the causes of the Union disasters at Bull Run and Ball's Bluff. In the Senate the radical leaders disagreed among themselves as to the nature of the committee—some considering it futile to explore the causes and asking for an agency that would put pressure on the President and the generals to conduct the war in the manner the agency determined. Several other Republican senators opposed a congressional investigation of military activities as a dangerous innovation, and Senator Lafayette S. Foster of Connecticut denounced it as an invasion of the

[6] *Ibid.*, pp. 134-142.
[7] This account of the joint committee is based largely on the careful, scholarly work of T. Harry Williams, *Lincoln and the Radicals* (1941); the quotation is from p. 63.

President's powers as commander in chief, and predicted that it would lead to confusion in the army: "We cannot have men in the field fighting a battle, and have them here in our committee rooms testifying as to who was to blame for a disaster." Finally, Senator John Sherman of Ohio successfully urged the creation of a "committee of inquiry into the general conduct of the war."[8]

The House accepted the bill embodying the suggestion without debate. Although those who had advocated the committee had asserted that its only purpose would be to advance the war effort, it was very soon turned into an instrument to advance the aims of the radicals. It consisted of four members from the House and three from the Senate, with Senator "Bluff Ben" Wade of Ohio as chairman. Not one of the seven had had military training or experience, but that deterred none of them from investigating military operations and passing judgment on military plans and strategy. The committee pressed Lincoln to remove generals who were not to its liking, especially Democrats and conservatives, and appoint persons of its own choosing. It demanded information about plans, insisting that the Army had no right to withhold such information; officers refusing to comply with the demands met with committee disfavor. Subordinates were encouraged to criticize the actions of their superiors. Secret meetings were supposed to be the rule, but information was divulged whenever it would work to the advantage of the radical machine. The sessions with Lincoln were often stormy; when the President felt that his position was strong he resisted the demands, but at other times he was obliged to yield. In only one area, that of procurement of military supplies, did the investigations contribute to the war's success. The committee's role is summed up by Williams as follows:

> It represented a full-throated attempt on the part of Congress to control the executive's prosecution of the war. In another and more realistic sense, the Committee was the implemented agency by which the radical faction hoped to direct the military struggle for the attainment of its own partisan ends. The bold and skillful machine politicians of the Committee were determined that it should be more than a mere fact-finding body. Wade announced that its function was to secure for Congress, and the radicals, a dominating voice in the conduct of the war and the formulation of war policies.[9]

[8] *Ibid.*, pp. 62-63.
[9] *Ibid.*, p. 71.

Lincoln himself is reported to have said to Ward Hill Lamon:

> I have never faltered in my faith of being ultimately able to suppress this rebellion and of reuniting this divided country; but this improvised vigilant committee to watch my movements and to keep me straight, appointed by Congress and called the "committee on the conduct of the war," is a marplot, and its greatest purpose seems to be to hamper my action and obstruct military operations.[10]

Exposés and Scrutiny: 1869-1900

During Ulysses S. Grant's eight years in office, congressional investigations soared. The high water mark was reached in the last two years of his second term, when the Democrats captured control of the House and an unprecedented resolution was adopted authorizing its standing committees on appropriations, foreign affairs, military affairs, and several others to conduct investigations of executive departments within their respective jurisdictions.[11] Special committee inquiries had been in process also. Altogether, between 1869 and 1877, Congress undertook thirty-seven inquiries into charges of maladministration. The large number was in part a response to the widespread charges of corruption and fraud and in part a genuine effort to seek remedies for poor administration and to achieve economy and efficiency. However, the investigations did little to restore the prestige of Congress, some of whose outstanding members had been involved in the Crédit Mobilier scandal. The following administration, that of President Hayes, was noted for its honesty and efficiency and witnessed a comparative cessation of inquiries.[12]

The first of the special committees of the Grant period was the Joint Select Committee on Retrenchment (1869-1871), headed by Senator James W. Patterson of New Hampshire, a former member of the House from a rural district and a man without executive experience, who was later recommended for expulsion from the Senate because of his involvement in the Crédit Mobilier scandal. The committee inquired into offices that could be abolished, salaries that could be reduced, persons unnecessarily employed, and expenses that could be curtailed. Con-

---

[10] Quoted in J. G. Randall, *Lincoln the President: Midstream* (1952), p. 134.
[11] Wilfred E. Brinkley, *President and Congress* (1947), pp. 169-170, citing *Congressional Record*, 44th Cong., 1st sess. (1876), p. 414.
[12] *Ibid.*, pp. 169-171.

cerned with economy rather than administrative reform, it gave particular attention to the customs service or delved into specific transactions, such as the lease of real estate or the sale of a revenue cutter. "Although invited to make recommendations on the reform of the civil service, the committee refrained from this unpleasant task."[13]

The Patterson joint committee was followed by a Senate committee whose duty "was to examine the several branches of the civil service 'with a view to the reorganization of the Departments,' a phrase that carried a connotation much less than a later generation was to understand."[14] The chairman was Senator George S. Boutwell, who as a House member from 1863 to 1869 had been a leading member of the radical Republicans; he had also been a governor of Massachusetts, Commissioner of Internal Revenue under Lincoln, and Grant's Secretary of the Treasury from 1869 to 1873. To start the committee business off, Boutwell had personal conferences with heads of the departments and agencies and then submitted a set of questions to each of them. According to Leonard White, the committee succeeded no better than the Patterson group in "advancing the art of administration. Its purpose appears to have been more constructive, but it quickly became lost in details that overshadowed any likelihood of a deeply ranging inquiry."[15]

In the third year of President Hayes' term, the Senate tried again to bring about improvement in the details of administration. This time a committee asked the departments to suggest changes in the laws that would contribute to economy and efficiency and to propose other improvements. White has summarized the committee's work thus:

> Although the Senate resolution suggested, if none too clearly, the concept of management in broad terms, the agencies failed to respond in this frame of reference. The committee recommendations, like those of its predecessors, were concerned with immediate practical detail. They revealed no sense of management or of system. The conclusion to be drawn was that this type of procedure was not likely to be productive of ideas other than those parochial in their application.[16]

Complaints about delays in the handling of department business continued to mount. In 1887 the Senate appointed another committee, with Senator Francis M. Cockrell of Missouri as chairman, "to inquire

---

[13] Leonard D. White, *The Republican Era* (1958), pp. 84-85.
[14] *Ibid.*, p. 86.
[15] *Ibid.*
[16] *Ibid.*, p. 87.

into and examine the methods of business and work in the Executive Departments." The departments were called upon to furnish the committee with detailed information about their work, procedures, business transacted each year, arrearages, internal organization, number of employees, and various other data. The volume of facts that resulted swamped the committee, which had no staff. Its subsequent report said much about unnecessary forms, duplication, useless papers, excessive employees, office methods, and laxness, but had no general remedies to prescribe for these shortcomings. Nearly all of the bureau chiefs blamed their difficulties on the lack of clerks; the committee, however, insisting that the remedy was not more clerks but greater efficiency, proposed longer hours of work—a formula that found little favor with the departments.

Next, the committee hit upon the device of asking two of the largest departments, Treasury and War, to set up departmental committees to consider and revise the methods of business. This appears to be the first recognition by Congress that the task of improving the organization and management of the departments could be performed by the agencies themselves.[17] Most of the recommendations of these departmental committees were put into effect by administrative action. The only legislative achievement of the Cockrell committee was a bill authorizing the departments, with the approval of a joint committee of Congress, to dispose of useless papers; the bill became law on February 16, 1889.[18]

Complaints about administrative delay and inefficiency were still rife. In 1893 Congress established a joint commission, headed by a seasoned House member, Alexander M. Dockery of Missouri, to make another inquiry into department operations and methods. The Dockery Commission was authorized to employ not more than three experts and to secure details of employees from the executive departments. Three outstanding accountants, including Charles W. Haskins and Elijah W. Sells, leading pioneers in the "modern" science of accountancy, were engaged. The commission issued numerous staff studies recommending many improvements in specific work methods and accounting procedures, and a good deal of useful legislation resulted, but it had almost nothing to say "of the art of administration." Once more little had

[17] *Ibid.*, pp. 87-89.
[18] See Oscar Kraines, "The Cockrell Committee, 1887-1889," *Western Political Quarterly*, Vol. 4 (December 1951), pp. 583-609, especially pp. 600-601.

been added to "the meager store of recorded doctrine. . . . The experts . . . transferred little of their expertness . . . to their study of government."[19]

World War I and the Harding Administration

The next spurt of investigations by Congress occurred at the end of World War I, after the Republicans captured control of the House in the 1918 election. During the ensuing 66th Congress approximately 250 resolutions were introduced calling for alleged mismanagement of the war effort to be investigated by special or standing committees; 51 of them were approved. By the time of the 1920 election, however, the public had tired of the futile inquiries.[20] The investigating activities of Congress subsided—but not for long.

The new surge of inquiries involved not only what was termed "the greatest political scandal of this or any generation"[21]—the juggling of the Teapot Dome and Elks Hill oil leases—but also a number of other cases of fraudulent dealing. When the 1923 and 1924 investigations by Senate committees of various aspects of the Harding administration were over, two members of the original Harding Cabinet had been forced out of office—one because of proven charges of corruption, the other because of incompetence—and a former member was also found corrupt; the head of the Veterans' Bureau had been dismissed, and would later be sentenced to prison; and several lesser government officials had been shown to be involved in dealings that later brought grand jury investigations. Echoes of the furore resounded in other investigations and court trials during most of the untainted Coolidge administration.[22]

Suspicions of wrongdoing in various departments of the government

[19] White, *op. cit.*, p. 91.
[20] "If the Civil War Committee . . . had been dangerous . . . the committees after World War I were futile." See Jonathan Daniels, *The Man of Independence* (1950), p. 222.
[21] Comment of Cordell Hull. Although Hull was at the time chairman of the Democratic National Committee and understandably partisan, the statement is hardly an exaggeration.
[22] The following account draws on the doctoral dissertation of William W. Young, "Congressional Investigations of the Federal Administration" (University of California, 1955), Chap. 5.

had flourished all through the first year of Harding's incumbency. In 1922 attempts to authorize investigations of the administration were blocked in the House by the Republican majority under tight party control, but in the Senate the Democrats and insurgent Republicans, who together constituted a majority, were able to force the issue. On April 29, 1922, a resolution introduced by Senator Robert M. La Follette of Wisconsin authorizing the Committee on Public Lands and Surveys to investigate the entire subject of the leases of naval oil resources was passed by the Senate without a dissenting vote. The chairman of the committee was Senator Reed Smoot of Utah, a conservative Republican, but Democrat Thomas J. Walsh, Senator from Montana, took charge of the investigation, and for a year and a half proceeded alone to make an analysis of the lease of the Teapot Dome reserve and all of the facts relating to it.

When the oil lease hearings were opened in October 1923, about two months after President Harding's death, Walsh was prepared to conduct a thorough examination of the witnesses. At the outset the inquiry was concerned with the legality and expediency of the leases, but evidence reached Walsh that former Secretary of the Interior Albert B. Fall, who had earlier been in financial straits, now seemed to have a great deal of money, and with some trepidation he followed this lead until conclusive evidence was secured of the bribery of Fall by Harry F. Sinclair and Edward F. Doheny in the form of loans. The case rocked the country from one end to another. Fall was later convicted of accepting a bribe. Secretary of the Navy Edwin Denby was forced to resign for his incompetence in permitting the naval reserves to be transferred to the Interior Department, and for entering no objection to the leases.

On the heels of this inquiry came an investigation of Attorney General Harry M. Daugherty conducted by a special committee headed by Senator Burton K. Wheeler of Montana, which exposed the full corruption of the "Ohio gang" and led President Coolidge to request Daugherty to resign. In all, as a careful student of the investigations of the period has reported,

    . . . a blizzard of congressional investigations swept the national Capital. . . . Scarcely a corner of the administration escaped inquisition. . . . Upwards of two-score inquests were instituted by Congress, through its committees, into the official behavior of the executive branch of the national government.[23]

When the charges of corruption among the members of the Cabinet and other high officials began to be aired, a loud protest was raised in the press. The *New York Times* called Senators Walsh and Wheeler "assassins of character"; the *New York Tribune* labeled them "scandal-mongers." A law school dean denounced them in even more severe terms: ". . . senatorial debauch of investigations—poking into political garbage cans and dragging the sewers of political intrigue . . . the level of professional searchers of municipal dunghills."[24] The investigating committees were charged with taking testimony from disreputable characters, airing rumors and gossip, admitting irrelevant charges, conducting "fishing expeditions" for partisan advantage, and, in general, not following the procedures and rules of evidence of a court. It is true that many voluntary witnesses had been permitted to testify without proper screening, but there could be little if any doubt that the findings were supported by the evidence.

Other critics claimed that the investigations had monopolized the attention of the Senate at the expense of more important legislative business. Senator William E. Borah called upon the committees to end the inquiries so that the Senate could return to its main duty. Various proposals were made to curb congressional investigations and to require the committees to function more in accordance with the rules of a court of law—to all of which Professor Felix Frankfurter of Harvard Law School replied:

> The procedure of congressional investigation should remain as it is. No limitations should be imposed by congressional legislation or standing rules. The power of investigation should be left untrammeled, and the methods and forms of each investigation should be left for the determination of Congress and its committees, as each situation arises. The safeguards against abuse and folly are to be looked for in the forces of responsibility which are operating from within Congress, and are generated from without.[25]

[23] George B. Galloway, "The Investigative Function of Congress," *American Political Science Review*, Vol. 21 (February 1927), p. 47.

[24] John H. Wigmore, "Legislative Power to Compel Testimonial Disclosure," *Illinois Law Review*, Vol. 19 (February 1925), pp. 453-454.

[25] "Hands Off Investigations," *New Republic*, Vol. 39 (May 21, 1924), p. 330.

Recent Trends

After the sensations of the mid-1920's, the wave of investigations receded, but within a few years it began to build up into the surge that by the 1950's established the investigative function as a major activity of Congress, especially in the Senate, and one of the most potent forms of control over the executive departments. The rate of growth, however, always followed an uneven course, conditioned by various factors such as wars and other national and international events, by changes in policies, personnel, or rules in the House and Senate, and especially by the party balance between White House and Capitol Hill. The rate has usually expanded in periods when a majority in either house was in opposition to the President, especially when the President was weak or surrounded himself with an incompetent Cabinet, and receded when the President commanded the support of a majority in both houses.

During Franklin D. Roosevelt's first term few investigations of administration were conducted, but a number of inquiries were instituted to advance the President's program in various fields. In his second term, Congress began looking into the activities of a number of the newer agencies, among them, in 1938, the Works Progress Administration (the Sheppard committee) and the Tennessee Valley Authority. The WPA investigation uncovered political manipulation of work relief in certain states, and was partially responsible for the later passage of the Hatch Act; the investigation of the TVA led to a divided report along party lines, but nevertheless cleared the agency of charges of maladministration. In 1943 the House of Representatives set up the Smith committee—the Select Committee to Investigate Acts of Executive Agencies beyond the scope of their authority—which issued a series of severely critical reports on such agencies as the Office of Price Administration, the War Labor Board, and the National Labor Relations Board.

The Truman Committee

After the United States entered World War II, several inquiries were made into the mobilization of the country for defense. The most important of these was conducted by the Truman committee. Taking heed of the lesson to be learned from the Committee on the Conduct of the Civil War, Senator Harry S. Truman of Missouri steered the investigation away from any attempt to pass judgment on military policy and operations. Instead, the committee worked closely with the defense departments and war agencies, in an effort to expedite industrial mobilization and production; it sought to discover and put a stop to wasteful practices rather than to capture headlines. It was careful of its facts and most of its recommendations had already been put into effect before it published its findings. Consisting largely of freshman senators who were able to devote much of their time to the investigation, the group worked hard to ferret out practices that were injuring the war effort.

Perhaps no congressional committee in the history of the country was ever more effective in bringing about needed improvements in administration and large savings in money, personnel, and materiel. The great speed with which industrial production for war was put into high gear, as well as the rapid expansion of the military facilities, required enormous expenditures within a short period of time. Customary procedures and safeguards were streamlined in the interest of speed; as a result, shocking waste and faulty administration were widespread. It was this type of situation that the Truman committee undertook to investigate, and it did so boldly, demanding improved management, more careful planning, the exercise of greater prudence and better judgment, and the avoidance of waste. It is of interest that the British Parliament utilized a similar National Expenditures Committee to check on the huge wartime expenditures, with similar results.

Many factors contributed to the Truman committee's success. The chairman was well equipped to direct such an inquiry; an able staff was recruited; investigations were conducted in an eminently fair manner; the committee secured the cooperation of the executive departments by working with them, avoiding sensational charges, and checking the facts before giving out any reports—and as a result it had the support of the administration, and its work was warmly endorsed by the heads of the departments whose activities it investigated. It is hardly necessary to point out that some of these factors were due in large part to the fact that the country was at war, and would seldom be present in peacetime. Nevertheless, the committee's conduct of its investigation can stand as a model of usefulness.

The Investigation Explosion

The very great and continuing expansion of congressional investigations in the postwar period was due to a number of factors. When the Republicans captured control of Congress in 1946, it was virtually a political obligation to set about discrediting the Democratic administration through investigations—with an eye to the 1948 elections. Deterioration of United States relations with the Soviet Union in the first few years after the war's end generated concern about the dangers of communism throughout the country, and brought about a climate of suspicion in which a number of large-scale investigations of communist infiltration and allied subjects were mounted. President Truman's second term afforded his opponents in Congress—in both parties—the opportunity to exploit conflict-of-interest scandals for partisan advantage. The return of the Democrats to control of Congress after the first two years of the Eisenhower administration again set the stage for a further increase of investigations. (However, the fact that, even when the Republicans controlled both houses during the first two years of the Eisenhower administration, investigations continued in large numbers suggests that congressional inquiries had become more a habit than a political necessity.)

As pointed out at the beginning of this chapter, the "legislative oversight" provisions of the Legislative Reorganization Act of 1946 gave great impetus to investigations by directing every standing committee of Congress to conduct a continuous review of the work of agencies under their jurisdiction. In addition, both the House and the Senate Committee on Expenditures in Executive Departments (later changed to Government Operations) were authorized to conduct investigations of any government activity. All standing committees of the Senate were given authority to subpoena witnesses, to require the production of papers, and to spend up to $10,000 during each Congress. Four standing committees of the House—Appropriations, Government Operations, Un-American Activities, and Rules—were granted the authority to subpoena witnesses and call for papers; other House committees were required to secure special authorization of investigations before they could exercise these powers.[26]

[26] 60 Stat. 832.

The increase in committee staffs authorized by the act enabled the standing committees to exercise far greater oversight of the departments than formerly. In recent years certain committees, especially House and Senate Government Operations and the House Un-American Activities, have been concerned almost wholly with the conduct of investigations, and the Senate Judiciary Committee and the House Appropriations Committee have carried on many large-scale investigations. The other standing committees, however, have used their staffs largely on legislative matters and have employed special staffs when undertaking investigations.

Although statistics on the number of congressional inquiries are not a valid measurement of the investigative activity of Congress, since investigations may vary so greatly in importance, the numerical increase over the years since 1789 provides interesting food for thought. From 1789 to 1925, 285 investigations were conducted by Congress (not including those not officially reported); of these, 100 were conducted between 1919 and 1925.[27] From 1929 to 1938, 146 were authorized.[28] In the first session of the 79th Congress, just preceding the passage of the 1946 Reorganization Act, at least 50 inquiries were voted.[29] A majority of all investigations up to and including those last mentioned were carried on by special or select committees; after 1946, of course, the proportion conducted by standing committees was enlarged. The 82d Congress (1950-1951) was responsible for 236 probes, the 83d, 215. Corresponding statistics for later years are not available, but the continuously mounting cost of investigations (see below) indicates there has been no decline.

Cost of Investigations

In the earlier history of Congress, as we have seen, most investigations were conducted without special funds and without the aid of staff assistants. The total cost of the Senate's investigative activity during the decade 1910-1919 was $330,000. House expenditures were even

[27] Galloway, op. cit., p. 48.

[28] M. Nelson McGeary, "Congressional Investigations: Historical Development," University of Chicago Law Review, Vol. 18 (1951), p. 425. See also McGeary's book, The Developments of Congressional Investigative Power (1940).

[29] Floyd M. Riddick, The United States Congress: Organization and Procedure (1949), p. 27.

less, since during this period the Senate conducted most of the important investigations. For the next seven years, from 1920 to 1926, the Senate total was $1,053,500; $290,000 of this was spent in 1925, at the height of the investigations of the Harding administration.[30] There was little further increase through 1940, when the Senate spent $170,267 for inquiries, but during the next decade the expenditures mounted rapidly, especially after the passage of the Legislative Reorganization Act. In 1952, $1,639,040 was used—almost ten times the 1940 figure.

As indicated by the tabulation below of investigation funds voted to committees, the leaps-and-bounds increase generated by the 1946 act has continued. The totals cited include the annual $10,000 that each standing committee of the Senate and the Select Small Business Committee automatically receive and the special authorizations for investigations by House and Senate standing committees and several select and special committees. They do not include the funds for each of the two Appropriations Committees, which together annually receive around $900,000, or those for six joint committees (including the Joint Atomic Energy Committee), which amount annually to around $1 million, a large proportion of which is used for investigations.[31]

	Authorized	Spent
83d Congress (1953-55)	$ 8,175,394	$ 5,354,681
84th Congress (1955-57)	9,309,205	7,062,407
85th Congress (1957-59)	12,118,280	9,717,797
86th Congress (1959-61)	15,463,520	11,653,231

The committees which received the largest amounts for investigations in the 86th Congress were as follows:[32]

Senate

Judiciary	$3,192,500
Interstate and Foreign Commerce	1,161,020
Appropriations	380,000
Government Operations	915,000
Foreign Relations	705,000

[30] The statistics were placed in the *Congressional Record*, Vol. 67, Pt. 4, 69th Cong., 1st sess. (Feb. 17, 1926), p. 4159, by Senator Warren, chairman of the Senate Appropriations Committee.
[31] See *Congressional Quarterly Almanac*, Vol. 11 (1955), p. 502; Vol. 13 (1957), p. 773; Vol. 17 (1961), p. 995. (The 1961 spending figures are given as of Dec. 31, 1961.)
[32] See *ibid.*, Vol. 17 (1961), pp. 994-995.

House

Government Operations	$1,040,000
Appropriations	500,000
Interstate and Foreign Commerce	750,000
Un-American Activities	654,000
Public Works	475,000

The above figures relate only to special appropriations for investigations and do not include the expenditures for committee staffs and other items, part of which should be included in the cost of investigations. The appropriation for the regular staff of the two houses in 1960 totaled over $40 million. In addition, personnel are often borrowed from the departments and executive agencies without reimbursement. The Comptroller General's Office reports the loan of staff to congressional committees involving approximately a half million dollars of staff time annually, only a small part of which is reimbursed.[33] Similar reports are not available for the FBI and various other agencies from which investigating staff is often borrowed. It should be noted also that the largest share of the cost of investigations is that of the executive departments in assembling the requested data and in preparing for department presentations. Even a seemingly simple inquiry or questionnaire submitted by an investigating committee or its staff may require months of work by the departments concerned. As with an iceberg, only a small part of the cost of investigations is visible.

The phenomenal rise in the funds authorized for inquiries since the end of World War I is highly significant. Even more than the number of investigations, it indicates that the investigative process has become an increasingly important aspect of the work of Congress and is considered by Congress itself as one of the most potent means whereby it can exercise control over administration.

The Authority of Congress
To Require Information

The power of Congress to conduct investigations relating to the conduct of the executive departments has never been successfully challenged throughout the history of the country. In the famous case of *Kilbourn* v. *Thompson* (1880), the Supreme Court narrowly construed

[33] See Comptroller General, *Annual Report . . . 1959*, p. 274.

the congressional authority to inquire into private affairs not directly related to legislation and to punish recalcitrant witnesses for contempt, but the case did not concern the power to investigate the conduct of the executive departments.[34] The latter power was affirmed in the case of *McGrain* v. *Daugherty* (1927), when the Supreme Court held that Congress could compel Mally S. Daugherty, Ohio banker and brother of the former Attorney General, to testify.[35] Interpreting broadly the investigative powers of Congress, the Court in unanimous decision held: ". . . the two houses of Congress . . . possess not only such powers as are expressly granted to them by the Constitution, but such auxiliary powers as are necessary and appropriate to make the express powers effective."[36]

The Issue of Executive Discretion

The power of the President—and of departments, acting under his instructions—to withhold confidential papers called for by Congress and its committees and to refuse to disclose the nature of consultations by the President with other executive officers has been at issue many times, beginning with the St. Clair investigation in 1792. The general rule on which President Washington and his Cabinet determined ("the Executive ought to communicate such papers as the public good would permit, and ought to refuse those the disclosure of which would endanger the public") has stood as the best statement of principle under which a President exercises discretion in responding to congressional requests for executive papers and testimony. In 1796, Washington applied the principle when he refused to submit to the House the correspondence with and instructions to John Jay regarding the treaty negotiated with England; many later Presidents followed the precedent.

The right of a President to withhold information when he considers its disclosure would be contrary to the public interest has often been challenged in Congress, but so far has held its well-established ground. The issue became particularly heated in 1948 after President Truman ordered that loyalty investigations of federal employees were to be treated as confidential and hence would not be supplied to committees except with the specific approval of the President. A joint resolution

[34] 103 U. S. 168.
[35] 273 U. S. 135.
[36] *Ibid.*, p. 173.

was introduced by the House, directing executive departments to make available to congressional committees any information deemed by them to be necessary for their work, but it was not acted on by the Senate. There were several later occasions when Truman and executive officers acting under his directions refused to supply requested information; one of the most notable of these was the refusal of General Omar Bradley in 1951 to divulge the conversations between President Truman and his advisers concerning the removal of General Douglas MacArthur.[37]

Conversations and communications between the President and members of his Cabinet and other top executive officials and advisers have usually been regarded as confidential, but from time to time Congress has asked for this type of information. In 1833, when the Senate requested President Jackson to transmit to it a paper alleged to have been read to his Cabinet concerning the removal of deposits from the United States Bank, he indignantly replied:

> The Executive is a coordinate and independent branch of the Government equally with the Senate, and I have yet to learn under what constitutional authority that branch of the legislature has a right to require of me an account of any communication, either verbally or in writing, made to the heads of departments acting as a Cabinet council. As well might I be required to detail to the Senate the free and private conversations I have held with those officers on any subject relating to their duties and my own.[38]

One of the most sweeping presidential directives instructing executive officers to withhold such communications from congressional committees was issued by President Eisenhower during the McCarthy investigation of Fort Monmouth in 1954. In a letter to the Secretary of Defense the President stated:

> Because it is essential to efficient and effective administration that employees of the executive branch be in a position to be completely candid in advising with each other on official matters, and because it is not in the public interest that any of their conversations or communications, or any documents or reproductions, concerning such advice be disclosed, you will instruct employees of your Department

[37] Many similar instances are cited in a 1954 memorandum of the Attorney General; see *Congressional Record*, Vol. 100, Pt. 5, 83d Cong., 2d sess. (May 17, 1954), pp. 6621-6623; see also Vol. 101, Pt. 9, 84th Cong., 1st sess. (July 26, 1955), pp. 11458-11462.

[38] Quoted in *Congressional Record*, Vol. 67, Pt. 4 (Feb. 25, 1926), p. 4549.

that in all their appearances before the subcommittee of the Senate Committee on Government Operations regarding the inquiry now before it they are not to testify to any such communications or to produce any such documents or reproductions. This principle must be maintained regardless of who would be benefited by such disclosures.[39]

The issue arose again in 1958, when the International Cooperation Administration declined to furnish the General Accounting Office and investigating committees of Congress with copies of confidential evaluative reports on its operations in Laos, Pakistan, and certain other countries. Congress countered the following year by attaching an amendment to the Foreign Aid Authorization Bill requiring the ICA to supply all documents, reports, etc., requested by the GAO or by committees. Although President Eisenhower signed the bill, he added a statement that the amendment could not "alter the recognized constitutional duty and power of the Executive with respect to the disclosure of information, documents, and other materials," and declined to put the amendment into effect.

A principal reason for presidential refusals to supply informal communications was first voiced by Thomas Jefferson in 1807 when he declined to submit to the House certain papers in his possession concerning the Burr conspiracy:

> It is chiefly in the form of letters, often containing such a mixture of rumors, conjectures, and suspicions as renders it difficult to sift out the real facts and unadvisable to hazard more than general outlines. . . . In this state of the evidence, delivered sometimes, too, under the restriction of private confidence, neither safety nor justice will permit exposing names.[40]

Evaluation of Investigations

The importance of legislative investigations of administration was eloquently stated by Woodrow Wilson in his classic study of Congress written in 1883-1884—a time when the Congress was ill equipped to carry out this function:

[39] *Congressional Record,* Vol. 100, Pt. 5, 83rd Cong., 2d sess. (May 17, 1954), p. 6621.
[40] James D. Richardson, *Messages and Papers of the Presidents* (1899), Vol. 1, p. 412.

It is the proper duty of a representative body to look diligently into every affair of government and to talk about what it sees. It is meant to be the eyes and the voice, and to embody the wisdom and will of its constituents. Unless Congress have and use every means of acquainting itself with the acts and disposition of the administrative agents of the government, the country must be helpless to learn how it is being served. . . . The informing function of Congress should be preferred even to the legislative function.[41]

Inquiries into administration are a major part of the work of Congress today. They are essential if Congress is to legislate wisely; they are equally important as a means of checking on the work of the departments and of holding executive officers responsible for administration. They provide a necessary—but not the only—safeguard against executive mismanagement and abuse of authority, and the improper use of public funds. The possibility of a congressional investigation acts as a constant deterrrent against improper and unauthorized executive acts; however, since it may also cause executive officers to be unduly cautious and timid, unwilling to take necessary risks or to put innovations into effect, the result may be a wooden and inefficient administration.

Administrative incompetence, faulty administration, and occasionally corruption of executive officers have not infrequently been exposed by investigation; nevertheless, investigations in this area are subject to serious weaknesses. Spurred on by the prospect of publicity and party advantage, committees have often conducted such inquiries with more zeal than discretion, and have been guilty of unfortunate excesses and failure to act in a judicial manner. Undoubtedly, capturing headlines has been at times of more interest to members of committees than ascertaining facts.

Galloway's 1927 study of congressional investigations summed up the weaknesses as follows:

At best, congressional investigation is a blundering, crude, clumsy, and tedious process for getting at the truth, formulating criticism, or achieving effective control. It is an expensive business, though it has on occasions saved the country many times its cost. It is time-consuming, dragging on interminably and diverting the attention of committee members from their other legislative duties. . . . When the facts are finally and fully determined, the matter has lost its news

[41] Wilson, *Congressional Government* (1913 ed.), p. 303.

interest for the public. Inquiry is an instrument unsuited to frequent or continuous employment and justified only by grave circumstances.[42]

Partisanship

Large-scale investigations of alleged mismanagement or improper activities on the part of executive officers are likely to be greatly influenced by partisan considerations. It is not uncommon for such an inquiry to result in reports that divide along party lines, with pro-administration members of the committee absolving the officers of blame, and anti-administration members finding the charges sustained. Partisanship is also often responsible for the initiation of investigations and greatly affects the manner in which they are conducted. According to one student of the process, "A partisan approach is almost inevitable, because the committees are nearly always established to prove or publicize some point of view. As a result, friendly witnesses are allowed free rein and those who hold opposing views are routed and discredited as quickly as possible."[43]

That an investigation can be conducted in a nonpartisan manner was notably proved by the Truman committee during World War II and by its successor, the Senate Preparedness Subcommittee, but it must be said that these constitute somewhat exceptional examples. In Great Britain investigations of administration, whether by parliamentary committees or by Tribunals of Inquiry, are strictly nonpartisan, and their findings are usually accepted without question. Given the nature of the American political system, however, it is doubtful that congressional investigations can ever be divorced from partisanship, except in time of war.

Investigations have often been instituted at the behest of a minority of Congress, even in some instances by a few members who are not interested in a bona fide inquiry into the facts but wish to advance the point of view of a special interest group. For example, the late Senator Patrick A. McCarran of Nevada launched an inquiry into alleged abuses in the administration of grazing lands in 1941, for the sole purpose of preventing any increase in grazing fees. Failing to secure the

[42] "The Investigative Function of Congress," American Political Science Review, Vol. 21 (1927), p. 66.

[43] James A. Perkins, "Congressional Investigations of Matters of International Import," American Political Science Review, Vol. 34 (1940), p. 289.

adoption of an amendment to the Taylor Grazing Act that would prohibit the Grazing Service from raising fees without the approval of the
district advisory board, McCarran accomplished the same purpose by
the threat of an investigation whenever the Service attempted to raise
fees. In 1944 he introduced a resolution, which the Public Lands Committee passed unanimously, demanding that no increase be made in
grazing fees until the committee had completed its investigation. The
Grazing Service found itself caught between opposing committee pressures—the House appropriations subcommittee demanding that the
Service increase grazing fees and threatening to slash its budget if it
did not do so, the Senate Public Lands Committee strenuously opposing any increase in fees, and urging reduced appropriations to the Service to avoid any justification for an increase. The Senate investigations
were used intermittently until 1947 to mobilize the stockmen in their
opposition to increased fees when any attempt was made to raise
them.[44] Similarly, the Forest Service has been investigated at various
times when it attempted to institute regulations and policies opposed
by the stockmen.[45]

A study of nine major investigations of foreign affairs between 1919
and 1940 indicated that "five . . . grew out of the personal predilections
of certain congressmen." Senator Key Pittman of Nevada, for instance,
on behalf of the silver mining interests, conducted an investigation in
1930 of the reduced trade between the United States and China, believing that it was due to the depreciated price of silver in relation to
gold. Senator Albert B. Fall of New Mexico, who had long advocated
intervention in Mexico, launched an investigation in 1919, with the support of Americans who had large holdings in that country, to force such
a policy on the administration.[46]

Effects on Agencies

Investigations at times place a heavy burden of work on executive
departments and agencies. When an agency is being investigated, its
officers must put aside other duties and give virtually full time to the

[44] See Phillip O. Foss, *Politics and Grass: the Administration of the Taylor Grazing
Act* (1960), pp. 179-185.

[45] See Bernard DeVoto, "Sacred Cows and Public Lands," *Harper's Magazine,*
Vol. 197 (July 1948), pp. 44-55.

[46] See Perkins, *op. cit.*, pp. 285-287.

investigation. Important decisions are postponed, morale suffers, and the work of the whole agency is apt to be disrupted. Even when no special inquiry is under way, department heads and other top officers must spend a considerable amount of time testifying before various committees, and even more in preparing for such testimony.[47] When a large-scale inquisition involves charges of mismanagement and maladministration, the work of the agency may be seriously harmed. Many of the charges that are aired may later prove to be wholly unfounded, but in the meantime the agency has suffered a serious loss of public confidence.

Dr. William Alanson White, former head of St. Elizabeths Hospital in Washington, D.C., the federal institution for the treatment of the mentally ill, has recorded his observations of the three full-scale congressional investigations the hospital endured during his administration. Each investigation was concerned with charges of maltreatment of patients and other allegations of mismanagement—charges that were dispelled after lengthy probing. In his temperate and thoughtful account, Dr. White tells of the great tensions which resulted from the interrogation of disgruntled employees and the airing of rumors, suspicions, and grievances—real or fancied—and of how the work of the hospital was disrupted. Each time, however, the outcome of the inquiry strengthened the institution by dispelling the unfounded charges that had been bandied about and enabled it to secure renewed support by Congress. Dr. White commented, "If one is attempting to do a good job honestly and effectively he need have little fear" of the investigating process.[48]

Congressional investigations are a drastic remedy for administrative shortcomings, though at times a necessary remedy. To avoid unwarranted use of a process that is so likely to disrupt the work of the executive agencies, Congress and its committees should make it a practice to institute preliminary inquiries before a full-scale investigation is undertaken. The functions performed by executive departments and agencies are too important for them to be made the football of partisan politics through unnecessary inquisitions.

[47] See Cabell Phillips, "Congress Inquiries Keep Cabinet Officers on the Run," *New York Times* (Feb. 15, 1959), Section 4, p. 7.
[48] *White: The Autobiography of a Purpose* (1938), pp. 92-93.

Inefficiencies

Unless the persons in charge of an investigation have sufficient expert knowledge of a given subject and the necessary available time to conduct a thorough inquiry, the investigative process is an inefficient method of legislative oversight. The few notably successful investigations have been conducted under able leadership and with competent staff assistance. As the activities of government become more complex and technical it is increasingly difficult for members of Congress, already overburdened with legislative and other duties, to acquire the detailed knowledge of a subject and to devote the amount of time that is required for a thorough investigation. Increasingly, investigating committees are forced to place great reliance upon their staffs. One of the merits of the Royal Commissions of Inquiry used in Great Britain is that the persons in charge can be selected for their special qualifications and for their judgment and objectivity, thus assuring a competent inquiry and well-considered findings. Members of these bodies usually devote a large amount of their time to an inquiry.

Most congressional investigating committees usually place great reliance on public hearings as a means of fact-finding. In public hearings, much of the testimony is irrelevant and repetitive and thus of slight value, unless the interrogation of witnesses is skillfully conducted by persons who are fully informed on the subject matter. Hearings need to be preceded by thorough staff work, and witnesses need to be carefully selected to avoid wasting the time of the committee. Though public hearings have their place in legislative inquiries, in many instances other means of fact-finding would be more effective.

The overlapping and duplication of jurisdiction that is a feature of congressional committees may result in the simultaneous investigation of one agency by a number of different committees and subcommittees. In 1957 and 1958, for example, civil aviation was the subject of inquiries of various types by the following: subcommittees of both the Senate and the House Committee on Interstate and Foreign Commerce; two appropriations subcommittees that pass on the appropriations of the Department of Commerce; a special Subcommittee on Legislative Oversight of the House Committee on Interstate and Foreign Commerce; both the Senate and the House Committee on Government Operations; the Senate Judiciary Committee; a special subcommittee of the House Armed Services Committee; and several other appropriations subcommittees. No less than twelve subcommittees were concerned with the work and policies of civil aeronautics agencies.[49]

The splintering of responsibility for inquiries into administration among numerous congressional committees and subcommittees weakens the control that Congress might otherwise exercise, and provides the departments with many legislative controllers. In theory each of the committees is expected to exercise a somewhat different type of control, but in practice questions of program, policy, finance, and efficiency cannot be neatly divided, and when inquiries are undertaken by any one of the various committees they are likely to touch upon all aspects of the work of the department. Investigations need to be more effectively controlled by each house, not only to prevent their misuse but also to assure that inquiries are fairly and efficiently conducted.[50]

Proposed Reforms

Critics of congressional investigations have frequently and urgently recommended that Congress delegate certain types of investigations to other bodies. It is significant to note that the British Parliament, which developed the function of investigation to a fine art and was the "Grand Inquest" of the nation, today conducts relatively few investigations; other bodies are used for this purpose. Preliminary to Parliament's enactment of major legislation, Royal Commissions of Inquiry look into important social, economic, and political problems. "It is probably true to say that since the early part of the 19th century hardly a social, economic, or political statute of any importance has been drafted and introduced into Parliament otherwise than as a result of recommendations of a Royal Commission of Inquiry."[51] Similar commissions are used in Sweden and some other countries for nearly every important legislative reform.

The British government also uses Departmental Committees, which

[49] See Emmette S. Redford, "A Case Analysis of Congressional Activity: Civil Aviation, 1957-58," *Journal of Politics*, Vol. 22 (1960), pp. 228-258.

[50] See Lindsay Rogers, "Congressional Investigations: The Problem and Its Solution," *University of Chicago Law Review*, Vol. 18 (Spring 1951), pp. 464-477.

[51] Herman Finer, "The British System," *University of Chicago Law Review*, Vol. 18 (Spring 1951), p. 554.

are appointed by the government but whose members do not receive a commission from the Crown, to inquire into legislative problems preliminary to the submission of bills to Parliament for its consideration. Investigations of charges of misconduct by officials are conducted by Tribunals of Inquiry, which require the approval of both houses of Parliament. A tribunal is usually headed by a distinguished judge, and may include members of Parliament and others; it possesses the same powers, rights, and privileges as a high court, and conducts proceedings in a judicial manner, with the assistance of counsel. These bodies have been uniformly fair, discriminating, and thorough; their findings have been accepted by Parliament and the public. Appointed to the tribunals by the Crown or the government, the members are chosen for their ability, public esteem, and reputations for fairness and objectivity. The government would be severely criticized if its appointed tribunal did not command public confidence.

The commission system used in New York State is often cited by those who urge Congress to delegate the inquiry function. The governor of New York is authorized by the Moreland Act of 1907 to appoint a commissioner or commissioners, when he so chooses, "to examine and investigate the management and affairs of any department, board, bureau, or commission of the State"; substantial funds are appropriated by the legislature to pay the expenses of such investigations. Commissioners are authorized to subpoena persons and records and to swear witnesses, and can employ counselors and investigators. Their reports are made to the governor for submission to the legislature. Commissioners have usually been men of standing, with reputations to preserve. Professor Lindsay Rogers, who once served as a Moreland Commissioner, reports: "Such men were careful to provide themselves with efficient investigators and counsel and did not seek headlines. Their inquiries have ranged over the whole field of New York State's administration." The legislature has rarely been hostile to such inquiries, and on occasions has called off its own investigation when the governor appointed a commissioner to probe the same subject.[52]

Congress has not looked kindly upon proposals that it delegate part of its investigative function, though on occasion it has created special commissions of inquiry—such as the 1955 Commission on Government Security—and has also participated in joint legislative-executive com-

[52] See Rogers, *op. cit.*, *University of Chicago Law Review*, pp. 471-472.

missions of inquiry, among them the two Hoover Commissions. The reluctance of Congress to go farther in delegating the function or to give the President a general investigative authority comparable to that of the governor of New York is politically understandable, as Senator George Wharton Pepper of Pennsylvania noted in 1931. Such action, he said, would involve the "surrender of a most effective political weapon. . . . The last thing that is desired by the promoters of such an inquiry is the calmness and detachment of a judicial tribunal."[53]

However, it is likely that in the future Congress will be obliged to make increasing use of other bodies to conduct certain types of investigations, partly because the pressure of legislative work does not allow the ranking members sufficient time to direct thorough inquiries, and partly because of the limitations and inefficiency of the present practice for certain areas of inquiry. The enactment of a federal law similar to New York's Moreland Act, authorizing the President to appoint commissions to inquire into charges of maladministration and improper conduct of public officers, would lead to more efficient investigations in this area. Congress would, of course, retain its power to investigate such charges, but might possibly rely in many cases on the commissions' investigations, as the New York legislature has become inclined to do.

It has frequently been proposed that the House and Senate should adopt a code of procedure for their investigating committees, to protect the rights of witnesses and to avoid the excesses that have led to widespread criticism of the investigative process.[54] The House has adopted such a code for its committees, and a number of Senate committees have individually set up their own rules. No code or set of rules, however, is wholly effective, for in the last analysis the actions of an investigating committee are determined by its members, as Senator J. W. Fulbright has pointed out:

> In order to investigate effectively, a congressional committee must have within the field of inquiry assigned to it a virtually unrestrained delegation of this vast congressional power. As a practical matter, this means that the power to investigate is wielded by individuals, not by institutions. . . . This is . . . at once both the weakness and the strength of our legislative processes.[55]

[53] Pepper, *Family Quarrels* (1931), pp. 181-182.
[54] See Galloway, *The Legislative Process in Congress*, Chap. 24.
[55] Fulbright, "Congressional Investigations: Significance for the Legislative Process," *University of Chicago Law Review*, Vol. 18 (Spring 1951), p. 442.

The proper use of the investigative power by a congressional commit-tee depends on the committee's traditions and the self-restraint of its members rather than upon rules of procedure.

It has also been proposed that the Senate and the House each es-tablish more effective controls over the initiation of full-scale investiga-tions. There is hardly a committee or subcommittee in either house which today does not carry on several investigations at every session of Congress. The chairman of the House Rules Committee announced in 1955 that his committee thereafter would scrutinize carefully all re-quests for authorization of special investigations to ascertain exactly what was to be investigated, whether other investigations would thus be duplicated, and whether such inquiry was needed.[56]

In the past, investigations have often been instituted by a minority of members to promote a policy which did not command the support of the majority, or to hamper the administration of programs and poli-cies which Congress has previously approved. Controls are needed to prevent the harassment of the administration for personal or partisan purposes and unwarranted attacks on the policies of the government; they are needed even more to make sure whether proposed investiga-tions are necessary and whether the probable results will justify the cost, the burden placed upon the executive departments, and the in-terference with other legislative functions. Only Congress itself can bring about the reforms in the investigative process that are most needed—the exercise of restraint and the establishment of more effec-tive internal controls.

[56] See the remarks of Representative Howard W. Smith, *Congressional Record*, Vol. 101, Pt. 1, 84th Cong., 1st sess. (Jan. 26, 1955), pp. 778-779.

10

Conclusions

IN THIS CONCLUDING CHAPTER we shall summarize and discuss the major findings of the earlier chapters and, in addition, compare legislative control of administration in the United States and Great Britain. Despite the fundamental differences in the constitutional systems of the two nations, some comparisons will be useful, though it is not suggested that the institutions and practices of one would necessarily be suited to the other. The British Parliament, it must be noted, has had longer experience than any other legislative body in exercising control over the executive. If the controls appear inadequate to the American reader, it must be recalled that they are part of a parliamentary form of government in which ministerial responsibility is a cardinal principle.

Congressional control of the executive departments and agencies is primarily applied prior to executive action. As we have seen, Congress exercises this pre-control in several ways: by passing detailed statutes which authorize (and restrict) the specific activities that may be carried on by the departments; by prescribing the internal organization of the departments and often the procedures and work methods to be used; and by requiring committee approval of certain executive decisions before they are put into effect. In addition, the appropriations committees exercise a large amount of pre-control over department activities through detailed appropriation acts, committee reports, and informal understandings with department officers, as well as subsequent consultations before obligations are incurred.

Parliamentary control of the executive in Great Britain, in contrast, is essentially a post-control, and consists in holding the ministers and the permanent heads of departments accountable for their policies and administration. It does not curtail executive discretion or require executive officers to share responsibility with legislative committees, and there is no attempt to dictate day-to-day executive decisions, for this would defeat the responsibility of the ministers for the conduct of the departments. Nevertheless, by holding the ministers accountable, especially in the question period, and by making the permanent heads of departments answer to the Public Accounts Committee for any expenditure that is questionable, the House of Commons exercises a continuous control that is pervasive and effective.

The form which legislative control of the executive takes in any nation depends primarily on the constitutional framework, but evolves from there along with the evolving history and traditions of the legislature and the political system. The American Constitution's provision for coordinate and separate legislative, executive, and judicial branches made a continuous struggle for power between the legislative and executive branches inevitable. In the history of the country the pendulum has swung from one side to the other, depending in part on the political strength of the President, the leadership of Congress, the needs of the time, and the public support which the President and the Congress are each able to command at any given time. In recent years Congress has greatly increased the size of its professional staff and has developed new means of exercising control over the departments, but in view of the tremendous growth of the federal departments and the increasingly technical character of their activities, it may be questioned whether the actual control by Congress today is as great as it was in the early 1900's.

Although the perennial tug of war between Congress and the Executive branch is due basically to the constitutional division of powers, it is also a part of the power struggle of the two major political parties and of coalitions and other organized groups. Members of the President's party customarily defend his prerogatives against attack, while his opponents press for greater congressional control, appealing to the institutional loyalty of members to Congress. Opponents of a government program often attempt to saddle it with restrictions and controls that will hamper its activities, while those who favor the program seek adequate authority for the executive officers. The outcome usually turns on whether the opponents have sufficient strength to force the adoption of crippling restrictions and controls.

The strongest legislative control is imposed when the political opponents of the President have the upper hand in Congress; the control recedes when the President has the support of the House and the Senate leadership and of the chairmen of committees. The bureaus may sometimes be found siding with Congress rather than with the President, preferring the looser control of congressional committees to the tighter and more continuous control of the department heads and the President and his staff.

The amount of control which Congress exercises over the executive departments is related to the amount of control exercised by the President. During the latter part of of the nineteenth century the bureaus and departments had few contacts with the President, and it was the committees of Congress rather than the President that supervised them. Since the beginning of the present century, however, the President's role as head of the Executive branch has been greatly strengthened, especially during the terms of Theodore Roosevelt, Woodrow Wilson, and Franklin D. Roosevelt. The first major step to increase the administrative authority of the President was the passage of the Budget and Accounting Act of 1921, which authorized him to review and revise the department estimates and to submit his budget for the entire government to Congress. The act provided him with a budget staff, but placed the Bureau of the Budget in the Treasury Department, though subject to the direction of the President. Under this arrangement the Bureau failed to develop as an effective staff agency of the President, but in 1939, following the recommendations of the President's Committee on Administrative Management, it was moved into the newly formed Executive Office of the President, and at the same time the President's staff was substantially increased.

During World War II the President's staff was further increased, to aid him in coordinating the war effort. In 1946 Congress established the Council of Economic Advisers in the Executive Office of the President, and at intervals during the next ten years several other central staff agencies were added. In 1949 the first Hoover Commission recommended further strengthening of the President's staff, but criticized the practice of creating the staff agencies by law, stating that the

President should have discretion in organizing them. The greatest increase in personnel came in the Eisenhower administration with the establishment of a chief of staff and various other units and advisory councils.

The increased role of the President as administrative chief, however, has not lessened the control that Congress and its committees exercise over the executive establishment. Essentially, congressional and executive controls are not repugnant but complementary to each other and should be carried on in close cooperation. The primary aim of congressional controls should be to galvanize the internal disciplines of the Executive branch, since there are many forms of control that can be exercised effectively only from within the Executive branch itself. Congressional committees, however, usually look with suspicion on the supervision of the executive departments by the President's central staff agencies.

The Legislative Veto

In recent years Congress has discovered new means of exercising control over the executive. The legislative veto, first used to permit Congress to set aside executive reorganization plans of the President, was extended after 1939 to other executive actions. The 1939 Executive Reorganization Act, which became the precedent for subsequent legislative veto legislation, required a concurrent resolution passed by both houses to set aside the President's reorganization plans, but later acts permitted either house to veto executive decisions by simple resolution. The next step, which was not long delayed, was to grant the same authority to individual committees of Congress. If the committee veto becomes a permanent part of legislative-executive relations and is widely used, it will bring about a fundamental change in our constitutional system, placing executive agencies under the supervision and direction of congressional committees. Presidents Eisenhower and Truman both vetoed a number of bills because of committee veto provisions, but both accepted such provisions when attached to urgently needed legislation.

According to the classic theory of separation of powers, a legislature enacts the laws and an executive branch executes them, but this theory is an obvious oversimplification of an intricate relationship. The legislature's interest in policies and programs does not cease when it enacts legislation, for legislation goes only part way in determining government policy. It is administration that endows the content of laws with meaning, and it is the appropriate function of the legislature to check on the execution of the laws to ascertain whether policies are faithfully and effectively carried out, to hold the executive officers responsible for administration, and to determine whether new legislation is needed. Congress, however, especially in recent years, has been seeking a more direct means whereby it (or its committees) can share with executive officers the responsibility for executive decisions. "The weight is no longer on the initial insertion of statutory details or upon judicial review. Rather, the legislative body itself seeks to be continuously a participant in guiding administrative conduct and the exercise of discretion."[1] Congressional committees have long exercised a continuing informal control over executive decisions by requiring department officers to consult with them prior to certain actions and by oral instructions to the departments during the course of hearings. Recently this informal control has been given legal sanction through laws providing for the committee veto of certain executive decisions.

The factors that influence the decisions of legislative committees are often quite different from those that influence department heads. The department head is expected to take into account government-wide policies, the program of the President, how a particular action will affect the policies and operations of other departments and whether it will promote the national interest. He should be prepared to accept responsibility for the policies and actions of his department when they are attacked in Congress or elsewhere. This responsibility has a sobering effect upon his judgment. His decisions are ordinarily not his alone, but the product of conferences in which many specialists and administrators participate; practical considerations of administration and timing are given great weight. Department decisions are subject to review, consultation, and clearance by other government agencies affected, and often by the central staff agencies of the President. Committee decisions, on the other hand, are based on considerations in which provincial, partisan, and personal factors often play key parts.

[1] Arthur Macmahon, "Congressional Oversight of Administration: The Power of the Purse," *Political Science Quarterly*, Vol. 58 (1943), p. 162.

Committee participation in executive decisions, especially when formalized to the extent of giving the committee the final determination, divides responsibility for administration and in essence enables a few members of Congress, who are accountable only to their own constituents, to direct department activities.

In contrast, the committees of the British Parliament take no part in executive decisions, for this would be regarded as contrary to the basic principle of ministerial responsibility and make it impossible for Parliament to hold the minister accountable for the actions of the department. The British House of Commons does not have standing committees for the various major fields of legislation, as Congress does. The Public Accounts Committee, the single most important agency of the House of Commons for controlling the executive, does not consider expenditures until after they have been made and the accounts are examined. The permanent secretary, who answers to the committee, never consults with it prior to making expenditures, and both would consider it highly improper for him to do so, but he must be prepared to defend before the committee any expenditure or action that may be questioned by the Comptroller and Auditor General.

Legislative Control Through Statutes

There has been an increasing tendency in recent years for Congress to enact detailed statutes authorizing the activities of the departments, prescribing their internal organization, and regulating their procedures and work methods. As various surveys of federal administration have pointed out, unnecessarily detailed legislation is harmful to good administration, for it deprives executive officers of the discretion which they must have if they are to be held responsible for the performance of the agencies which they head, and imposes rigid and often unsuitable procedures, which soon become obsolete. Under such legislation executive agencies are unable to adopt improved methods and keep abreast of rapidly changing technical developments.

Authorization of programs for one year, or at most two years, is another means which Congress has used in recent years to augment its control. When an agency is thus forced to return frequently for a new authorization, it presumably becomes more amenable to committee direction and supervision. It is, in effect, put on good behavior, for if the legislative committee finds the program displeasing, it has ready means to curtail or modify it. Although justified for questionable or highly temporary activities, the annual authorization places great handicaps on administration, for it prevents advance planning and makes it difficult to build a competent staff.

Statutes creating bureaus and offices within executive departments and agencies have several unfortunate effects. The bureau is put on a statutory pedestal and removed to some extent from responsibility to the department head. The determination of the major features of executive organization is a proper concern of the legislature, but the internal organization and assignment of duties within executive establishments is essentially an executive function.

Recognizing the difficulties in reorganizing the Executive branch by legislation, Congress has delegated a limited reorganization authority to the President, subject to the legislative veto. The recent executive reorganization acts, however, have unfortunately trimmed the President's authority by providing that either house may set aside his reorganization plans. The change in the form of the legislative veto has greatly weakened what once appeared to be a practicable procedure to enable the President and the Congress to work together in effecting needed executive reorganization.

The tendency of Congress to enact detailed statutes prescribing the procedures and methods to be followed is clearly seen in legislation relating to the civil service. Prior to 1930, Congress followed the course of enacting into law only the general policies relating to the federal service, delegating the task of issuing detailed rules and regulations to the President and the Civil Service Commission. In recent years, however, it has passed many highly detailed statutes regulating almost every aspect of personnel administration, the effect of which has been to hamper rather than to strengthen the civil service. In contrast, the British Parliament has left the regulation of the civil service to the Treasury, except for the retirement system, which is regulated by statute.

That detailed statutes regulating the work of the departments are passed by Congress is due in part to the fact that there is no central control agency in the federal government comparable to the British Treasury to which Congress is willing to delegate supervision of the administration of the departments. The Bureau of the Budget performs many of the same functions as the British Treasury, but does not command the same confidence of the legislative body which the Treasury has acquired after several centuries of watching over the work of the departments. The reluctance of Congress to delegate greater control functions to the Bureau of the Budget is understandable, because ours is a government of divided powers, and the Bureau is regarded as an arm of the President. Instead of turning to the Bureau to investigate administrative problems and to exercise needed central controls over the departments, as Parliament turns to the Treasury, congressional committees generally view the Bureau with suspicion and regard it as a rival rather than as a central agency that it may utilize.

Legislative Control of the Budget

In no other area does legislative control of administration in the United States and Great Britain differ so widely as in the control of the budget. Even the term "budget" is used differently: in the United States it refers primarily to the spending program of the President, while in Great Britain it refers to revenue measures, and the vote of funds to the departments is referred to as "supply."

It is a basic constitutional principle of both countries that no taxes may be levied or public funds spent without authorization by the legislature, but the manner in which the executive and the legislative branches cooperate to pass upon fiscal matters is wholly different. In fact, the differences are so great that it may be questioned whether a comparison is useful, yet several American states have budgetary systems which in some respects are similar to that of the British government. The methods by which Congress passes on the President's budget are not necessarily inherent in a government with divided powers. They have been revised from time to time, and doubtless will be subject to further change.

Congress exerts its greatest control over the executive departments in authorizing their programs (which is a financial as well as a policy determination), and in voting appropriations. The control exercised by the large House and Senate Appropriations Committees, largely through their numerous subcommittees, is more continuous and detailed than that of any other committee, and probably more so than that of any other national legislative body. The control is not limited to finance; the subcommittees review the policies and operations of the departments, their work methods and accomplishments, their estimates and plans, and on the basis of this review recommend the appropriations for the next fiscal year. Although their recommendations are subject to revision by the full committee and Congress itself, few changes are made except by the other house, and these are usually compromised in conference.

A basic feature of the federal government's financial system is that Congress is free to make any changes that it wishes in the financial proposals of the President. It may increase or decrease his estimates; it may strike them entirely, and add other items not requested by him; it may attach such conditions and restrictions to appropriations as it determines. It also instructs the President what to put in his budget requests by authorizing legislation that prescribes, often in considerable detail, the programs that the government may conduct, and in many instances commits the government to future expenditures. Individual members of Congress are free to introduce bills or motions that add to the expenditures of the government, and have a greater voice in finance than the individual members of any other major legislative body in the world.

A basic defect in the organization and procedures of Congress in passing on the budget is that responsibility is hopelessly divided among numerous committees and subcommittees, each considering only a small part of the finances of the government. Appropriations are passed on separately by a dozen or more subcommittees in each house, and fifteen or more appropriation bills are passed at different times; revenue measures are considered by another set of committees; and, finally, authorizations of government activities and expenditures are passed on by the various legislative committees of both houses. As a result, Congress passes upon finance in numerous separate bills and at different times, but never considers the entire budget, including revenues, at one time.

This defect has been widely recognized and many reforms have been proposed, but the present organization and procedures of Congress in passing upon fiscal matters are so firmly established that any change will be difficult to accomplish. Any reform will necessarily have to be built upon the present system, and it is safe to say that no change will be made until the need for it is generally accepted. Yet the tremendous size of the federal budget and its importance to the national economy, the imperative need for the wise management of federal finance, and the widely recognized weaknesses of the present fiscal system of the government will force, sooner or later, a fresh and broad-gauged consideration of the entire budgetary system of the government. A joint legislative-executive commission, with representation of outstanding citizens, is needed to conduct an inquiry into the federal budgetary system, including all aspects, executive and legislative, and to recommend improvements which will correct the obvious defects in the present system, strengthen financial management, and, hopefully, facilitate greater cooperation between the Congress and the Executive branch.

IN GREAT BRITAIN, a major constitutional principle of the financial system is embodied in the rule that the House of Commons adopted in 1713, stating that the House will not entertain any motion to raise taxes or to vote funds which places an obligation on the Exchequer, except a motion by a minister of the Crown. By this self-denying ordinance the House of Commons has restricted itself to reducing the estimates of the government, although in fact it makes no change at all. It has also established the rule that it will authorize no new activities which would place a drain on the Exchequer unless they are proposed by the government; the effect of this is to place unquestioned responsibility on the government for finance. The ministers, who are the heads of the executive departments, are also the leaders of Parliament. They present and defend their budgets directly to the House of Commons without the intervention of a parliamentary committee. Parliament invariably votes the supply estimates of the government without any revision. All votes on finances are treated as votes of confidence, hence any change in the budget voted by Parliament would bring about the overthrow of the government.

The House of Commons has declined to establish a standing committee to examine the estimates and recommend reductions, although the use of such a committee has been frequently urged during the last hundred years and has been considered by several select committees. The Select Committee of Estimates (which has never been made a standing committee, but is created annually) does not examine the estimates in detail and does not recommend any revision of them. Its function is to inquire into administration with a view to recommending economies, and thus it examines the estimates only as incident to its inquiries. The government has consistently opposed the establishment of a committee which would recommend revisions of the budget estimates, taking the position that such a committee would weaken the responsibility of the ministers and of the Cabinet for finance, and would not lead to economy. Members of Parliament, as a rule, believe that no purpose would be served by having a parliamentary committee examine the estimates that have already been examined and revised by the Treasury.

Parliament, however, does debate the budget at length. Twenty-six days are set aside for debate on supply. The opposition party is permitted to select those parts of the budget which it wishes to debate, and the government must be prepared to defend not only its fiscal policies, but the budget and administration of particular departments and activities that come under attack. Although the budget is adopted without change, the debate serves to educate and inform the public about fiscal affairs and the administration of the departments. The Cabinet would not dare to present a budget that it could not defend against attack by the Opposition. Its responsibility for the sound management of government finances is inescapable.

Parliamentary control of the budget in Great Britain is thus fundamentally different from that exercised by Congress; it does not provide for a detailed examination of the budget by a parliamentary committee, and does not result in any revision of the budget submitted by the government; it relates to the fiscal policies of the government rather than to appropriations for specific activities. To outsiders it might appear that Parliament has abdicated its control of fiscal affairs, but it cannot be doubted that the finances of the British government are well managed, regardless of which party is in office. Individual members of Parliament are prohibited from proposing new or increased expenditures, and hence are not expected to secure expenditures of benefits to their districts. Similarly, special-interest groups are unable to lobby in Parliament for special activities of benefit to them and must take their demands to the government, which is more likely than the legislature to turn them down. The unquestioned responsibility of the Cabinet for the fiscal affairs of the government is the keystone of the British financial system.

Legislative Control of Expenditures

Control of expenditures involves the means taken by the legislature to check on how public funds have been used, to assure that they have been properly accounted for, have been used only for legally authorized activities and for the purposes for which they were voted, and are in conformity with laws and regulations. This form of control is accomplished through an independent audit of the accounts of the departments, the results of which are reported to the legislative body for its consideration.

The control of expenditures is one of the most important of the executive controls in the hands of the House of Commons; it is exercised through the Public Accounts Committee, which receives and examines the audit reports of the Comptroller and Auditor General. It is a post-expenditure control. Neither the Comptroller and Auditor General nor the committee has the power to disallow expenditures or to order restitution of moneys improperly or illegally used. The only authority of the Comptroller and Auditor General is to lay his findings before Parliament, which refers them to the Public Accounts Committee, and the only power of the committee is to report to Parliament. Nevertheless, the examination of the accounts and activities of the departments by the committee has far-reaching effects on administration. Any questionable activity, any uneconomic use or waste of public funds, any practice that is not in accord with accepted procedures, and any shortcomings in accounting or financial administration discovered by the auditors may be brought before the committee for its attention.

The accounting officer of each department, usually the permanent secretary, must appear before the committee and defend the actions of the department that have been questioned. The committee's findings and recommendations, though not legally binding on the departments, are customarily accepted and carried out under instructions from the Treasury. The effects of this form of control are to require the departments to exercise diligence and frugality in their expenditure of public funds, and to make sure that they are in conformity with laws and regulations. Since all government activities involve the use of public funds, this control applies to all administration. If it does not assure that administration will be competent and efficient, it at least provides protection against unauthorized, uneconomic, and improper uses of public funds.

The control of federal expenditures in the United States is handled in an entirely different manner. Although Congress in the early days of the Republic often established committees to examine the accounts and to check on the department expenditures, these were never effective, largely because there was no independent audit to serve as the basis for their examination. In 1921, Congress established the General Accounting Office, headed by an officer responsible to Congress—the Comptroller General; failing, however, to recognize the distinction between the function of accounting and that of auditing, it vested both functions in this office. As a result, the U. S. Comptroller General has devoted his efforts primarily to the settlement of accounts and to his accounting functions, which are inconsistent with the functions of an auditor.

The granting of executive functions to the Comptroller General has often been criticized as being contrary to sound financial organization, and as depriving the President and the executive departments of essential executive controls. Efforts to revise the system have been unavailing, however, because Congress is unwilling to curtail the authority of its own agent, although it has frequently exempted certain executive acts from his control. The effect of the system is to deprive executive officers of the discretion which they should have in the choice of methods and procedures to carry on their activities, and to impose on them outside legal rulings which govern and often hamper the conduct of their work.

It has often been proposed that the Comptroller General should be limited to the function of conducting a post-audit of the department accounts and reporting the findings of his audits to Congress, and that Congress should establish an accounts committee similar to the British committee to receive and act upon these reports. Several states have recently adopted auditing systems of this type, but Congress has not looked with favor upon the proposal.

The effectiveness of the British Public Accounts Committee depends largely on its long tradition for nonpartisanship. Its chairman is drawn from the opposition party, and the committee devotes its attention almost wholly to questions of economy, the prudent use of public funds, and the financial practices of the departments, refraining from partisan attacks on the administration.

It may be doubted whether an accounts committee of Congress would be able to divorce its activities from partisan considerations. Nevertheless, the present auditing system of the federal government has basic faults that indicate the need for a revision of the system and the establishment of more effective means whereby Congress can exercise control over expenditures and check the financial management of the departments.

Legislative Oversight of Administration

Congressional oversight of administration is highly diffused, being exercised by all standing committees, with much overlapping and duplication of responsibility. Each department and executive agency is subject to supervision and investigation by at least six congressional committees. The largest amount of supervision of the departments is exercised by the Appropriations Committee of each house, and the numerous appropriations subcommittees. The Senate and the House Government Operations Committees have jurisdiction to inquire into the operations of all executive departments, and have become large-scale investigatory agencies, often working at cross purposes with the legislative committees. Several other standing committees, among them the Post Office and Civil Service Committee of each house conduct investigations touching upon the activities of all departments.

The number of investigations conducted by Congress has greatly increased in recent years. Investigations and other forms of inquiry are conducted by every standing legislative committee and by most of the subcommittees. Thus, inquiries are often duplicated and committee jurisdictions overlap confusingly. For Congress, the result is a splintering of its responsibility for legislative oversight that sharply reduces the effectiveness of investigation as a tool and often permits departments to play off one committee against another. The departments, in turn, are subjected to conflicting directives, as well as excessive demands for information.

Congressional investigations of administration, and especially of charges of mismanagement or misconduct of executive officers, are seldom free of partisanship. Many result in divided reports, the members of one party absolving the executive officers of any serious blame for shortcomings, and those of the other party finding them guilty of misconduct or incompetence as charged. This obvious partisanship seriously impairs the utility of the inquiry, except as a weapon of party warfare; the public is more likely to be confused than informed by such conflicting findings. Yet even highly partisan investigations may at times serve a useful purpose in bringing about needed corrections of administrative abuses or mismanagement. However, the grosser forms of corruption and maladministration that have been exposed in the past have fortunately all but disappeared from the federal government. The greater need today is for inquiries designed to bring about improvements in organization and management, and in this area the typical investigation has not been notably successful.

The British Parliament, which has been called the Grand Inquest and which was the first national legislature to conduct investigations, today conducts few inquiries except those relating to its own procedures. It has only two committees that regularly inquire into administration—the Public Accounts Committee and the Select Committee of Estimates—each with well-defined functions. No government has been willing to permit the establishment of a parliamentary committee to gather information with which to attack it. If an investigation is demanded, the government is called upon to institute an inquiry. If the subject relates to broad social and economic problems, a Royal Commission of Inquiry will probably be appointed, whose members are chosen for their high qualifications and standing as well as their objectivity. If charges of misconduct of public officials are to be investigated, a Tribunal of Inquiry, headed by a prominent judge, will be instituted; and if problems of administration are to be investigated, an interdepartmental committee of top-ranking civil servants, chosen for their special qualifications, will be appointed. The government is responsible for its selection of the persons to conduct these various forms of inquiries, and would be subject to serious attack in Parliament if the appointees were unqualified or unsuitable.

Although the British House of Commons conducts few investigations of administration, it has other means of inquiring into the work of the departments. Parliamentary questions are used to inquire into administrative actions that have given rise to public complaint, often forcing the departments to make corrections. Congressional hearings are similarly used in the United States, but they are sporadic and limited to a few members, whereas parliamentary questions are continuous while Parliament is in session and questions may be put by all members. Congressional hearings provide a more thorough inquiry into a few administrative problems, while parliamentary questions permit a limited inquiry into all aspects of the work of the departments.

Congressional investigations of administration need to be reformed, not because of the criticisms that have been made of various specific investigations, but rather because they are ordinarily inefficient and ineffective. Investigations of the work of the departments conducted by the standing committees of Congress incident to the consideration of legislative policies and appropriations have been carried on without the fanfare of publicity and, for the most part, with reasonably high standards. But special investigations of charges of maladministration, mismanagement, and corruption have often been highly charged with politics. The obvious solution is to provide other machinery whereby the latter type of investigations may be carried on competently, and on a nonpartisan basis, assuring findings that will be generally accepted. The President should be authorized, as is the governor of New York under the Moreland Act, to institute such inquiries when there are charges against public officials. The President would be subject to serious criticism if he failed to appoint to such commissions of inquiry persons of outstanding competence, prestige, and ability. Provision should also be made for outside inquiries into administrative management of the government, another area in which congressional inquiries have not been effective. By authorizing the President to institute inquiries in these areas Congress would not give up its authority to look into any aspect of the work of the government, but would provide supplemental machinery which would in some types of investigation be more effective.

The Role of the Legislature

We come back to what was said in the first chapter of this study: legislative control and oversight of the executive departments and agencies is one of the most important functions of modern legislatures. It is the means by which the legislature is assured that its policies are being faithfully and efficiently carried out, by which it may hold executive officers to an accounting for their stewardship, and by which it learns of the effects of legislative policies and is thus able to make necessary statutory revisions. Important legislative policies and programs are of little effect unless they are effectively administered. However, it should be recognized that it is not the function of the legislature or of its committees to direct and supervise the administration, or to dictate executive decisions. Legislative control is not an end in itself; it is most salutary when it strengthens rather than supplants executive direction. Unless it is exercised with wisdom and restraint and with due regard to the executive function, it may defeat the very purpose for which it is instituted. Too much "looking over the shoulder" of executive officers, whether public or private, is always harmful. Legislative oversight needs to be adequate—but should not become excessive or encroach upon the executive function.

Legislative control should strengthen and enforce the responsibility of executive officers for the management of the agencies which they head; it should seek to galvanize the internal disciplines of the executive establishment rather than to impose external controls; and it should set the general direction and limits of policy. It is not the function of the legislature to participate in executive decisions or share responsibility with executive officers, for which it is ill equipped, but rather to check on the administration in order to hold the officers in charge accountable for their decisions and for management and results. Executive officers should thus be held to account for any failure to carry out legislative policies, for any mismanagement or misuse of public funds, and for any improper, unauthorized, wasteful, or imprudent expenditures The knowledge that they will thus be held accountable not only for the legality but also for the prudence of their actions will act as a powerful deterrent against laxity, poor management, or improper actions. On the other hand, participation by a legislative committee in executive decisions ordinarily tends to absolve the executive officers from future accountability.

Congress has failed to utilize some of the most salutary and effective forms of legislative control of administration. This is notably true in its failure to establish a public accounts committee to receive and act upon audit reports of its independent auditing officer, using these reports as a means of enforcing the responsibility of the principal executive officers for proper accounting and financial management, and for their uses of public funds. In Great Britain the control of expenditures through the audit has been found to be a highly effective instrument of surveillance which touches upon every administrative act, and goes far beyond questions of legality and regularity of expenditures. If effective means are developed whereby executive officers may be held to a strict accounting, many of the other restrictions and limitations that are harmful to good administration may be abandoned as unnecessary.

CONGRESS SHOULD RECONSIDER the whole problem of legislative oversight of administration, including its own organization for oversight and the various means utilized. The present practice has developed more as an accidental by-product of the legislative functions of Congress than by design. The responsibility for oversight of the individual departments and agencies is divided among numerous committees, resulting in a large amount of duplication and overlapping, and the lack of any clear responsibility. Heavy drains are placed upon the time and energy of the heads of departments and other executive officers by reason of the numerous congressional committees to which they must report and explain their actions. Legislative oversight of administration, properly conceived and carried out, is a safeguard against lax, inefficient, and inept administration; but excessive controls, often written into law to correct abuses of years ago and continued long after the need has passed, may hamper rather than improve administration. The practice which has grown up in recent years for congressional committees to share executive responsibility with the officers in charge of departments and agencies by the exercise of a committee veto of executive decisions is one which especially should be carefully assessed before it becomes a permanent fixture of executive-legislative relations.

A joint committee of the Congress or a joint legislative-executive commission is needed to re-examine the essential meaning of the oversight responsibility placed on Congress by the Constitution and to conduct a searching inquiry into legislative control of administration, the various forms it has taken, and its effect on executive action and responsibility. The task will not be easy; the subject is as large and complex as it is important to the future of the country. But if such an inquiry produces greater understanding of the mutuality of legislative and administration problems, it may lead to an increasing cooperation between Congress and the Executive branch through which legislative oversight will be strengthened where it is needed and the kind of controls that hamper administration will be reduced. This cooperation is essential if the United States government is to perform the ever increasing tasks modern society places upon it.

Index

Agricultural Conservation Program, 87, 88, 90, 93

Agriculture Adjustment Act of 1938, 93

Agriculture, Department of: appropriations to, 92, 96-97; budget growth of, 65; control of by detailed statute, 20; General Accounting Office and, 151; policy controversy with House Agricultural Appropriations Subcommittee, 87, 88

Alien Registration Act of 1940, 210-11, 241

American Farm Bureau Federation, 87

Appropriation bills: committee reports accompanying, 97; in conference committee, 100; in the House, 97-99; in the Senate, 99-100; itemized and lump sum, 49-51, 91, 92; proposals for different procedures, 107-26; provisions of, 92-97; restrictions of on departments, 94-97, 106; weaknesses of, 68, **106**

Appropriations committees, 69-75; creation of, 53; membership of, 69-70; relationship of with Bureau of the Budget, 124-26; relationship of with General Accounting Office, 152; relationship of with legislative committees, 54, 86-87, 96, 101, 122-23; staffs of, 72-75, 106; supervision of departments, 292; tasks and importance of, 47, 53, 54, 68-69, 70, 79-80, 279, 286-87; use of committee veto requiring "come into agreement," 230-31; use of committee veto requiring committee approval before funds appropriated, 232-33; use of committee veto terminating government business, 226-30; weaknesses of, 66-67, 79, 110, 121-22

Appropriations process: budget carry-overs under, 91, 115-16; comparisons of with Great Britain, 95, 125n; development of, 46, 47, 48n; deficiency appropriations under, 52, 57, 106; dispersion of responsibility of among legislative and appropriations committees, 53, 54, 55; weaknesses of, 68, 95, 101-03. *See also* Budget.

Appropriations subcommittees: activities of House Agriculture, 87-89; allocation of funds, 79-86; assignments to, 71-72; in the Senate, 72, 75-79; investigations, as a form of, 88-90; knowledge of members of, 101; of number of personnel, 201; over administrative policies, 86-88; reliance of on formal hearings, 75-79, 87, 124-26; requiring consultation in advance of department actions, 89, 90, 214-15; staffs of, 75, 101, 117; supervision by of departments, 90, 292; tasks and importance of, 69, 70, 71, 94, 97, 286-87; use of hearings, 87; weaknesses of, 65, 72, 106, 110

Armed Services. *See* Defense Department.

Armed Services committees, 26, 220-25; House, 27-28, 30; subcommittees review of Defense Department real estate transactions, 222-23

Articles of Confederation, 16

Atomic Energy Act of 1946, 38, 211, 236-37

Atomic Energy Commission, 237-38

Attorney General, office established, 18

Auditing system: comparisons of with Great Britain, 152-58, 159, 161, 296; distinguished from business or internal audit, 128, 143; essential conditions of effective system, 128-29; his-

299

Classification Act of 1923, 166, 170, 175, 176

Cockrell, Francis M., 256-57

Commission on Organization of the Executive Branch of the Government. *See* Hoover Commission.

Committee chairmen: comptroller general staff used by to conduct investigations, 161-62; former right of to exercise legislative veto, 225; influence of, 12, 161, 214-15

Committee on Administrative Management, 169-70, 171-72, 208, 281

Committee veto: advantages of, 246-47; approval of actions before funds appropriated under, 230-33; come into agreement by, 224, 230-31; constitutionality of, 224, 229, 231, 242-45, 282-83; development of, 217-38; objections to, 243-44; real estate control by, 217, 220-25, 230; request of advance reports under, 233-38; termination of government business enterprises in 1955 by, 226-30. *See also* Legislative veto.

Comptroller General: appointment of, 131; auditing accounts of executive officers, 139-44; auditing as distinguished from interpreting laws, 234; criticisms of, 146-47, 160, 291; establishment of office of, 60; legal interpretations of, 144-47; power of settlement, 144, 158; prescription of principles and control of accounting standards in executive agencies, 136-37; proposed modifications of, 132-35, 146-47, 160; ruling of on employee training, 180-81; staffs of used by committee chairmen, 161-62, 266; statutory exceptions of, 147-48. *See also* General Accounting Office.

Conference committee, 61, 69, 100

Consolidated Appropriations Act: advantages of, 109; objections to, 109-10

Constitution of the United States: checks and balances of, 3-5; congressional powers authorized by, 4, 12-13; presidential powers granted by, 17, 239-40, 242; Senate confirmation of presiden-

tial appointees required by, 199; separation of powers, 3-5, 11, 12, 45, 125-26, 160-61, 205-06, 242, 249-50, 280, 282-83

Constitutional Convention of 1787, 11, 12, 16, 48n, 239-40

Continental Congress in 1775, 175

Coolidge, President Calvin, 259

Council of Economic Advisers, 281

Courts, James C., 72

Crédit Mobilier scandal, 255-56

Daugherty, Harry M., 259

Daugherty, Mally S., 267

Davis, Jefferson, 110

"Decompetition program," 226-30

Defense, Department of: control of by committee veto terminating business enterprises, 226-30; control of by legislative veto, 208-10, 217, 219-30; reorganization of, 24-30, 209-10; ropewalk business of, 226-30; use of committee veto on real estate transactions of, 217, 220-25, 230

Defense Reorganization Act of 1958, 25-30, 209-10

Deficiency appropriations, 52, 57, 106

Dirksen, Everett: and agricultural appropriations restrictions, 94; and committee veto, 231

Dockery Act, 130

Dockery Commission, 257-58

Doheny, Edward F., 259

Dworshak, Henry C., 76n

Economy Act of 1933 (Title IV), presidential power of reorganizing departments by executive order granted by, 207

Egger, Rowland, 125

Eisenhower, President Dwight D.: bills signed by with protest, 229, 232; creation by of Career Executive Committee, 185-86; Department of Agriculture policies, 88; increase in personnel under, 282; on government employee training, 181; on loyalty program, 197; on withholding information, 37, 268-69; opposition to "come